P9-DMT-085

SHADES OF DEVIANCE

A primer on crime, deviance and social harm

Edited by Rowland Atkinson

Routledge
Taylor & Francis Group

LONDON AND NEW YORK

First published 2014
by Routledge
2 Park Square, Milton Park, Abingdon, Oxon, OX14 4RN

and by Routledge
711 Third Avenue, New York, NY 10017

Routledge is an imprint of the Taylor & Francis Group, an informa business

© 2014 Rowland Atkinson, selection and editorial material; the
contributors, their individual chapters

The right of Rowland Atkinson to be identified as author of this work has
been asserted by him in accordance with sections 77 and 78 of the
Copyright, Designs and Patents Act 1988.

All rights reserved. No part of this book may be reprinted or reproduced or
utilised in any form or by any electronic, mechanical, or other means, now
known or hereafter invented, including photocopying and recording, or in
any information storage or retrieval system, without permission in writing
from the publishers.

British Library Cataloguing in Publication Data
A catalogue record for this book is available from the British Library

Library of Congress Cataloging-in-Publication Data
Shades of deviance : a primer on crime, deviance and social harm / edited by
Rowland Atkinson.
pages cm
1. Crime. 2. Deviant behavior. 3. Criminal behavior. I. Atkinson, Rowland.
HV6025.S453 2014
364 – dc23
2013031352

ISBN: 978-0-415-73322-9 (hbk)
ISBN: 978-0-415-73323-6 (pbk)
ISBN: 978-1-315-84855-6 (ebk)

Typeset in Bembo and ITCStoneSans
by Cenveo Publisher Services

Dedicated to my dearest LLB and LGJ,
and to all my friends.

CONTENTS

CONTRIBUTORS

Craig Ancrum is a Senior Lecturer in Criminology at Teesside University. His research interests include contemporary drug markets, criminal culture and ethnographic methods.

Nicole Asquith is a Senior Lecturer in the School of Humanities and Social Sciences, Deakin University, Australia, and Associate Senior Research Fellow with the Tasmanian Institute of Law Enforcement Studies. She is the co-author (with Rob White and Fiona Haines) of *Crime and Criminology* (Oxford University Press, 2012), and co-editor (with Isabelle Bartkowiak-Théron) of *Policing Vulnerability* (Federation Press, 2013).

Rowland Atkinson is Reader in Urban Studies and Criminology at the Department of Sociology, University of York. He is the co-editor of *New Directions in Crime and Deviancy* (Routledge, 2013, with Simon Winlow) and *Securing an Urban Renaissance* (Policy Press, 2007, with Gesa Helms), and has written extensively on urban social problems and disorder.

Andrea Beckmann is a critical criminologist and social pedagogue who has published widely on consensual SM, representations of 'body', contexts of education and critical pedagogies. Her work with Charlie Cooper was subsumed under the category of 'cultural criminology' in the *Oxford Handbook of Criminology* (2012).

Mike Brogden has retired from the post of Professor of Criminal Justice at Queen's University Belfast. He is the author of many texts in socio-legal studies, the latest (with Graham Ellison) being *Policing in an Age of Austerity: A Postcolonial Perspective* (Routledge, 2013).

Pat Carlen has published many books and articles on criminal and social justice. Awards include: 1997: the American Society of Criminology's Sellin-Glueck Award for Outstanding International Contributions to Criminology; 2010: the British Society of Criminology's Outstanding Achievement Award; 2011: an Honorary Doctorate from the University of Lincoln. A collection of selected works, *A Criminological Imagination: Essays on Justice, Punishment, Discourse* was published in Ashgate's Pioneers in Contemporary Criminology series in 2010.

Bruce M. Z. Cohen is a Senior Lecturer in Sociology at the University of Auckland, New Zealand. He has previously researched mental illness experience in his book *Mental Health User Narratives: New Perspectives on Illness and Recovery* (Palgrave Macmillan, 2008), and is currently writing on the process and forms of 'psychiatric hegemony' in neoliberal society.

Karen Corteen is Programme Leader for Criminology at the University of Chester. Her current work in progress focuses on popular victimology and her current research explores professional wrestling in the United States through a victimological lens (see her 2012 article, co-authored with Ajay Corteen, in *International Perspectives in Victimology*, 7, (1), 47–53). In 2007, with Alana Barton, David Scott and Dave Whyte, she co-edited *Expanding the Criminological Imagination* (Willan).

Teresa Degenhardt is Lecturer in Criminology at Queen's University Belfast. She works on the overlap between war and crime, politics and criminology, and in general on international criminology and feminist issues.

Walter S. DeKeseredy holds the position of Anna Deane Carlson Endowed Chair of Social Sciences in the Department of Sociology and Anthropology at West Virginia University. He has published 18 books and over 130 scientific journal articles and book chapters on violence against women and other social problems. In 1995, he received the Critical Criminologist of the Year Award from the American Society of Criminology's Division on Critical Criminology (DCC) and in 2008 the DCC gave him their Lifetime Achievement Award.

Molly Dragiewicz is Associate Professor in the School of Justice at Queensland University of Technology, Brisbane. She received the Critical

Criminologist of the Year Award from the American Society of Criminology's Division on Critical Criminology (DCC) in 2012 and the New Scholar Award from the American Society of Criminology's Division on Women and Crime in 2009.

Samantha Fletcher is a Lecturer in Sociology at Staffordshire University. Her research involves critical explorations of the changing forms of both coercive state power and manifestations of state violence in the context of recent forms of contestation, primarily with reference to the Occupy movement.

Anne Foley is Senior Lecturer in Criminology at Leeds Metropolitan University. She has researched the policing and victimisation of gypsies and travellers, as well as the informal systems of justice used by these communities. Her interests lie in understanding informal systems of justice among marginalised and 'forgotten' communities. Anne's expertise on gypsies and travellers has been called upon by local and national radio, as well as a number of NGOs.

Christian Garland is a writer and theorist, and a Fellow of the Institut für Kritische Theorie at the Freie Universität Berlin. He has taught at the Universities of Edinburgh, Bedfordshire and Warwick, and will return to a Ph.D somewhere in 2013.

Steve Hall is Professor of Criminology at Teesside University. He is essentially a criminologist with interests in philosophy, psychoanalysis, history and political economy. He is the author of *Theorizing Crime and Deviance* (SAGE, 2012), co-editor (with Simon Winlow) of *New Directions in Criminological Theory* (Routledge, 2012) and co-author (with Simon Winlow and Craig Ancrum) of *Criminal Identities and Consumer Culture* (Willan, 2008), and (with Simon Winlow) of *Violent Night* (Berg, 2006) and *Rethinking Social Exclusion* (SAGE, 2013, forthcoming).

Katherine Harrison is Senior Lecturer in Sociology at the University of Chester. She researches and teaches in the broad area of visual culture, particularly the work of iconic images in the construction of identity, memory and difference. She is currently working on 'hoodie horror' films and their role in producing new discourses of social class in Britain. Katherine is series editor of *Issues in the Social Sciences* (University of Chester Press).

Mark Hayes is Senior Lecturer in Criminology and Politics at Southampton Solent University. He has published academic material on a wide variety of subject areas, including fascism, the New Right, Irish republicanism, political ideology and football. Mark was a member of Anti-Fascist Action and is currently working on a book about the extreme right and fascism in Britain.

Steven Hirschler is a Researcher within the Department of Politics and the Centre for Applied Human Rights at the University of York. His primary area of research is the privatisation of asylum housing, while he is also involved in teaching criminology.

Mark Horsley is in the process of completing a Ph.D on Cultural Motivations for Consumer Borrowing at Teesside University. He recently finished a stint as a fixed-term Lecturer in Criminology and Criminal Justice at the University of the West of Scotland.

Keith Jacobs is Professor of Sociology at the University of Tasmania, Australia. He is also a recipient of an Australian Research Council Future Fellowship award (2012–16) to investigate key problems in Australian housing policy making. He is currently writing a monograph for Reaktion Books entitled *Housing: a Post War History*.

Bob Jeffery is Senior Lecturer in Sociology at Sheffield Hallam University and his research interests include class inequalities, urban studies, political economy and research methods. His current research focuses on the dynamics of the 2011 English riots.

Sarah Kingston is Senior Lecturer and Course Leader of the undergraduate BA (Hons) Criminology degree at Leeds Metropolitan University. Her recent books include *Prostitution in the Community: Attitudes, Action and Resistance* (Routledge, 2013) and (co-edited with Kate Hardy and Teela Sanders) *New Sociologies of Sex Work* (Ashgate, 2010).

Karen Lumsden is Lecturer in Sociology at Loughborough University and has a Ph.D in Sociology from the University of Aberdeen. Her research interests include crime and deviance, youth culture, car culture, policing, social networking and qualitative methods. She is the author of *Boy Racer Culture: Youth, Masculinity and Deviance* (Routledge, 2013) and has published in journals including *Sociology, Policing and Society* and *Qualitative Research*.

Anne-Marie McAlinden is a Reader in the School of Law, Queen's University Belfast. Her publications include *The Shaming of Sexual Offenders: Risk, Retribution and Reintegration* (Hart Publishing, 2007) and *'Grooming' and the Sexual Abuse of Children* (Oxford University Press, 2012).

Robert MacDonald is Professor of Sociology at Teesside University. Currently, his research focuses on social exclusion, poverty and youth. His most recent book, co-authored with Tracy Shildrick, Colin Webster and Kayleigh Garthwaite, is *Poverty and Insecurity: Life in Low-pay, No-pay Britain* (Policy Press, 2012).

Joanne Massey is a Senior Lecturer in Cultural Criminology at Manchester Metropolitan University. Joanne's Ph.D thesis 'Public Space and the Rebuilding of Manchester' focused on the regeneration of an area of central Manchester (now known as the Millennium Quarter) after the 1996 IRA bombing. Her research interests include public space, urban regeneration, gentrification, youth culture, subculture, popular culture, media representations, communities and urban studies.

Gareth Millington is Lecturer in the Department of Sociology, University of York. He is the author of *'Race', Culture and the Right to the City: Centres, Peripheries, Margins* (Palgrave Macmillan, 2011).

Mark Monaghan is a Lecturer in Social Policy and Crime at the University of Leeds. His main research area follows the scientific and political battles through which policy decisions are made in the area of illicit drugs. His recent monograph *Evidence versus Politics: Exploiting Research in UK Drug Policy Making?* was published in 2011 by Policy Press.

Cassandra A. Ogden is Senior Lecturer and Programme Leader for Sociology at the University of Chester. She has recently co-edited (with Stephen Wakeman) a book entitled *Corporeality: Body and Society* (University of Chester Press, 2013) and annually co-organises the international conference *Theorising Normalcy and the Mundane*. Her research adopts a critical disability lens to interrogate both illness experiences and ideas of normalcy surrounding the body.

Georgios Papanicolaou is Reader in Criminology at Teesside University. His research interests include the political economy of policing and the social organisation and regulation of illicit markets, particularly in a transnational context. His book *Transnational Policing and Sex Trafficking in Southeast Europe: Policing the Imperialist Chain* was published by Palgrave Macmillan in 2011.

Tina G. Patel is a Lecturer in Criminology at the University of Salford. Tina's research and teaching interests relate to 'race', exclusion, police and violent behaviour, and her published work includes the book *Race, Crime and Resistance*, published in 2011 by SAGE and co-authored with David Tyrer.

Nathan W. Pino is Professor of Sociology at Texas State University in San Marcos, where he conducts research on sexual and other forms of extreme violence, and policing and police reform in an international context. In addition to numerous academic journal articles, he is co-editor (with Michael D. Wiatrowski) of *Democratic Policing in Transitional and Developing Countries* (Ashgate, 2006); and co-author (with Graham Ellison) of *Globalization, Police Reform and Development* (Palgrave Macmillan, 2012).

Nicoletta Policek is a Senior Criminology Lecturer at the University of Lincoln. Her current research is on the gendering of global justice. Publications include works on the policing of outdoor sex work, criminalisation of HIV transmission and rape as a weapon of mass destruction in conflict zones.

Scott Poynting is Professor in Criminology at the University of Auckland, New Zealand. He is co-editor (with David Whyte) of *Counterterrorism and State Political Violence* (Routledge, 2012) and (with Richard Jackson and Eamon Murphy) of *Contemporary State Terrorism* (Routledge, 2010); and co-author (with Greg Noble, Paul Tabar and Jock Collins) of *Bin Laden in the Suburbs* (Sydney Institute of Criminology, 2004).

Michael Puniskis is a Researcher at Middlesex University in the Department of Mental Health and Social Work. His doctoral work examined the effects of weather on crime and policing in London. He is a part-time Lecturer in the Department of Criminology (also at Middlesex University) and Associate Lecturer for the Open University.

Tara Lai Quinlan is a lawyer and researcher interested in policing, terrorism, gentrification and discrimination issues. Ms Quinlan is also a Ph.D

Candidate at the London School of Economics and Political Science, and received a Master of Laws from King's College London and a Juris Doctor from Northeastern University School of Law, Boston.

Patricia (Paddy) Rawlinson is a Senior Lecturer in Criminology at Monash University, Melbourne. She has conducted extensive research and published on crime, corruption and political economy in former communist states. She is the author of *From Fear to Fraternity: a Russian Tale of Crime, Economy and Modernity* (Pluto Press, 2010), and is currently conducting research on violence, the state, medical issues and the pharma-industry.

Thomas Rodgers is based in the Department of Sociology at the University of York. His research focuses on digital and social media, political economy, the historical development of video-games, and questions of social harm and gaming more broadly. He is particularly interested in how economic value is extracted from player populations.

Prem Sikka is Professor of Accounting at the University of Essex. His research on accountancy, auditing, tax avoidance, tax havens, corporate governance, money laundering, insolvency and business affairs has been published in books, international scholarly journals, newspapers and magazines.

Oliver Smith is Lecturer in Criminology at Plymouth University. His recent work focuses on the changing relationship between ageing and 'youthful' consumption practices in urban spaces.

Sarah L. Steele is Fellow, Lecturer and Director of Studies in Law at Christ's College, University of Cambridge, where she conducts research on transnational crimes including trafficking, death tourism and the organ trade. She is an Adjunct Research Associate of Flinders University, Adelaide, and a Research Associate at the Cambridge Centre for Applied Research in Human Trafficking (www.ccarht.org).

Terry Thomas is Visiting Professor in Criminal Justice Studies at Leeds Metropolitan University. He has written widely on sexual offending and the 'management' of sex offenders in the community, including the books *Sex Crime: Sex Offending and Society* (Willan, 2005) and *The Registration and Monitoring of Sex Offenders: A Comparative Study* (Routledge, 2011).

He spent six months in the USA on a Leverhulme Trust grant looking at services to sex offenders.

Philippa Tomczak is writing a Criminology Ph.D thesis at the University of Manchester, funded by a School of Law Scholarship. Her research examines the penal voluntary sector and the relationship between punishment and charity. She won the 2012 John Howard Postgraduate Essay Prize.

James Treadwell is Lecturer in Criminology in the School of Law, University of Birmingham. He is a noted criminological ethnographer who has written on a range of criminological topics including football violence, drug use, violent crime and masculinity in a number of leading academic criminology journals. He is also the author of *Criminology* (SAGE, 2006) and *Criminology: the Essentials* (SAGE, 2013).

Waqas Tufail is Lecturer in Criminology at Manchester Metropolitan University and is currently completing his doctoral research on the role of policing within community safety partnerships. His research interests centre on issues of class, ethnicity and urban marginalisation.

Craig Webber is a Senior Lecturer in the Department of Sociology, Social Policy and Applied Social Science at the University of Southampton. His main research interests are in youth crime and justice, policing, criminological theory, media and crime, crime and technology, and social psychology and crime.

Rob White is Professor of Criminology at the University of Tasmania, Australia. Recent books include *Crimes against Nature* (Willan, 2008), *Environmental Crime: A Reader* (Willan, 2009), *Global Environmental Harm: Criminological Perspectives* (Willan, 2010), *Transnational Environmental Crime* (Routledge, 2011), *Climate Change from a Criminological Perspective* (Springer, 2012) and *Environmental Harm: An Eco-justice Perspective* (Policy, 2013).

Emma Wincup is currently Director of Student Education in the School of Law at the University of Leeds. Her research interests relate to interconnections between crime and social policy, and she has particular interests in drug policy, resettlement and homelessness. Her current work focuses on the regulation of (deviant) behaviour through welfare reform.

Simon Winlow is Professor of Criminology at Teesside University. His major works include *Badfellas* (Berg, 2001) and, as co-author, *Bouncers* (Oxford University Press, 2003, with Dick Hobbs, Philip Hadfield and Stuart Lister), *Violent Night* (Berg, 2006, with Steve Hall), *Criminal Identities and Consumer Culture* (Willan, 2008, with Steve Hall and Craig Ancrum) and *Rethinking Social Exclusion* (SAGE, 2013, forthcoming, with Steve Hall).

Steve Wright was Head of Manchester City Council's Police Monitoring Unit and Director of the Omega Research Foundation. He co-authored the report 'Crowd Control Technologies' (European Parliament, 2000) and is now Reader in Applied Global Ethics at Leeds Metropolitan University.

Maggie Wykes is a Senior Criminology Lecturer at the University of Sheffield. Her current research is on sexual violence in South Africa. Her publications deal with subjects including crime news, the West case, stalking, paedophilia and masculinity, for example *Violence, Gender and Justice* (SAGE, 2009), co-authored with Kirsty Welsh.

INTRODUCTION

Shades of deviance, crime and social harm

Rowland Atkinson

We might begin by imagining a robbery on a street, a man attacking someone else to steal an item, perhaps a wallet or an iPod. The attack is swift but vicious, designed to stun and create total domination over the victim, to ensure success and a rapid escape. Now let's think about why this event might have happened. It could be that the assailant was desperate for money because he had lost his job, then his home after being unable to keep up with the rent. Surfing friends' sofas and with few options, in desperation he plans a theft to try and raise some money. Another story we can imagine is that our assailant is a pretty unpleasant person who has always used aggressive body language and even violence when it suited him and in order to get his way. With little self-control and a powerful self-image as a dominant male he happens to spot a weak-looking young man, there is no one else on the street and he finds a sense of exhilaration in being able to take his prize while inducing a sense of fear and dread in his victim, someone weaker than himself.

Now let's scale up a little. Let's imagine, as is the case in many societies today, that most people have valuable consumer items that are must-have objects; something that to be without seems almost strange. But these are also societies of massive inequality in which a significant section of the population cannot meet their immediate needs and effectively have no disposable income but are nevertheless subjected to the same kinds of advertising and social pressures to conform. These factors may have meant that the robbery happened, at least in part, because of the pressures of living in such a society, with an assailant feeling under pressure to get something he could not through conventional means. Such observations help to highlight the fact that all rule-breaking, violence and crime happens for diverse and complex reasons – psychological, opportunistic, social (questions of masculinity, violence and social pressure) and economic. Social life is messy and close examination of worrisome problems like these requires critical thinking and careful analysis; yet, so often, what we see instead are sensational headlines and analyses around us, with little contextualisation that might help us to understand *why* terrible things happen and what we might thereby do about them.

Shades of Deviance is a wide-ranging guide to a number of issues that are harmful and worrisome but also, as we shall see, often victimless and complex in their causes and impacts. Let's start with a quick exercise. Take a look at the list of chapters indexed in this volume and ask yourself, is each one a *crime* (you may or may not know the answer to this basic question in each case)? Now ask yourself, do I actually think it is wrong or harmful? Finally, consider what you are basing any of your personal judgements on – research evidence, media headlines? It is very likely that you will disagree that some problems are designated as crimes to be punished through the criminal justice system while others you may feel are under-recognised by policing and crime control agencies. The problem you have is due in large part to the fact that social rule-breaking of all kinds cannot be observed from some neutral position. To say that something is wrong because it is illegal is a circular argument; we need to ask why a particular action is wrong and for whom and why these perspectives are as they are. Our views on crime and deviance of all kinds take place in social contexts with varying customs and norms applied by discrete social groups that may themselves be unequal in their power to act to prohibit them (a reason that problems like environmental or white-collar crime have often been neglected). This makes for frustration, but also the development of criminology as an exciting field of rich discovery and analysis when taken on with an open mind.

As some have argued, to show an interest in deviance is more than a little deviant in its own right, particularly when we approach socially taboo topics like paedophilia or trying to understand motives for the use of extreme violence. By deviance we are referring here to 'banned or controlled behaviour which is likely to attract punishment or disapproval'

(Downes and Rock, 2011: 23) and criminologists therefore profess a direct interest in many of the things that make many people uncomfortable, scared and angry. Our exposure to the media on a daily basis generates powerful images that we internalise and which influence our impression of how dangerous and risky the world is outside our front doors. These images also affect our daily routines (the places and people we might seek to avoid) and personal beliefs about what should be done. Are 'legal highs' a major problem? How are we to understand attacks on vulnerable people, such as the elderly? Why would someone set a bomb to kill innocent people, stab someone in a fight or murder a spouse? These are the kinds of questions that criminologists seek to tackle, but they are also incredibly important questions because condemnation and prisons alone do little to prevent people being harmed in the first place – we need to understand why crime occurs in order to be able to reduce harm to victims and to right wrongs of diverse kinds.

What can criminology do?

The great criminologist Stan Cohen once reduced questions and anxieties about crime to the following simple summary: 'The stuff of criminology consists of only three questions: Why are laws made? Why are they broken? What do we do or what should we do about this?' (1998: 9). Yet in making this clear he was also arguing that the project of criminology (in essence the study of crime) was deeply flawed because such questions are often posed in the wrong way, usually by those in charge of the crime control system and without understanding the social conditions that tend to produce such problems in the first place. In short, we need to engage with these wider factors to produce comprehensive and convincing accounts of negative, anti-social, aggressive and damaging behaviour and provide effective answers and thinking on the problem of crime.

There is, of course, much alarm and irrationality in thinking about crime, a crime 'complex' in which we are fixed on searching out criminals and punishing them and often remain deeply afraid of crime; journalists, politicians and the public more generally often submit to alarmist and sensationalist impressions of the level of crime (often called a moral panic). Yet we must also recognise that becoming the victim of assault, rape, bullying, abuse, fraud, among many other serious crimes, creates lasting and often permanent mental and physical scars (Young, 1999). Explaining such acts by reference to social inequality or childhood histories is unlikely to satisfy victims and injured parties. Seeing crime and deviant behaviour as social constructions (see below for an explanation) should not prevent us from understanding the way that hurt runs throughout society, or that injury from aggressive, predatory and neglectful behaviour tends to impact most heavily on the poorest in society; nor should it prevent us from thinking about how to respond to and prevent crimes and harms (Elliott, 1985). Thus we always need to disentangle the question of scale and measurement (to what extent is 'X' a problem?) from that of whether most criminal and deviant acts are unproblematic because they rely on social reactions to make sense. Let's consider an example. We may suggest that the response to paedophilia has been one of massive panic and over-reaction by news media and the public while at the same time highlighting the traumatic harms that such actions generate (cyber bullying and gangs can be analysed in a similar way).

The primary focus of sociological treatments of crime is to understand the sources of individual motives and social and contextual influences that may make crimes more or less likely. Though this is a gross simplification it helps us to begin to see how a sociological approach is different from one in which, for example, the criminal justice system alone is seen as the most important answer to the problem of crime (Lea, 2002), given its focus on picking up the pieces after the event. So criminologists have argued that acquisitive crimes (such as burglary or robbery) are more likely at times of economic stress or personal hardship, or in highly une-qual social systems in which envy or need may drive such crimes (Lea, 2002; Young, 1999). However, a major challenge for criminology today is understanding how and why many forms of crime are falling despite increasing inequality and a drop in public support for social insurance (pensions, welfare payments, and so on). Sociologists will say that at the very least we need to focus on different kinds of crime rather than some catch-all category to understand what is happening, while also focusing on long-term trends to check on where we stand today (much crime is lower now than in the mid-1990s but about as high as at the beginning of the 1980s, when it was already at unprecedented post-war levels).

Many issues remain the subject of heated public debate, particularly where there is not widespread consensus on what to do about such issues. For example, what should be done about drug prohibition? Does it matter if people speed in their cars (most confess they do, despite under-standing the dangers to themselves and others) or if people pay construc-tion workers cash-in-hand to avoid paying tax? Should we be concerned or intervene if people decide to smoke cigarettes or become involved in sexual practices that might appear 'deviant' in some way? All of these issues raise questions about rules and legal injunctions that circulate in complex and uneven ways in our daily social lives. One of the main roles of this book is to offer insightful and critical profiles of a wide range of problematic, complex and criminal acts and issues to help readers re-think and clarify such problems.

One of the main principles of the disciplined study of crime is to pare back partial impressions and engage robustly with particular forms of criminal behaviour by asking searching questions. Such interests stem from a need to ask about the why, who and how of crime and deviance, to challenge superficial and value-laden arguments and engage with problems and issues that are often contested, complex and demanding – what are the roots of crime and harm and how can we respond to them? The basic point to make here is that there are many forms of rule-breaking, many with dramatic consequences for victims, but there are also questions of social power, bias and the production of harm to individuals, communities and environments that can all too often be ignored where criminologists follow only that which has been defined as criminal by the state (Quinney, 1965). We know that the state has tended to give precedence to property crimes and acts that are destabilising to markets and challenge personal freedoms while neglecting problems of policing, safety and harms to poorer and more marginal communities, for example (Reiner, 2007).

Harmful, deviant or criminal?

Understanding *why* behaviour is banned, legally prohibited or shunned is clearly an important, but also difficult, undertaking. There are few unambiguous answers to these questions and this problem lies at the heart of what is often called the sociology of deviance: to seek answers to the question of why people break social rules and why such rules exist in the first place. Social rule-breaking, the very idea of deviance, has many nuances, 'shades' or variations. This book picks up on a wide range of issues, from nudism and smoking through to homicide, hate crime and violence. While each of these acts is deviant, not all are illegal. Many of the themes we touch on might be judged to be relatively benign and unproblematic (some forms of drug taking or modes of dress, for example). On top of this complexity there are many problems that destroy livelihoods, human bodies and personal opportunities for development but lie outside the domain of the criminal justice, policing and legal systems, and which criminologists describe as harms (which should be turned into criminal acts by the state). Here we can include neglectful toxic waste dumping, dangerous counterfeit drug production or acts of war that may be contested and lead to civilian casualties. Even where such problems are against the law they may not be subject to effective monitoring or sanctions given their complexity or indeed their role in financial or political rewards to governments and the powerful (Hillyard and Tombs, 2007).

A key issue for those who study crime and deviance is the importance of recognising that such issues are socially constructed. What this means is that, while any act can be considered a break from conventional values or rules because of the way it is defined by those that perceive it, there is nothing intrinsic to any act that simply *makes* it a crime (to say that something is a crime because it is illegal does not help us to understand why it has come to be defined in this way). Take cannabis use in Amsterdam and the UK. Where one jurisdiction, Amsterdam, allows the regulated consumption of this substance, we find that in the UK it remains prohibited and those caught using it may be subject to criminal sanction. Such an example shows that in many cases it is not the act that is inherently problematic or self-evidently a crime, because we can observe that at different times and places sanctions and rules do or do not apply.

The idea that deviance is socially constructed and interpreted in these ways adds a great deal of complexity to a range of problems labelled as crimes. This can be seen in debates about how we can go about closely defining issues like harassment, abuse, legitimate violence in war, torture, rape and even murder. Protracted public debates around violence towards prisoners in Abu Ghraib, the question of what constitutes rape provoked by the Julian Assange case or issues of disability hate crime all show that what 'we' feel is problematic cannot be taken for granted. To focus on only one of these examples, we can see that torture has been vigorously defended by many in the UK and USA as a means of securing information to save lives, just as others claim that it reduces the moral mandate of those that use it and is a criminal act. Competing positions and ideas about rule-breaking and crime are regularly tested and debated in public but are also applied in practice by police officers, deliberated over in law courts and may result in individuals being held within a criminal justice system designed to punish people on behalf of the community.

What any community defines as problematic, the state as illegal and communities as transgressive may come to have a dramatic impact on the lives, liberties and life-courses of individuals caught up in these systems of control. The contested nature of criminal conduct can be elaborated using Émile Durkheim's discussion of an imagined community of saints (what he called 'exemplary individuals'). In such a society Durkheim argues that the pettiest of acts would then be judged as crimes and would be treated as such by the community. In this sense we can see how crime is both relative and a persistent feature of social groups and thus even a normal part of social life. On the other hand, such a perspective does help us to recognise that criminals are not an alien group of individuals but are, in fact, other members of our society. However, we may still continue to ask what is an acceptable or tolerable level of crime? Even if crime is declining, should we no longer be worried about violence, for example? It seems likely that most people would disagree, either because they may have a distorted view of the problem of crime by virtue of sensational media coverage or because they recognise the profound cost of physical, financial and other damage that stems from a wide range of acts.

To elaborate on these issues let us turn to the example of homicide for a moment, an act that most will view as self-evidently criminal. Yet things are more complex than this. If extreme provocation is involved the perpetrator may receive a sentence of manslaughter. If they were attacked in their home or killed someone while defending themselves from physical attack they are also unlikely to be seen as murderers, and if the killer is a soldier working for the state, then the killing of an enemy combatant, unless later deemed to have been a war crime, will not be met with punishment (in fact they are more likely to be lauded as heroes) (Currie, 2009). These examples show that even the most extreme use of violence and pain can generate differing responses; there are different 'degrees' of murder in the eyes of the community and judicial systems that depend on complex contextual factors such as a person's intentions, their experiences in particular situations, their mental capacities, their long-term experiences (in the case of abused spouses killing abusive partners) or in the wider political theatre of action (in the case of war). While murder appears to be a self-evident form of extreme deviance that requires dramatic action the reality is more complex.

Following and disobeying social rules

We can find a variety of rules outside the court and beyond the powers of those who police us. It is far from being the case that only laws compel us or encourage us to behave in particular ways. Communities may apply varying sanctions to those deemed to have broken rules. Telling off truanting school children, gossiping, shaming disreputable individuals within the community and asking people to pick up litter are all examples of this. Many aspects of our behaviour and dress are controlled by the social groups we are part of: schoolboys are told to wear their ties correctly; male office workers are required to be clean-shaven; landlords request that their tenants keep their homes tidy; and having coloured or spiky hair may invite public censure by others in the street. Reactions such as these form the basis of complex attempts in daily social life to bring others into the common framework of what is seen to be desirable, civil, appropriate or correct. Such rule systems are remarkably complex and often defy us when we attempt to codify them. We can see that much social control operates at a subtle level which we internalise (this contention is the basis of what is known as 'control theory'): we wear our tie straight because we would see not doing so as breaking convention and do not want to invite the reprimands of our boss; we are civil to other people so as to be seen as a good member of the community; we don't swear in public because we are not that 'kind' of person, and so on.

It is worth thinking about who the 'we' is when I say that *we* don't accept a particular form of behaviour. Are we in fact, to be more accurate, referring to a particular class within society that enjoys particular power over other people's behaviour? Is it a tendency for men or women to dislike something, or are there divisions of taste around age, ethnicity or sexuality that structure the definition of a particular form of rule-breaking? All of these things will be important, but so are particular social and spatial contexts. For example, hand-to-hand fighting is generally frowned upon (again, there are few hard and fast rules here) but we may still admire the skill of pugilists in a boxing ring, and expect to encounter, and take for granted, various forms of violence while at leisure in the night-time economy (Winlow, 2006); the killing of animals for fun is generally considered to be sadistic and worrisome but organised as a fox hunt there are many who enthusiastically support it. Other illustrative examples abound: smoking is now a crime inside a bar in many countries globally but is allowed standing outside (and there are many who would like to criminalise this as well!); shouting in a lecture will mean you are stared at or thrown out; not shouting at a football match may look as if you are 'doing' such a social experience wrongly. Examples such as these show that social structures (such as class and gender), social contexts (the built environment and its design) and social change (in the form of social attitudes and laws) are all involved in denoting a particular act as a deviation from accepted social practices or criminal laws.

Another key feature of deviance is the way that social reactions, whether in the form of public censure, police treatment, media portrayals or the involvement of politicians offering moral sentiments, shape the identity of the person or group who deviates (Presser, 2009). Interesting things appear to happen to people who are persistently defined as offenders by those with the power to wield such labels. Shoplifters, youth offenders and others considered to be beyond the pale of what society deems appropriate may find that such labels further their social exclusion or lead to a defiant reaction around which their deviant identity becomes more entrenched. These processes raise interesting questions about how we can effectively condemn problematic behaviour without deepening it still further, but it seems increasingly clear that even if such processes are not simply about bolstering criminal identities then contact with increasingly punitive criminal justice and prison systems helps generate more violent and excluded inmates.

Another trend over time is for more and more laws to be passed that generate the possibility for more people to be seen as deviant and criminal. This process of criminalisation includes prohibitions around anti-social behaviour, policies that tie the hands of the judiciary ('three strikes' laws, the use of Anti-social Behaviour Orders in the UK), the increasing use of prisons for ever more trivial forms of criminality and the massive proliferation of new laws that create a tendency towards incarceration, the expansion of policing systems and the criminalisation of the poor and minority groups (Simon, 2009). In this respect alone the outlook appears bleak, with a kind of anti-sociological perspective (lacking reference to social and economic conditions and forces) increasingly capturing public debates on what to do about crime in the popular media and political life. Instead of moving towards explanation and the resolution of conditions that fuel crime (inequality, basic poverty and issues around education, employment and housing conditions) the direction of travel is very much the opposite way, and at great speed. Cuts to municipal services, disinvestment in the economy and jobs, threats to almost all sections of welfare spending and stalling national economies continue to generate massive zones of risk and harm to local (usually poorer) communities to whom the 'risk versus reward' calculations of involvement in the illicit drugs trade, shows of masculine violence and forms of theft, resale and counterfeit all become viable or even acceptable methods of existence. Thus crime and deviant behaviour become as it were both the engine and exhaust of societies today (Lea, 2002).

Crime and harm

A point that many critical criminologists seek to make is that a broader interest in the idea of harm and human damage, through violence, neglect, abuse, and conditions and systems that produce such damage, necessarily widens our concern from only looking at things prohibited in law (DeKeseredy, 2012). It is easy to resort to the lazy reasoning that something is wrong because it is designated a crime by the state, but there are many examples of problems that either are not labelled as crimes or are ineffectively policed, but which generate severe human and ecological harm. The great triumph of feminist criminological research has been for societies to begin to take domestic violence and abuse seriously. We now recognise that large numbers of women are damaged physically or killed by violent partners each year and around a quarter of all women experience abuse during their lifetime, and yet this is after so many years in which these problems were sidelined as domestic matters that were not part of the role of the police (Walby and Allen, 2004). Times change, and now we take this issue more seriously

What we might call the 'crimes of the powerful' – money-laundering, insider share dealing, fraud and the manipulation of markets – rarely feature among the state's primary crime concerns, despite possessing the power to be hugely harmful on a global scale. For a whole host of reasons, forceful policing and legal injunctions are comparatively rare, especially when compared with street crime, welfare fraud and other rather more mundane forms of criminal conduct. While part of the reason for this is the real difficulty of pursuing and prosecuting white-collar criminals, there may also be a significant class bias within government and our legal system that problematises crimes against property and considers white-collar and corporate crime to be relatively trivial in comparison (Hillyard and Tombs, 2007).

Critical criminology focuses on the need to contextualise crime, deviance and harm in relation to social forces, structural inequalities and imbalances of power and control (DeKeseredy, 2012). Such criminology is alert to human damage (to bodies, communities, environments, and to human potential) and to violence wherever it exists, drawing criticism towards perpetrators and systems that generate such damage. Living in a growth economy impels us towards the production of armaments for sale without moral equivocation, and it generates irrevocable and unsustainable damage to environments and species and thus to ourselves and to less politically and economically powerful states, societies and communities. Our entirely unsustainable attachment to the current model of economic growth is presided over by a political system that favours an on-going expansion of corporate and military action as new revenue streams are sought and states manoeuvre in preparation for the coming crises in energy and resources (Chapters 47 and 52 are relevant here). Most importantly perhaps these societies are characterised by increasing investment in punishments and control, rather than the resolution of those social and economic contradictions that produce entrenched forms of violent crime and wayward behaviour as well as the harms of poor education, unemployment, malnutrition and exposure to other dangers (Currie, 2009; Young, 1999).

Critical criminology alerts us to these structural and persistent conditions and forces us to remove our blinkers and acknowledge how we ourselves are located within a system that is violent on a number of levels. Many societies tacitly, or sometimes overtly, support the use of violence against women. They are aggressive economic units involved in on-going, low-intensity wars for resources globally, they tolerate some despots while destroying others, they encourage extraction of natural resources along a headlong pathway to global misery and destruction and, not least, they take delight in representations of crime and violence as the very mainstay of their entertainment systems. Daily life is replete with news, books, Hollywood films and video games that offer us the repeated imagining and observation of assault, torture, human terror, sudden death, humiliation and bodily destruction (Presdee, 2000).

The remit of criminology expands when we realise that we must not ignore the multiple layers of harm and damage that occur in daily social life but are not captured by the term 'crime' or legal rules. To the extent that we acknowledge such harms we are drawn to analyse new patterns that tended to be sidelined in the past. We need to understand how such forces act to increase human and community insecurity, from the increasing use of prisons to the failure of drug prohibition (even as the middle classes and elites swallow such goods themselves, enjoy the profits of industries set up to repress 'evil' drug gangs or run banks that launder the profits of drug cartels). Financial services have similarly allowed corporations to reduce essential tax burdens needed to provide effective policing and health agencies capable of reducing harm in societies. Thus such acts can be viewed as crimes to the extent that tax evasion has the indirect effect of starving public support for family life, health and education and other forms of social insurance that militate against excessive inequality or the risks of ill health or unemployment that are themselves major motors of criminal enterprises.

Criminologists are interested in the mainstream problems of how crime might be reduced, controlled or softened, but also in offering something useful to communities by proffering explanations of and insights into why people become involved in genuinely harmful acts. Locking up or putting to death those who have gone on an orgy of killing may be an understandable response, but more important is how we can understand and seek to prevent atrocities in the future. It is this desire to contextualise and understand crime and harm that binds together the diverse contributions in this volume.

Bibliography

Cohen, S. (1998) *Against Criminology*, London: Transaction Publishers.

Currie, E. (2009) *The Roots of Danger: Violent Crime in Global Perspective*, Columbus, OH: Prentice Hall.

DeKeseredy, W. (2012) *Critical Criminology*, Abingdon: Routledge.

Downes, D. and Rock, P. (2011) *Understanding Deviance: A Guide to the Sociology of Crime and Rule-breaking*, Oxford: Oxford University Press.

Elliott, E. (1985) *Confronting Crime: an American Challenge*, New York: Random House.

Hillyard, P. and Tombs, S. (2007) From 'Crime' to Social Harm? *Crime, Law and Social Change*, 48, 1–2, pp. 9–25.

Lea, J. (2002) *Crime and Modernity: Continuities in Left Realist Criminology*, London: SAGE.

Presdee, M. (2000) *Cultural Criminology and the Carnival of Crime*, London: Routledge.

Presser, L. (2009) The Narratives of Offenders, *Theoretical Criminology*, 13, (2), pp. 177–200.

Quinney, R. (1965) Is Criminal Behaviour Deviant Behaviour? *British Journal of Criminology*, 5, (2), pp. 132–42.

Reiner, R. (2007) *Law and Order: an Honest Citizen's Guide to Crime and Control*, Cambridge: Polity.

Shanafelt, R. and Pino, N. (2012) Evil and the Common Life: towards a Wider Perspective on Serial Killing and Atrocities, in Winlow, S. and

R. Atkinson (Eds) *New Directions in Crime and Deviancy*, Abingdon: Routledge, pp. 252–73.

Simon, J. (2009) *Governing through Crime: How the War on Crime Transformed American Democracy and Created a Culture of Fear*, Oxford: Oxford University Press.

Walby, S. and Allen, J. (2004) *Domestic Violence, Sexual Assault and Stalking*, London: HMSO.

Winlow, S. (2006) *Violent Night: Urban Leisure and Contemporary Culture*, London: Berg.

Young, J. (1999) *The Exclusive Society*, London: SAGE.

PART I

Acts of transgression

This opening section deals with a range of behaviours and issues that cross social conventions, codes and laws in general terms. These issues range from those that would be unlikely to raise public concern and yet which are, in particular locations or social contexts, designated as beyond the law or social convention (such as jaywalking and nudism) to others which, like vandalism and cheating, generate deeper concerns and stronger responses because they cross widely held public beliefs about what is damaging or fair. All of the acts here are considered more or less problematic, depending on the social, economic, cultural, ethnic and national contexts in which they occur. Perhaps more importantly debates about the legality or acceptability of certain behaviours, such as prostitution and public street protests, demonstrate how deviant behaviour is generated in large part by the social reaction of groups and individuals who are witness to it. Protest is not a crime, nor is it illegal (in many national contexts), but it receives highly varied local and specific responses in line with what policing agencies and politicians deem to be the right response.

This section then highlights a major theme within studies of social deviance: that such behaviour is often tolerated and the subject of arguments and contests between social groups with more or less power and interest in the legality or desirability of particular acts. So the chapters here focus on behaviours that may not always be illegal but which some-times do receive criminal or police sanctions in order to control a sense of appropriateness, civility or notions of shared decency and respectabil-ity. So in the case of vandalism we find examples of damage to property that offend or worry some people while taking on the status of acts that excite or bring status to those within the groups that perform them. Similarly young people loitering may be seen as an indicator of social disorder and something that generates anxiety, while being a logical response by often very bored young people. So this is not to say that these issues are harmless or trivial, but rather that we need to focus on the deeper complexity and forces that some see as criminal and others as relatively benign conduct.

1

JAYWALKING

Gareth Millington

To jaywalk is to step into the road at a point other than a designated pedestrian crossing or, if starting from a crossing, to step out without the go-ahead from an automated 'WALK' signal. The offence originates in the USA, where jaywalking is deemed to be an unlawful act, although crossing the road 'inappropriately' is also a crime in Australia, parts of the Asia Pacific, Poland and Singapore (where you may even be unlucky enough to receive a three-month prison sentence). Yet even in the US restrictions diverge between states, with penalties varying considerably and different cities regulating jaywalking with differing levels of intensity. Los Angeles, for example, is known to take jaywalking very seriously and fines are common, whereas the New York Police Department have tended historically to adopt a more lenient approach. Even Rudolph Giuliani's diktat to clamp down on minor incivilities in the late 1990s failed to motivate police officers to penalise the legions of New Yorkers historically resistant to the tyranny of automotive traffic. In fact it was still so rare to be caught jaywalking that a *New York Times* article from 1998 began with the sardonic announcement that 'A jaywalking ticket has been issued in New York City'. Yet while jaywalking appears to be a pedestrian crime – in more ways than one – it owes its existence to one of the most significant urban conflicts of the twentieth century, the struggle for the street between pedestrians and motorists.

The word originates from the Midwest. It is a compound term, from the word 'jay', referring to a naive country person, out of place in the city, and 'walk'. The inference was that 'jaywalkers' were more accustomed to cutting across fields and strolling down lanes and lacked the savvy to know how to walk in the city. As Peter D. Norton (2007: 342) explains, the first public appearance of jaywalking was in the *Chicago Tribune* in 1909, where an article claimed that the new craze for 'pleasure driving' motor vehicles in the city would cause little harm were it not for careless pedestrians who stepped in the way of automobiles and caused accidents. Despite its insulting etymology, the subsequent criminalisation of jaywalking can now be seen as pivotal in the transformation of the American city from a centripetal space dominated by verticality and density to a sprawling, inhuman space characterised by vast highways and dispersed suburbs. As Clay McShane explains in *Down the Asphalt Path: the Automobile and the American City*, there was considerable accord between wealthy motorists and city planners who regarded the car as the basis of a more ordered city and realtors who realised that automobility increased suburban property values.

At the beginning of the twentieth century city streets in the US were shared by a variety of users including pedestrians, horse-drawn vehicles, pushcart vendors and children at play. Automobiles disrupted the tacit street order achieved by these users and it was the car – or 'devil wagon' – that was initially considered to be out of place. In poorer city neighbourhoods that lacked parks and playgrounds, residents objected fiercely to the presence of automobiles and attacks on motorists and their vehicles were not uncommon. As McShane (1994: 177) explains, at the sharp end of the battle between pedestrians and automobile owners there were clear overtones of class warfare. Although the legitimacy of the presence of motor cars on public streets was vigorously questioned, their obvious speed and power made people cautious about crossing the street or allowing their children to play there. In the early decades of the century, pedestrians found sympathy in high places, as authorities, judges and juries became concerned about the increased risk of being injured by cars. There was also indignation that city folk, especially children, were forced to relinquish an important aspect of their freedom of movement. As such many cities imposed pre-motor age speed limits of eight or nine miles per hour or laid brick-built speed bumps across streets in order to slow down 'speed maniacs' or 'joy riders'.

If cars were to legitimate their dominance over urban streets then the streets themselves had to be recast in the popular imagination as thoroughfares for motor vehicles. It had to be demonstrated that pedestrians, children and horses lacked any special claim to the street. An important part of the ideological battle taken on by the American Automobile Association and National Automobile Chamber of Commerce was the education of pedestrians in the new art of 'road safety'. The belief of these associations was that pedestrians injured in collisions with cars were rarely innocent victims. The obfuscation of the central conflict between pedestrians and motorists under the more inclusive rubric of 'road safety' was shrewd in that it offered a rebuttal to suspicions that it was motorists rather than pedestrians who were acting irresponsibly. It was the dissemination – often in schools – of information on the dangers of jaywalking and the public construction of the reckless jaywalker that were crucial in shifting public opinion. As Norton (2007: 350) explains, it was Los Angeles that led the way, supporting both legal measures that enhanced the rights of motorists and the implementation of technical devices such as crossings that restricted the freedom of pedestrians. The Los Angeles Police Department even discovered that rather than fining jaywalkers it was more effective if they brought attention to their deviant behaviour by blowing whistles, thereby heaping public shame on 'irresponsible' pedestrians. The automobile lobby also appealed to modernity. They argued that the presence of automobiles on streets was an indication of progress, growing societal affluence and American society's reasonable preference for private rather than public forms of transport. The automobile and motor age street, they claimed, were here to stay.

The contradiction at the heart of jaywalking between the rights of pedestrians and those of motorists continues to reveal the pernicious influence of class (and 'race') in urban America. In April 2010 in Atlanta an African-American woman named Raquel Nelson was convicted and sentenced to three years for 'vehicular homicide'. Having returned from a lengthy two-bus trip to Wal-Mart laden with groceries and facing an additional half-mile walk to cross at a marked crossing, Nelson and her three children crossed a five-lane highway in order to get from the bus stop to their housing complex on the other side of the road. As they crossed Nelson's 4-year-old son was tragically killed in a collision with a drunk driver who had three previous hit-and-run charges. Astonishingly the driver received a lesser sentence than Nelson, just six months. Despite the century-long dominance of the automobile in urban planning it should not be forgotten that many people cannot afford cars or choose not to pollute the environment. Instead they rely on public transport and often live in housing severed from amenities by massive highways that contain minimal crosswalks for fear they might interrupt and slow the traffic. Just as at the start of the twentieth century, jaywalking continues to offer a perilous form of conflict between people and machines in the streets.

References

McShane, C. (1994) *Down the Asphalt Path: the Automobile and the American City*, New York: Columbia University Press.

Norton, P. D. (2007) Street Rivals: Jaywalking and the Invention of the Motor Age Street, *Technology and Culture*, 48, (2), pp. 331–59.

Watch:

Man with a Movie Camera (1929), documentary film, directed by Dziga Vertov. Soviet Union: VUFKU.

2

PROSTITUTION

Teresa Degenhardt

Prostitution refers to exchanging sexual activities for money. The ways that sex is sold and bought encompass myriad acts, people and places, but this complexity is often denied in society at large, with suppressed moralities producing dystopian views. Although often associated with women selling sex to men, of course men can sell sex to other men and to women; transsexuals can sell and buy sex as well. However, the majority of prostitutes are female and the majority of users are male. Thus, the practice of selling sex for money has to be read against women's social and economic positioning in different countries.

Although prostitution used to be considered the form of deviance par excellence for women, unlike other forms of deviance, it is 'accepted' – an acceptance evident in its being referred to as 'the oldest profession'. Even today, women may capitalise on their bodies to enter the job market or to make a good marriage, but may not do so in exchange for money. In the latter case, they become 'deviant', 'immoral' or 'victims'. Women are generally expected to enter stable heterosexual relationships and have children; prostitutes are deviants from the traditional role of women as wives and mothers. And yet, this deviance is inextricably linked to the ways women are constituted as essentially 'bodies' and essentially 'accessible'. Thus, prostitution represents both a form of deviance and the paradigm upon which female sexuality is built and regulated.

Apart from the gender dimension, there are two other crucial aspects to consider when analysing prostitution. One is the marketisation of society, whereby human bodies (and sex) have become valuable commodities in a consumer society; the other is that sex has traditionally been regarded as a private, albeit central, characteristic of human subjectivities. These factors have made prostitution a moral problem – a simplistic (and dystopian) way to approach the issue. It stigmatises sex workers, enabling their further exploitation; as deviants, they are ostracised from society, thus much more likely to accept protection from pimps and criminal organisations, and far less safe.

Prostitution is most often associated with its most visible form: street prostitution. But prostitution can be managed elsewhere in more formal locales, including flats or organised brothels, hotels, saunas and bars. It can be advertised as various kinds of services, such as 'body massage', through the media and on the Internet. Economically, it can be quite lucrative, as in the case of escort services, a section of the market which often involves higher income clients, or poorly paid, as in the cases of drug addicts and undocumented migrants, who are arguably among the most vulnerable. At one end of the spectrum, some women say they have used their earnings to pay their university fees. At the other, the vulnerable section of the market is poorly paid and often subjected to violence by clients, but also by the police and by some sections of the general public who may abuse them when they see them on the streets. What is often missing in the depiction of sex workers is that their vulnerability is not due to this peculiar job, but to the conditions in which they work.

By and large, selling and buying sex is regulated by four different policy models: regulationism, decriminalisation, legalisation and prohibition. These models, which are rarely applied in their pure forms, reflect how prostitution is conceptualised within particular national cultures and reveal the power of a country's lobbying groups (Matthews, 2008). For instance, in the UK, prostitution itself is not a crime, but many related activities are criminalised (regulationism), including soliciting, loitering, kerb crawling (approaching other people from or near a vehicle for the purpose of prostitution), paying somebody who is subjected to force to provide sexual services and formally running a brothel. In the Netherlands and Germany sex work is legal; sex workers pay taxes and enjoy a number of rights such as pensions, health insurance and unemployment benefits (legalisation and regulationism); in other countries such as Sweden, Norway and Iceland, such work is illegal, but clients may be fined or arrested (prohibitionism).

Interestingly, opposing policies have been promoted by feminist groups. Some feminists support regulative policies, arguing that women who work in the industry should have their rights protected. Others argue that prostitution constitutes a form of violence against women and should not be allowed. Indeed, prostitution is a divisive issue. Some see it as the symbol of women's subordination and victimisation in a patriarchal society. Others say the regulation of prostitution is a form of sanctioning alternative desires and lifestyles in accordance with a prevailing bourgeois morality (Phoenix, 2013), with bad effects on those working in the field. While the former view links prostitution to trafficking and sexual exploitation, either criminalising women or portraying them as victims, the latter perspective understands migrant sex workers as agents searching for a better life in a strongly unequal world (Augustin, 2007). In this latter view, migrant sex workers' vulnerability is due not so much to their current working practices as to prior forms of exclusion such as the state's exclusionary citizenship and working policies. The crucial issue for these different views is whether it is better for women to fight prostitution as a patriarchal institution which contributes to maintaining women's subjugation, or to side with women from economically disadvantaged countries who are working in the sex trade as a way to improve their lives.

References

Augustin, L. (2007) *Sex at the Margins: Migration, Labour Markets and the Rescue Industry*, New York: Palgrave.

Matthews, R. (2008) *Prostitution, Politics and Policy*, Abingdon: Routledge.

Phoenix, J. (2013) Sex Work, Sexual Exploitations and Consumerism, in K. Carrington, M. Ball, E. O'Brien, and J. Tauri (eds) *Crime, Justice and Social Democracy*, New York: Palgrave Macmillan.

Watch:

Vivre Sa Vie (1962), film, directed by Jean-Luc Godard. France: Panthéon.

3

NUDITY

Rowland Atkinson

The naked human body provides a rich area for discussions of social deviance and a useful means of identifying the way that sanctions are shaped by cultures, historical eras and specific contexts. Before we consider these issues we should note an important distinction. Nudity broadly refers to the act of being publicly naked; naturism, on the other hand, takes nudity as part of a broader philosophy in which individuals and groups adopt particular attitudes to dress and to social life that see nudity as desirable and authentic. Today British Naturism, the representative body in the UK, claims that there are four million naturists in the UK.

The casting of naturism as a form of deviance, given over-simplified associations with eroticism or exhibitionism and breaking of conventions around the wearing of clothes, misplaces the aims of those involved in this lifestyle. For one thing naturism is fundamentally about a freeing from such regulations and, far from being concerned with erotic practices or sexual availability, underlines a concern with a simpler lifestyle, a return to nature and healthier forms of unrestricted living. Yet public nudity raises anxiety, the designation of illegality because of social conventions about dress and the presentation of sexual organs in public, and is generally deemed to be inappropriate, sexually arousing or alarming (Andriotis, 2010). Such responses are matched by legal prohibitions in most countries that make nudity a criminal offence that may attract arrest, a fine in court and even a prison sentence, though this tends to be in relation to the specific offence of indecent exposure (exposure of the genitals with the intent to shock).

Naturism has an established history with nudist beaches, hotels and resorts going back in some countries to the late nineteenth century. Yet the jokey treatment of nudist 'colonies' (some may remember Peter Sellers carrying a strategically placed guitar in a nudist colony while investigating in one of the *Pink Panther* movies) and continued innuendoes and levity around the subject suggest that most cultures view such liberated conduct as a form of mild deviance, yet one that does not invite censure, primarily because it tends to take place in self-regulated or domestic settings (Schrank, 2012). Status and sexuality are encoded in our clothing and naturists seek to move away from these cultural codes (see Chapter 13); the term 'textilist' has been used by naturists to refer to those who are non-naturists. Dressing behind towels on beaches is a common sign that many naturists view as an indication of prudery and perhaps the idiocy of social rules that force a modesty and unnecessary control of our public lives. From the naturist perspective the majority of people are thus locked into modes of dress and self-presentation that are divorced from our relationship to nature.

Nudity raises interesting questions about modes of dress, fashion and highly gendered assumptions about what is appropriate or acceptable within society. This can be seen very clearly in religious strictures around the degree to which the (almost always female) body should be clothed. New debates in some European countries have questioned rules like the wearing of the hijab, seen by some as emancipation from the gaze of men and an important tradition, and by others as a form of repressive dress code imposed by men and an alienating mode of dress given common modes of dress in European cities. These complex examples highlight the social, cultural, gendered and traditional rule structures that deeply influence how we dress ourselves in public and private spaces.

Context plays an important role in determining social reactions to public nudity. For example, while the *Puppetry of the Penis* stage show has been a huge success in theatres the exposure of one's genitals in a public park would be likely to end in an arrest or, at the least, public alarm. Similarly nudity during organised yoga sessions, in the theatre or during political demonstrations and consciousness-raising activities (naked cycling runs), do not generally attract censure (Carr-Gorm, 2012).

A range of other issues can be connected to the issue of nudism as a form of social deviance. People 'dogging' public sexual exhibitionists have gained attention in recent years, yet even here clear rules are shared within such groups (including taking home any litter). Mooning, the act of exposing one's buttocks, has long been associated with showing disrespect, though it is also done for fun or to generate a shock response in 'respectable' audiences. Skinny dipping seems to be an activity that many non-self-proclaimed nudists enjoy as fun in its own right and as a slightly risqué experiment in social conventions that can feel liberating. Streaking, on the other hand, refers to the humorous tradition at some sports events in which an individual quickly strips and runs on to a sports field or court. On a very different level we have seen the use of imposed nudity on US prisoners of war to humiliate and demotivate those involved (notably the pictures that emerged at the Abu Ghraib facility in Iraq).

Toplessness highlights how even modes of partial undress, specifically in relation to women, raise controversy among both men and women. Some beaches permit toplessness among women (with some groups of women campaigning against the double standard and implicit deviance assumed in codes that forbid such practices) while the 'Page Three' phenomenon of a topless model appearing daily in *The Sun* newspaper continues to arouse significant controversy and disagreement between those who see it as a casualised form of sexual representation and those who see it as something akin to a tradition. Partial nudity can be placed within broader social debates about what constitutes erotic or sexualised forms of bodily display: debates about nakedness in proliferating strip clubs, the meaning of emancipated forms of conduct given the clear sexual interest and profits to be derived from such activities and questions about the boundaries of pornography and artistic appreciation. Such debates continue to be a minefield of moral opinion, sexual politics and corporate influence, with even the topic of public breastfeeding generating on-going disagreement.

References

Andriotis, K. (2010) Heterotopic Erotic Oases: The Public Nude Beach Experience, *Annals of Tourism Research*, 37, (4), pp. 1076–96.

Carr-Gorm, A. (2012) *A Brief History of Nakedness*, London: Reaktion.

Schrank, S. (2012) Naked Houses: The Architecture of Nudism and the Rethinking of the American Suburbs, *Journal of Urban History*, 38, (4), pp. 635–61.

Watch:

Naked States (2000), film, directed by Arlene Nelson. USA: HBO.

4

BEGGING

Philippa Tomczak

Begging can be defined as the act of requesting money from passers-by in a public place, without offering a service in return (Fitzpatrick and Kennedy, 2001). Since begging is widespread across cities globally, it may be accepted as a normal aspect of everyday urban life. In fact, begging is a symbol of social exclusion that merits attention. While people who beg are often reviled and seen as deviating from what is considered acceptable in public spaces, they are frequently victims themselves: of crime, of economic deprivation and of social exclusion more broadly.

Modern moral panics in which a disproportionate reaction to begging has resulted have tended to be focused on two key themes: the idea of the *aggressive* beggar and that of the *bogus* beggar (Fitzpatrick and Kennedy, 2001). Regarding the former, begging is seen as requiring regulation; the very presence of beggars here is seen to frighten or intimidate the 'respectable' public and beggars themselves are cast as threatening, violent, aggressive and abusive individuals (Walsh, 2004b; Hopkins Burke, 2000).

Although clearly undesirable and widely perceived to be a significant problem by the 'respectable' public, such aggressive begging appears to be seldom directly experienced by members of the public (Fitzpatrick and Kennedy, 2001), appearing to highlight a need to control those who do not fit conventional models of street life. Newspapers tend to focus on cases in which beggars may be bogus or fraudulent, preying on the gullibility of the public in order to earn 'easy money' – appearing to be in desperate need but faking disabilities; or they may have a home and claim benefits whilst using the proceeds of begging to buy drink and drugs, or may even be part of an organised begging ring (Walsh, 2004a; Fitzpatrick and Kennedy, 2001). There is, however, little empirical evidence to suggest that begging is a particularly lucrative way of life, or that it is experienced as a pleasant activity.

Those who beg are usually destitute, often having complex needs and a general background of deprivation and vulnerability (Walsh, 2004a; Fitzpatrick and Kennedy, 2001), with substance misuse problems common. Clear links thus exist between begging and homelessness, economic deprivation and social exclusion while social and familial support is often minimal. People who beg tend to report that they find it extremely humiliating and degrading, yet necessary to cover basic living costs. Such choices can also generate serious dangers, with beggars being at high risk of victimisation from both their associates and other members of society. Far from being a lucrative lifestyle choice, begging is in the vast majority of cases a *last resort* that generates intense humiliation and anxiety.

Whilst many police officers have a tolerant attitude to beggars, begging has at times been vigorously targeted through zero tolerance policing strategies, with the intention of 'cleaning up' the streets. The act of begging is technically an offence under the 1824 Vagrancy Act in England and Wales. More recent provisions (e.g. the Anti-social Behaviour Act 2003, the Crime and Disorder Act 1998) may also be used to control beggars and many cities in the USA have strict anti-begging laws and ordinances that make street homelessness difficult or impossible.

The rationale for such policing is based on the 'broken windows' thesis. This suggests that failure to check and control minor acts of deviance in a community (such as begging, graffiti, vandalism and public drunkenness) may ultimately result in increased criminal activity. High levels of these relatively minor incivilities can also lead to members of the community avoiding certain areas and types of people, or avoiding going out at night. As a result, the reduced number of capable guardians may exacerbate crime in such communities. Failure to check and control incivilities in a community can therefore give rise to the commission of more serious crimes in that community (Walsh, 2004a; Hopkins Burke, 2000).

However, the effectiveness and legitimacy of zero tolerance initiatives that target beggars is questionable. Such policies target and effectively criminalise some of the most deprived and disadvantaged members of society for the crime of being visibly poor and homeless, only displacing them to another area. The criminalisation and incarceration of beggars comes at great expense to the taxpayer while providing no solutions to the causal health, welfare and social problems of poverty that generate these problems in the first place.

Begging appears to challenge conventional social rules about how public space should be used and this sometimes generates anxiety or a sense of nuisance. Restricting access to public spaces or criminalising begging is increasingly considered necessary to protect the interests of the public, whose activities may be disturbed, or the interests of businesses, whose trade may be disrupted.

Yet the uncomfortable response of society at large belies the fact that such acts are generated by desperation, poverty and intense social marginality. People who resort to begging do so out of desperation as well as retaining legitimate human rights and interests – they are amongst the most disadvantaged and vulnerable of citizens and are worthy of tolerance and compassionate consideration.

References

Fitzpatrick, S. and Kennedy, C. (2001) The Links between Begging and Rough Sleeping: A Question of Legitimacy?, *Housing Studies*, 16, (5), pp. 549–68.

Hopkins Burke, R. (2000) The Regulation of Begging and Vagrancy: A Critical Discussion, *Crime Prevention and Community Safety*, 2, (2), pp. 43–51.

Walsh, T. (2004a) Defending Begging Offenders, *Queensland University of Technology Law and Justice Journal*, 4, (1), pp. 58–76.

Walsh, T. (2004b) Who Is the Public in Public Space?, *Alternative Law Journal*, 29, (2), pp. 81–6.

Watch:

Trading Places (1983), film, directed by John Landis. USA: Paramount Pictures.

5

CHEATING

Oliver Smith

> **Cheat:** *[no object]* act dishonestly or unfairly in order to gain an advantage: *she always* **cheats at** *cards. [with object]* gain an advantage over or deprive of something by using unfair or deceitful methods; defraud: *he had* **cheated** *her* **out of** *everything she had.*
>
> *(Oxford English Dictionary)*

The concept of cheating can be connected to concerns with crime and deviance on a number of levels. The central idea at the heart of common definitions of cheating is the notion of breaking commonly accepted social or game rules in order to gain an advantage unfairly. Accusations of cheating have been levelled across the class spectrum. For example, tabloid newspapers regularly call for neighbours to turn in those considered to be benefit cheats (see Chapter 29), while public outrage at fraudulent accounting practices has been focused on professionals in the upper echelons of major corporations (see also Chapters 31 and 50). Similarly condemnation of cheating now involves rule-breaking global brands who are commonly lambasted as 'tax cheats' for employing tactics designed to avoid paying large amounts of corporation tax in the United Kingdom. This chapter focuses on two examples of cheating: that found in sport and the rise of the market in student cheating in universities.

The revelations of cheating by the seven times winner of the Tour de France, Lance Armstrong, highlight many of the personal and cultural issues surrounding deviance within sport. His fall from grace was an undignified affair, culminating in an admission of guilt on live television. Rumours of doping – using performance enhancing drugs to gain an unfair advantage over other competitors – had been circulating since the late 1990s, though these were vigorously denied. For a long time it appeared that Armstrong, a cancer survivor, philanthropist and sporting idol, was untouchable. His elevation to global fame came on the back of a return from serious illness to global domination of his sport. His involvement with the Livestrong Foundation ensured that he transcended the world of cycling, with further rewards from promotions via Nike sponsorship, Hollywood cameos and charity work.

In the presence of Oprah Winfrey, Armstrong confessed he had embarked on a decade of performance enhancing drug use involving teammates, doctors on the payroll of the team and the complicit involvement of a number of major figures in cycling, in a case that threatened to puncture the sport in its marketable and corporatised ascendancy. Perhaps most interesting of all, he claimed that after looking up a definition of the word 'cheat' he felt that the word did not describe his actions.

Several criminological concepts might help us to understand Armstrong's actions. First, the promise of fame and fortune point towards an explanation of cheating wherein social actors feel a sense of strain that develops between their current position and the culturally proscribed goods or status positions they would like to achieve in life. Theorists like Merton (1938) would perhaps suggest that for Armstrong to achieve the cultural goals of wealth, fame and influence, he had to innovate in response to these pressures. Second, we might look to the work of Sykes and Matza (1957) who might look to his 'Oprah' interview as evidence of somebody seeking to deny that they broke the rules (the denial of his responsibility); Armstrong before this had been guilty of denying that he had victimised those who had quizzed him about his doping. In short, for Sykes and Matza figures like Armstrong are regularly involved in deploying techniques that help to neutralise the sense that they have done wrong (I did it to create a level playing field, I didn't hurt anybody else in doing this).

However, a full consideration of cheating in sport benefits from thinking about the processes that motivate individuals to cheat. Here we might suggest that success comes as a result of being acknowledged by a communal network of social institutions, customs and laws. It is not enough for us to know that we are a great athlete; this fact must be recognized by this broader network of others who will confirm our status to us. This becomes achievable through the accumulation of gold medals, yellow jerseys and lucrative sponsorship contracts; through interviews on Sky Sports and the accumulation of high profile intimate partners.

Let us turn to the issue of cheating in universities and the revelation in 2012 that half of the students enrolled on a politics course at Harvard University had cheated. This case served to illustrate a growing issue facing lecturers and students; the subjection of universites to market forces has radically altered the landscape of higher education (see Chapter 46). For students, learning has become less of a journey of exploration and has taken on an element of hard-nosed instrumentalism. Increasingly the emphasis has shifted onto employability and universities strive to ensure that students leave with a set of transferable skills, a shift mirrored by the student approach to learning, where anything without a direct correlate to discernable practical outcomes is dismissed as boring or irrelevant.

The combination of market imperatives and bureaucratically defined targets has been described as symptomatic of 'market Stalinism'. Fee-paying students are rapidly morphing into customers, whereupon the balance of power changes and sanctions or threat of exclusion lose their teeth. Gaining a degree becomes a commodity purchased like any other, and the notion of 'reading' for a degree becomes increasingly divorced from student expectations. In short, higher education becomes increasingly about the destination, and less about the journey, so it should come as no surprise that for many the prospect of cheating makes practical sense and is conceived of as a kind of outsourcing by already capable students who do not see themselves as cheats.

The past decade has witnessed the emergence of two markets: that which provides students with increasingly sophisticated or bespoke forms of cheating, and the market in software and surveillance in order to identify cases of academic cheating. The first element of these burgeoning markets is represented by 'essay mills', companies offering bespoke essays to university students for a price. Students submit their assignment question and receive an original piece of work which they are then able to pass off as their own work. On the other hand, educational establishments are able to purchase myriad counter-plagiarism and anti-cheating services, resulting in a complex game of cat and mouse. Explanations focused on the acts of individual students fail to capture the fact that the benefits of cheating now outweigh the possible sanctions imposed by institutions more worried about the receipt of fees than condemning or searching out malpractice. Thus a pervasive encroachment of consumer capitalism reduces the level of prohibitions within the social order.

Cheating in sport and in student life reveals complex shifts in what is considered to be acceptable or problematic conduct. Economic and social forces have reshaped institutions and the goals of social actors, and generated the sense that all is permitted in trying to get ahead. Criminologists need to explore deviance from the starting point of these broader structural and cultural issues that profoundly affect individuals' propensity to engage in such behaviours.

References

Merton, R. K. (1938) Social Structure and Anomie, *American Sociological Review*, 3, (5), pp. 672–82.

Sykes, G. and Matza, D. (1957) Techniques of Neutralization: A Theory of Delinquency, *American Sociological Review*, 22, (6), pp. 664–70.

Watch:

Cheats (2002), film, directed by Andrew Gurland. USA: New Line Cinema.

6

LOITERING

Michael Puniskis

When an individual remains stationary in a particular public place for a period of time, with no apparent aim or purpose, such as sitting on a bench in the park or standing around waiting for a friend, this is generally acceptable behaviour. However, if one engages in the same activity with a few friends, perhaps hanging around in a car park or outside a store, then such group behaviour can transform an apparently benign act into something socially unacceptable – hanging about becomes the more suspect loitering, depending on the particular context. In some jurisdictions, especially in the case of the United States and United Kingdom, such acts have increasingly become prohibited under laws, as the arrestable misdemeanour offence of loitering, in which the violator is known as a loiterer. Consequently, engaging in this illegal activity may be punishable by fines, jail time, probation, community service or other sanctioning methods. In turn, new loitering laws have provided police with additional powers for controlling anti-social behaviour, which in some instances have been abused by discriminatory forms of policing and, in certain cases, have been deemed unlawful by the High Court.

Historically, contemporary anti-loitering laws can be traced back to medieval England, when statutes were enacted to ban what was perceived to be a growing public nuisance at that time – vagrancy. Otherwise known as 'vagabonds', 'beggars', 'wanderers' or 'hobos', among other names, these were people who, although often living in poverty, were otherwise capable of working; however some refused to do so or were unable to find work, and instead relied on the gratitude of others essentially to 'get by' and earn a living. Such behaviour and respective laws prohibiting this began to emerge following the Black Death bubonic plague pandemic, which devastated Europe in 1348, killing between 75 and 200 million people, including a third to a half of England's population. In the aftermath, countries struggled with floundering economies supported by limited manpower. In response, England began to create statutes specifically aimed at increasing the workforce, and therefore made a new offence for anyone who 'idled', refused to work or was otherwise unemployed; they were punished by branding, whipping or required military service. Centuries later, vagrancy laws similar to those of the English began to emerge in the United States, beginning in the eighteenth century; however these were even more vague and covered a wide range of deviancy and crimes. For example, anti-loitering laws were often used to break up protests during the Civil Rights era. Over the years, however, a number of these laws have been challenged and even overturned.

Today, anti-loitering laws are essentially means for controlling social behaviour, which give police the discretionary legal power to arrest anyone refusing to 'move along', if they are reasonably considered to be causing a public annoyance, danger or harm to nearby people or property. In some jurisdictions, an individual can also be charged with loitering if he/she is unable adequately to justify his/her presence, refuses or fails to provide identification if requested by police, or immediately flees the scene. For example, if a group of friends leave a social venue such as a pub or theatre and spend a few minutes chatting on the sidewalk with each other before dispersing, while this would technically be considered loitering, this activity would be unlikely to be penalised, given the existing circumstances. Of course, many people may have engaged, or may regularly engage, in such behaviour. However, if the group continued to congregate and socialise, becoming boisterous and disruptive to the quality of life in the immediate area, the police might eventually be called; they would then have the legal authority to order the group to disperse to a more appropriate venue or risk facing a fine or being taken into custody. The same rules apply to other forms of legitimate sidewalk activity; for example, street vendors during daytime hours who, although they may otherwise be calm and respectful, through their mere presence may obstruct sidewalks and therefore be considered to be loitering with no valid licence.

Interestingly, one can also be accused of loitering on the suspicions of another person.

In the United States, anti-loitering laws have been legally challenged many times over the years through a number of landmark cases, such as *City of Chicago* v. *Morales* (1999). This notable case involved Jesus Morales, who had been one of 42,000 individuals who were prosecuted and found guilty in 1993 in violation of Chicago's Gang Congregation Ordinance, which had been established only a year earlier to give police officers authority to order anyone to disperse from a particular area where an officer reasonably believed the person to be a gang member. Having been arrested in a city neighbourhood after ignoring orders from the police to disperse, Morales challenged his arrest, which eventually reached the Illinois Appellate Court, where only two of the eleven trial judges upheld the ordinance's constitutionality. In addition, the case was subsequently affirmed by both the Illinois Supreme Court and the United States Supreme Court, on the grounds that the Chicago ordinance had violated the Due Process Clause of the Fourteenth Amendment of the United States Constitution, stating that the law was an arbitrary restriction on personal liberties and so impermissibly vague in its wording that a person of ordinary intelligence would be unable to make a distinction between innocent versus illegal activity, as in the case of loitering (see Livingston, 1999 and Poulos, 1995 for further commentary).

Generally, however, loitering laws are often used to control and prevent potentially more serious forms of crime and deviance. Especially with regard to young people, anti-loitering ordinances are regularly implemented, for example to keep youths from congregating either in certain public areas during evening hours (which may disturb or alarm those in nearby homes and businesses) or in areas prone to crime, such as parks during night-time. In other situations, loitering laws are typically used, particularly in high crime areas, to deal with a number of troublesome public behaviours such as aggressive begging, public drunkenness, blocking of sidewalks, roadways or store entries, drug dealing, soliciting prostitution, street gambling, gang activities, intimidation and other behaviours that may be a nuisance to the public. These behaviours may include prowling, wandering around, yelling obscenities or even singing and being masked, disguised or unusually dressed with others in public. While police deal with many of these problematic behaviours, many business owners and shopkeepers also take an active role in processes of informal monitoring and loitering prevention, through signage placed outside their establishments prohibiting such activity. This is often done in order to prevent congregations of young people who are seen as potentially discouraging customers and thus negatively affecting sales.

References

City of Chicago v. *Morales*, 527 U.S. 41 (1999).

Livingston, D. (1999) Gang Loitering, the Court, and Some Realism about Police Patrol, *The Supreme Court Review*, pp. 141–201.

Poulos, P. W. (1995) Chicago's Ban on Gang Loitering: Making Sense of Vagueness and Overbreadth in Loitering Laws, *California Law Review*, 83, (1), pp. 379–417.

Watch:

No Loitering (2002), documentary film, directed by Ellen Frankenstein. USA: KTOO-TV.

7

VANDALISM

Christian Garland

'Vandalism' may be defined as the intentional damage or destruction of material objects or 'property', either as a straightforwardly criminal act or for political reasons. The term originates in the name of the fifth-century Germanic peoples the Vandals, whose notoriety for seemingly wanton acts of destruction reached its apex in the sacking of Rome (Lévy-Leboyer, 1984).

Vandalism in its contemporary context can take many forms, and there has been much sociological debate, and media scrutiny, regarding what it actually constitutes and the possible reasons for its manifestation. Among such explanations perhaps the most simplistic is the idea that such acts are a form of simple criminality – an explanation often favoured by politicians and the media. More complex interpretations delve into the deeper specific social and physical contexts of acts of vandalism in a search for more plausible and helpful reasons.

Acts of vandalism can easily, and frequently do, blur distinctions between individual 'criminality' and the performance of such acts by broader groups. Some acts are about 'being heard' or rather becoming 'visible', such as the destruction or defacing of property by socially marginalised youth, officially all-but-invisible, but made to be seen through such acts. Sometimes 'ordinary' vandalism may overlap with acts that take on a more 'political' tinge, such as the acts committed during an urban insurrection, what are more commonly termed 'riots'. In such circumstances, many different acts of 'vandalism' usually take place, from the burning of cars to the breaking of shop windows, sometimes with acts of 'looting' following – that is, the immediate removal of goods without payment. Isolated acts of vandalism, such as damage to prestige cars, like 'keying' the paintwork or smashing a window, are not normally reported, beyond the owner's insurance claim and informing police authorities. However, during rioting such acts become so widespread, and appear on such a scale, carried out by multiple perpetrators, that they assume a meaning beyond simple 'criminal acts'.

In the English riots of 2011 widespread vandalism was reported and while politicians labelled such acts as a simple form of criminality other commentators have suggested that the scale of such vandalism and looting and the social anger underlying such acts posed the possibility of much larger social and political rationales (Lewis *et al.,* 2011). Besides acts of 'vandalism' the riots were notable for the disparate forms that they took, highlighting the different motivations of participants. In London and other cities across the country, frustration and anger at the day-to-day situation participants found themselves in were expressed in acts of destruction as well as direct engagement with the police, but in addition to this, there were also opportunistic acts of indiscriminate destruction that could be said to have occurred largely because mob conditions allowed such acts – 'normal' social rules did not apply, and were thus freely broken. Such an observation is not to condemn these behaviours, but rather to suggest the need to understand why they occurred, and the contexts that tend to generate such behaviours.

Specific acts, when committed in isolation, are frequently disregarded as straightforward criminality, usually attributable to indifference to societal rules, such as the sanctity of private property under capitalism and/or resentment at exclusion from the acceptable means of attaining it. Examples of 'isolated' everyday vandalism include individuals or groups who may break the windows of a car without stealing or 'joyriding', but just for the act of damaging it, just as, less commonly, a vehicle may be set alight with no specific goal beyond the targeted act of destruction itself. Breaking windows, uprooting or breaking trees and destroying playground equipment are other examples; there may appear to be little apparent 'purpose' or meaning besides destruction so that such acts are seen variously as anti-social, criminal and often 'senseless' by wider society. It is likely that we need to learn more about the senselessness, boredom and humiliation that pervade the lives of many habitual or occasional vandals, since the search for quick and temporary thrills or the spectacle of destruction itself may drive such acts.

The final example of vandalism can be seen as 'political' in orientation, in which specific banks, retail outlets, brands or kinds of car are targeted for 'property destruction'. Such acts are a controversial method of militant protest (Katsiaficas 2006); the counter-globalisation summits have often produced mobilisations that have generated examples of specific, targeted vandalism in which windows of well-known banks and chain stores of multinationals have found the power of 'branding' turned back against them, as militants and an indeterminate number of additional protesters frequently join them in spontaneous but focused and highly politicised vandalism. It remains to be seen whether more forms of politically motivated vandalism will occur and whether perhaps such terms can be applied to the acts of cyber-activists targeting corporate websites.

References

Katsiaficas, G. (2006) *The Subversion of Politics: European Social Movements and the Decolonization of Everyday Life*, Oakland, CA and Edinburgh: AK Press.

Lévy-Leboyer, C. (1984) *Vandalism: Behaviour and Motivations*, Oxford: North-Holland.

Lewis, P. *et al.* (2011) *Reading the Riots: Investigating England's Summer of Disorder*, London: LSE and *The Guardian*. Available online at www.guardian.co.uk/uk/2011/sep/05/reading-riots-study-guardian-lse (accessed 2 March 2013).

Watch:

Over the Edge (1979), film, directed by Jonathan Kaplan. UK/USA: Orion Pictures.

8

PROTEST

Samantha Fletcher

The year 2011 saw a new wave of protest, resistance and contestation movements emerge across the world seeking to challenge the ideologies of the ruling elite and the inequalities those ideologies reinforce. The Occupy movement (note that in many parts of the world Occupy is often referred to as the (Un)Occupy or Decolonise movement), and related movements, have generated much critique or a sense of an alternative to the hegemony of capitalism. These forms of contestation against dominant neoliberal agendas have created forums for discussion about alternative futures. Yet such spaces, both physical and discursive, are threatened by ruling elites who seek to quash them through measures of control that are often justified by viewing protesters as deviant or dangerous. Their control over the designation of deviance for rioters and protesters is an important way through which elites seek to maintain the daily reality of capitalist accumulation and inequality.

Acts of dissent against social order have historically been labelled deviant and criminal acts; unionisation and/or political allegiance to socialism are good examples of this. Recent acts of dissent, such as those of the Occupy movement, have highlighted the continued commitment of the ruling elite to maintain a position of power by implementing harsh policing measures and constructing protesters as deviant through labels actualised via an assortment of state apparatuses. One way in which such processes occur is through legislation changes geared towards the criminalisation of acts of protest. Topical illustrative examples of this can be seen in the 2012 public security law reform announcements, planned for implementation in 2013, from the Spanish government where, amongst the many proposed changes, peaceful protests and occupations of public spaces have been marked as 'an attack against public order' (Hudig, 2012: 4). Similar examples of proposed law reform which criminalise acts of peaceful protest continue to be seen across Europe, most evident in countries hit hardest by austerity measures. This in turn can serve to legitimate increased militarisation of policing and conduct towards protest movements.

Alongside new proposed legislative reforms Occupy has seen the remobilisation of a number of already established laws in order to attempt to position the occupiers as deviant law-breakers. Examples of this include the requirement of a permit to amplify sound (which was responded to with the now well-known 'human microphone'), arrests for violations of a 150-year-old state statute which 'prohibits masked gatherings of two or more people, with the exception of masquerade balls' and further arrests for those found sleeping on site and thus breaking anti-camping ordinances (Khalek, 2012). Those involved in protest through these movements consistently find themselves cast as deviants and, as a consequence, find themselves watched, attacked and criminalised.

The construction of the dissenting protestor as deviant is not limited to the legislative changes discussed so far. Constructions of deviance also play a key role in what Antonio Gramsci described in 1929 as cultural hegemony. This describes the domination by the ruling elite through a manipulation of public perceptions, in this case the perception of what is publicly to be seen as deviant. The main tool utilised in this process of constructing the deviant is the mainstream media, itself an industry dominated by the ruling elite, which continues to position protestors as a threat. Despite a commitment to pursue solidarity, the '99 per cent' in its broadest sense is often divided through the multifarious ways the state exploits and reproduces constructions of deviance. This could be seen during the August 2011 UK urban unrest, in which those involved in the riots saw the mainstream media fail to contextualise the behaviour of those groups and instead label various persons as 'feral', among other criminalising modes of description. Thus the media helps to reinforce elite views by sidelining the legitimate grievances of protesters as a means of evading such critique.

Descriptions of capitalist systems as harmful and criminal remain virtually unheard in mainstream media. Thus deviance, as constructed by the ruling elite, positions these and other factions of the 99 per cent as a deviant threat and capitalism as a legitimate 'normalising' force. Harvey (2011) has employed a critical analysis of the unrest and declared capitalism as feral through its own far more consequential forms of theft, fraud and dishonesty. His analysis is in line with critical criminological perspectives that seek to refocus our attention from everyday street crime to state and corporate crime. The terminology often used in the mainstream media to describe members of Occupy has echoes of the 2011 UK urban unrest, with some depicted as a 'gormless rent-a-mob' and 'mad leftists'. All of this suggests that an uncritical media significantly assists in enabling the shared interests of the ruling elite to criminalise and shame members of these groups and those who might seek to join their agendas. This is in some contrast to the efforts of Occupy to challenge a process by which neoliberalism and inequality have come to be seen somehow as natural phenomena (Fisher, 2012).

Deviance is often perceived as disruption of stability; yet movements such as Occupy do not disrupt stability. In fact there is little stability to be found in current systems of capitalist accumulation where, to use the language of Occupy, wealth is amassed by the top '1 per cent' of world populations at the expense of the other '99 per cent'. Protest movements disrupt the *instability* of capitalism and seek to challenge underlying normalised values instigated by the ruling elite that governs our society. The ruling elite will continually seek to label opposition movements as deviant for its own gain. The points raised here regarding contemporary protest movements cover just some of the challenges faced by protesters who seek spaces to discuss and explore alternative futures and redress inequality and the social exclusion that this generates.

References

Fisher, M. (2012) Preoccupying: Mark Fisher, *The Occupied Times of London*, available online at http://theoccupiedtimes.co.uk/ (accessed 17 February 2013).

Harvey, D. (2011) Feral Capitalism Hits the Streets, *Counterpunch*, Weekend Edition August 12–14, available online at www.counterpunch.org (accessed 29 July 2013).

Hudig, K. (2012) European Governments Step up Repression of Anti-austerity Activists, *Statewatch*, 22, (1), 15–17, available at www.statewatch.org/ (accessed 2 October 2013).

Khalek, R. (2012) 12 Most Absurd Laws Used to Stifle the Occupy Wall St. Movement around the Country, available online at www.alternet.org (accessed 29 July 2013).

Watch:

Fault Lines – Occupy Wall Street: the History and the Survival (2010), documentary film. US: Al Jazeera America. Available online at http://topdocumentaryfilms.com/occupy-wall-street-history-survival/ (accessed 2 October 2013).

9

PUBLIC SEX

Sarah Kingston and Terry Thomas

Public or outdoor sex can take many forms, such as sexual intercourse between a 'loving' couple or strangers in a field or public toilet; group sex in outdoor 'swingers' parties where 'loving couples' openly engage in sex with other couples or single people; 'dogging', where single people or couples engage in sexual acts in public or semi-public places, or watch others doing so; prostitution, where sex workers and their clients engage in sexual acts in cars and car parks; or sex between prisoners in a prison cell.

Individuals and groups engage in public sex for a range of different reasons. For clients who buy sexual acts from prostitutes, research has demonstrated that some clients prefer to buy sex on the streets rather than indoors because it is more convenient, risky or adventurous (Sanders, 2008). For homosexual men who have sex in public toilets, evidence suggests that the opportunity to meet previously unknown sexual partners motivates their engagement (Church *et al.*, 1993). Convenience and risk have also been identified by people who engage in dogging, as it provides the space for voyeurs, exhibitionists and those who wish to partner-swap to do so in a free and convenient location (Bell, 2006). Prisoners sometimes engage in homosexual acts with other prisoners to release sexual 'tensions', despite not identifying as homosexual or engaging in such acts outside prison (Stewart, 2007).

For some, having sex in public is an active choice and is part of their sexual preference, whilst for others engaging in sexual acts in public spaces is a consequence of their circumstances and limited opportunities. Although for one person engagement in outdoor sexual activity may be romantic and spiced with risk and adventure, another's view of the same sexual act may be that it is an outrage to public decency. Thus, laws exist in some countries which seek to regulate public sex so that, in some instances, such conduct may be considered to be a criminal offence.

Today in many countries we have a fragmentary series of laws that govern sex in public places. However, arguments on what constitutes a public place and what constitutes causing 'distress or offence' (which has often been the basis of a criminal offence in this context) have highlighted the difficulty of trying to provide widely shared and understood definitions of these concepts. Thus the laws in some nations are patchy, unclear and ambiguous. For example, in the UK the Public Order Act 1986, section 5 has been used by the police to stop people behaving in a sexual manner in public because it is causing 'alarm or distress'. However, the Act makes no specific mention of sexual behaviour but does refer to 'insulting behaviour'. In the United States, public indecency laws can differ between states, and what is considered to be indecent behaviour is not explicitly stated in law. In addition, those who are meant to enforce such laws are able to exercise some discretion as to whether they will charge those found to be behaving in an indecent, offensive or lewd manner. Indeed, police officers themselves may not consider such activities to be offensive or indecent.

Public sex also comes with other associated risks. Having sex outdoors sometimes means that other people, who may find this offensive, stimulating or humorous, could impose on the sexual activity, prompting a range of responses. For prostitutes on the street, vigilante groups have been known to throw stones at sex workers and their clients. Couples have also been caught 'in the act' on CCTV cameras in cities and towns, and the images have led to ridicule and laughter or have ignited sexual arousal in those watching. The outdoors can also lead to other physical injuries and threats from animals or the physical environment, as one couple found out in Africa when they were mauled by a lion during the outdoor sex act. Public sex can in some instances be dangerous and risky, and can have grave consequences, not only for those involved, but also for those watching. For children who stumble across people engaging in sex acts in public, for instance, this may be a shocking experience.

Sex is an activity which many believe should be confined to private locations and consenting adults. Public sex, because of its very nature, challenges norms and values around appropriate and acceptable behaviour, and thus attempts have been made by law to control, manage and regulate these activities. Yet despite these social norms and legal rules, some people still choose to engage in sexual activities in public and outdoor spaces because of their sexual desires, while for others their constrained circumstances mean that private sex is not an option. Public sex also comes with many risks, not only in terms of the possibility of being charged with a criminal offence, but also the risks associated with having sex outdoors.

References

Bell, D. (2006) Bodies, Technologies, Spaces: on 'Dogging', *Sexualities*, 9, (4), pp. 387–407.

Church, J., J. Green, S. Vearnals, and P. Keogh (1993) Investigation of Motivational and Behavioural Factors Influencing Men who Have Sex with Other Men in Public Toilets (Cottaging), *AIDS Care*, 5, (3), pp. 337–46.

Sanders, T. (2008) *Paying for Pleasure: Men who Buy Sex*, Cullompton, UK: Willan.

Stewart, E. C. (2007) The Sexual Health and Behaviour of Male Prisoners: the Need for Research, *The Howard Journal of Criminal Justice*, 46, (1), pp. 43–59.

Watch:

Dogging Tales (2012), TV documentary, directed by Leo Maguire. UK: Channel 4 TV.

PART II

Subcultures and deviating social codes

Subcultures, systems of values located within marginalised groups distinct from wider society, continue to have a place in ideas about crime and deviance. Historically subcultures have been used by criminologists to help understand issues like gang membership among young people, which was often explained by virtue of the poverty of and discrimination directed towards particular ethnic groups in the USA, for example. The main proposition was that behaviour deemed to be delinquent, deviant and indeed criminal could be explained by the position of social groups and neighbourhoods. Over time sociologists believed that value systems arose in these social contexts, as a response to social conditions and lack of opportunity, which came to stand in opposition to the conventional norms found more widely. This might mean a greater preparedness to use violence or steal, or to reject norms that link educational performance to achievement in life more generally. There is still much in this perspective that remains influential in studies of deviance and crime today, but perhaps there is also greater acknowledgment of the complexity of social systems and contexts and an understanding that many such values are found more widely, while conventional codes are also commonly found in apparently deviant groups and poorer neighbourhoods. The growth and diversity of youth culture in the later twentieth century onwards, and the use of leisure pursuits and dress codes, showed how often young people responded to transitions in their lives by adopting particular speech patterns and clothing distinct from other groups in society as a badge and celebration of their youth and difference.

The chapters in this section reflect these strands of work as well as the importance of understanding how values in subcultures can drive social conformity and rule-following within social sub-groups (drug dealers conforming to the hierarchies of reputation and status within a neighbourhood, for example), while those involved appear socially different or deviant to anyone outside these groups. In the case of grassing and vigilantism we also see the profound importance of local social conditions and neighbourhood life which have a significant influence on attitudes to the police and to criminals. In other words, local social spaces may structure responses to the need for social control that may seem at odds with conventional methods of policing but which are generated by factors like economic opportunity, histories of contact with and treatment by the police and values focused on masculinity and respect.

10

GRASSING AND INFORMANTS

Craig Ancrum

Grass, snitch, nark, squealer, squawker, rat, stool pigeon…There are many names used to describe those who offer information to police. In official and sociological parlance there are at least as many definitions and some confusion over terms. 'Informant' is taken by some to refer to those who aid investigations as victims or witnesses whilst the term 'informer' pertains to those who are involved in criminal activities themselves. In the UK the Association of Chief Police Officers adopted the following definition of an informer as an individual:

> *normally of criminal history, habits or associates, who gives information about crime or persons associated with criminal activity, such information being freely given, whether or not for financial reward or other advantage. That individual having the expectation that his/her identity will be protected.*
> *(Billingsley, 2001: xiv)*

The common term 'grass' itself is derived from cockney criminal parlance. Policemen in London in the 1800s were known as 'grasshoppers', therefore someone who gave them information became known as a grass (Greer, 1995).

The use of informers by the police is fraught with ethical and procedural dangers. Accusations of collusion and police and thieves becoming too 'friendly' are common, often with good cause. In Britain, the Metropolitan Police in particular have come under scrutiny in the past. Hobbs (1988) discusses the 'entrepreneurial' culture among East End detectives and their felonious counterparts, with information and money exchanged both ways.

In criminal circles, to 'grass' is to break the most sacred of all taboos. In Sutherland's seminal 1937 work, *The Professional Thief*, he discusses the implications of informing or 'squawking' and claims that it is 'the greatest disgrace and the greatest hardship that can befall a thief' (Sutherland, 1937: 11). He speaks of the hatred and genuine disgust felt at the time towards informers and the informal sanctions imposed upon them for breaking the 'criminal code'. Whilst such outdated notions of 'honour among thieves' have been rightly challenged, there remains a culture among those involved in crime of not 'squealing'. Criminals in the UK notoriously and monotonously chant 'no comment' to any police enquiries, whilst their US counterparts 'claim the Fifth'. To stray from this routine and comply or, more tellingly, to be *found* to do so, is to risk social vilification, physical injury and, in some circumstances, death.

Possibly the most famous of all the grasses are the Mafia informers. The first of these to betray their peers in return for leniency was Joe 'the Rat' Valachi in the 1960s. Italian–American mob 'foot soldier' Valachi revealed the inner workings of Cosa Nostra to an enthralled America in a series of hearings aired live on TV. This first and very public betrayal opened the flood gates and there followed a string of Mafia operatives willing to do deals with the FBI. Most notable of these was Sammy 'the Bull' Gravano, who was responsible for bringing Mafia don John Gotti to justice in the early 1990s. In Britain, the armed robber Bertie Smalls created a legal precedent when in the early 1970s he offered to betray some of London's most violent and prolific criminals. In return for leniency for himself he supplied the Met Police with enough information eventually to jail 21 men for a total of 308 years, and was the first recognised 'supergrass'. Smalls became the most reviled figure in the UK 'underworld' and was said to have a one-million-pound contract hanging over his head. Perhaps surprisingly, he passed away peacefully in 2008.

Criminology has not tended to generate real engagement with informers themselves in research. Billingsley (2001) engaged with actual police informants in order to gauge their motivations. However, he primarily concerns himself with the management and 'handling' of the respondents, not their biographical details or how they became involved in crime. This is true of a lot of the existing academic literature on the use of 'Covert Human Intelligence Sources' – it largely sees those who inform as an expendable resource in a war against crime.

The significance of not grassing is perhaps most important of all to those in marginalised and 'crime rich' communities. For those locked in areas of permanent recession and exclusion, the 'no grassing rule' is a key aspect in negotiating the obstacles of life in such a precarious social position. Safety, status and the prospects of 'getting by' all depend on the staunch refusal of those in such locales to co-operate with the police or any other agents of the state. Of course, there is also large scale mistrust and resentment of the police at large in such a milieu and this enmity serves to reinforce the reticence to co-operate.

Historically, tensions between working class populations and the police have formed the backdrop to industrialisation and were exacerbated further by its post-modern demise. Initially, the unwillingness of the lower classes to inform served as both an inclusionary measure to reinforce solidarity and an effective form of protection from police oppression. This culture of silence has been cited as problematic for law enforcement attempting to police today's modern inner city neighbourhoods and the no informing rule remains an important cultural rule for many. Informers and law enforcement's reliance on them will doubtless continue to be a contested and controversial area of modern day policing.

References

Billingsley, R. (2001) Informer Careers: Motivation and Change in R. Billingsley, T. Nemitz and P. Bean (eds) *Informers: Policing, Policy, Practice*, Cullompton, UK: Willan.

Greer, S. (1995) Towards a Sociological Model of the Police Informant, *British Journal of Sociology*, 46, (3), pp. 509–27.

Hobbs, D. (1988) *Doing the Business: Entrepreneurship, the Working Class and Detectives in the East End of London*, Oxford: Clarendon Press.

Sutherland, E. H. (1937) *The Professional Thief, by a Professional Thief*, Chicago: University of Chicago Press.

Watch:

Fifty Dead Men Walking (2008), film, directed by Kari Skogland. UK/Canada: Brightlight Pictures.

11

VIGILANTISM

Mark Hayes

Vigilantism and 'informal' justice exist in the penumbra beyond the boundaries of formal, legal and state-led responses to crime and social disorder. As such they are particularly problematic, for a number of reasons. Empirical research is meagre and the issue raises critical questions about morality, power, authority and legitimacy. Even the language used to define this area of activity is contested, and efforts at taxonomic clarity are often hampered by pejorative assumptions about the moral utility of extra-legal social action. Moreover, the issue of vigilantism can elicit strong emotional responses, not least because of sensationalist coverage in the media and the serious human costs which are often incurred. The use of violence or the threat of coercion beyond the law is inevitably troubling, and raises anxieties about 'mob rule'. However, even the most cursory foray into popular culture will reveal the 'vigilante' as a prominent, often positive, motif in the popular imagination – the success of fictional representations, from *Batman* to *The A-Team* or *The Magnificent Seven*, reflects this interesting paradox.

Vigilantism is, in essence, the self-appointed maintenance of order and dispensing of justice, which often involves violence or the threat thereof. Vigilantism usually consists of the voluntary, premeditated planning by autonomous citizens of actions which use or threaten force in response to transgressions of accepted 'norms' in order to control crime and guarantee security in a given community. Vigilantism can be prescriptive (telling people what they should do) or proscriptive (telling people what they should not do); it can be individualistic or collective, (relatively) spontaneous or well organised, pro-active or reactive. Clearly the boundaries here are permeable and motives are notoriously difficult to discern and disaggregate, indeed vigilantes may have contradictory objectives. For example, activity which might be construed as principled political resistance against the state *and* the desire to defend the state as a consequence of its perceived deficiencies might both be defined as vigilantism.

The examples of Anti-Fascist Action (UK) and the Ku Klux Klan (USA) serve to illustrate the relative diversity of kinds of vigilantism. Using vigilante tactics can be found in movements which are either politically and socially progressive or reactionary, and vigilantism can thus constitute acts which are arbitrary, pathological, authoritarian, benign or indeed protective and liberating. In fact there is a huge number of diverse historical and contemporary examples which *might* fit the descriptive criteria, ranging from the 'rough music' of community punishments in agrarian England to the actions of the *Justiceiros* in Brazil, or the independent 'Guardian Angel' scheme which operated on the subways of New York. Each particular example contains a historical narrative in which we can identify specific contexts, causes and consequences. Therefore, given the protean nature of the phenomenon, generalisation and comparison is fraught with difficulty and labelling vigilantes often becomes a politically situated value judgement.

It is interesting to note that nations and regions which are undergoing significant political and social transition often experience acute conflict over the legitimacy of state-imposed sanctions designed to ensure social order and 'justice'. In this context, as the boundaries of state action are challenged and re-drawn, the activities of non-state actors are thrown into a much sharper light. The contemporary examples of Yugoslavia, South Africa and Northern Ireland are illustrative. In Northern Ireland, for instance, various paramilitary groups have, over a sustained period, dispensed an informal 'rough' retributive justice in their own communities, often with the compliance of local people. In predominantly Nationalist communities the Provisional Irish Republican Army (PIRA) engaged in 'punishment' beatings because the prevailing ethos amongst Catholics rejected the legitimacy of the state's overwhelmingly Protestant state police force, the Royal Ulster Constabulary (RUC). Meanwhile in Protestant communities groups like the Ulster Volunteer Force (UVF) and the Ulster

Defence Association (UDA) used similar 'punishments' to enforce local social control.

Punishments by the paramilitaries for alleged acts of crime and anti-social disorder in Northern Ireland have included warnings, the imposition of curfews, beatings, 'kneecapping', expulsion and execution. Republican paramilitaries even operated a tariff system with 'factors to be taken into consideration' such as age, previous behaviour and family background. This apparently summary justice was, in fact, quite well organised and required considerable logistical effort in terms of the organisation of personnel and commitment of resources. What was particularly disconcerting for politicians, policy makers and 'official' policing practitioners, eager to condemn such activity, was the fact that, certainly in Nationalist neighbourhoods, it was often community pressure that precipitated the punishments. Local people looked to the paramilitaries to provide an immediate, punitive response to criminality and anti-social behaviour. Significant sections of the Catholic community in working class areas therefore saw the paramilitaries as 'protectors' rather than the perpetrators of illegitimate violence.

An interesting aspect of this example is that, in the context of the Northern Ireland peace process, some paramilitary elements which had been involved in dispensing 'rough justice' have been at the forefront of contemporary restorative justice schemes which now emphasise inter-personal dialogue, negotiated reparation and re-integration of offenders back into the community. Such schemes are still controversial in the sense that they challenge the system of retributive justice dispensed by the formal legal framework of the state, and may even contain a transformative essence which prefigures a deeper debate about the legitimacy of certain forms of social control.

The examples given here confirm that popular, community-based initiatives are not necessarily at odds with concepts of natural justice, civic responsibility or active citizenship, and quite often an examination of the reality of vigilantism exposes a spasmodic and semi-structured response to the diminution of such concepts in the communities where it takes place. It is also worth remembering that the historical trajectory of the non-state provision of policing and justice precedes the efforts by governments to provide these services. Moreover, it might also be noted that the contemporary ascendancy of neo-liberal ideas and policy prescriptions has precipitated not only a de-centring of the state in many peoples' lives but has eroded the capacity of formal legal mechanisms to guarantee security and social stability.

Vigilantism has become, in certain contexts, the understandable reflex of those people left insecure and marginalised by inadequate state provision for a variety of possible reasons. In this sense the nature and form of vigilantism and 'informal' justice in the future will inevitably depend upon the functions dispensed by the state and the quality of distributive 'social' justice. Hence the proliferation of local, community-based responses to crime and social disorder, which inevitably reflect the diverse specificity of existing cultural and historical contexts, is certain to continue. It is an uncomfortable fact that although the violence of assorted vigilantes is disturbing to those who are preoccupied with formal legalistic methods and who are therefore committed to the utility of state structures, such acts often contain an ethical core which resonates in those communities where, at times, there are few reasonable alternatives.

Bibliography

Abrahams, R. (1998) *Vigilant Citizens: Vigilantism and the State*, Oxford, Polity Press.

Johnston, L. (1996) What is Vigilantism?, *British Journal of Criminology*, 36, (2), pp. 220–36.

Pratten, D. and Sen, A. (eds) (2008) *Global Vigilantes,* New York: Columbia University Press.

Watch:

The Molly Maguires (1970), film, directed by Martin Ritt. USA: Paramount Pictures.

12

SUBCULTURE

Joanne Massey

In cultural theory societies are understood to be structured around power relations involving more or less dominant groupings; relative dominance facilitates a position of cultural ideology or hegemony, the idea that the interests of ruling classes also become the ideas that dominate and influence society more generally. Yet even within the most culturally dominated societies we can locate counter- or subcultures, groups with norms that are at odds with, or different from, hegemonic ideas and values. Such subcultures often involve a range of practices linked with style (Hebdige, 1979) such as fashion, dress or taste in music that are used by particular groups to display political opposition or social difference from mainstream tastes or social values. Cultural studies and criminology share a concern with the study of deviance; the rise of cultural criminology has moved these concerns forward by investigating the styles and experiences of illicit subcultures and the criminalisation of such popular forms (Ferrell, 1999: 395).

In a sense anyone proclaiming membership of a subculture is deviant since they are choosing to express themselves in ways that go beyond or break generally accepted rules about how to live or other political values, and we can also locate subcultures who view themselves as lying outside mainstream society. Subcultures are delineated and defined by their opposition to mainstream culture; they are 'sub' in the sense that they are subterranean, lying under conventional social modes, and subordinated, in the sense of being subject to domination by or tension with prevailing social codes. Subcultural groups often appropriate elements of the dominant culture in order to subvert meaning and reclaim them as their own. Teddy boys reclaimed and transformed Edwardian style in an act of 'bricolage' while the mods used pills intended to treat neuroses as recreational drugs (Hebdige, 1979).

It is important to note that processes of subversion and resistance are not always unilateral. Capitalism has proved adept at incorporating displays of resistance and commodifying these for sale or the pursuit of profit, often forcing subcultures to adapt and adopt new codes or forms of taste. For example, graffiti, which began as a subversive and deviant activity, has been appropriated by corporations such as Nissan to advertise their Qashqai four-by-four car and Müller to advertise their range of children's yogurts. Both brands use graffiti as a backdrop when advertising their products. Similarly 'graffitti' artists like Banksy have adopted street art as a means of pursuing profitable careers that have been adopted by sections of the art establishment.

Birmingham's Centre for Contemporary Cultural Studies (CCCS), established in 1964 by Richard Hoggart, played a vital role in academic debate concerning subculture. It was here that Paul Willis wrote *Learning to Labour* (1978), observing how school prepares young people for employment and how working class boys opposed authority via a subculture of nonconformity in which 'skiving' and being tough, sexist and racist were prevailing values. However, such values were not a form of resistance to those in power in the way that Gramsci might argue. Instead their resistance was limited to the school, an institution that was preparing them for the world of work and the shop floor culture of the factory. Subcultures posing a challenge to the hegemony now include computer hackers, guerrilla gardeners, graffiti writers and gangs. However, if a subculture is to meet with Hebdige's (1979) criteria it should have a certain 'style' attached to it. Skateboarders, punks, emos, rockers, ravers, teddy boys, chavs and gangsta rap and parkour enthusiasts all fall into this category.

Emo is short for 'emotional punk' and stereotypically refers to teenagers who are often depressed, are rumoured to self-harm, have hairstyles that partially cover their faces and wear tight black jeans, Converse trainers and band T-shirts. They listen to music by artists such as Panic! at the Disco and My Chemical Romance, though many emos might dispute this. Subculture often involves the appropriation of public space. Massey (2011) highlights how large numbers of emos dominated space in Manchester city centre and had to legitimate their presence by establishing a peer youth work project giving them the right to be there. Thus they posed a challenge to the hegemony of the consumer economy of the city centre.

The subculture of 'chav' (from the Romani world 'chavi' for child, but also known as an acronym for 'council houses and violence') is interesting in that it has its own signifiers including Burberry, 'bling' and behaviour which 'for chavs consists in a combination of transgressive acts, mundane activities like hanging out on street corners, and expressivity through dress and style under "consumer capitalism"' (Martin, 2009: 125). The chav phenomenon is related to modes of cultural domination and resistance. On the one hand the term is seen as a mode of abuse or a wider collusion in practices of shaming those sections of society who are seen as deviant or dangerous (such as loitering, hoodie wearing youth groups) or operating at the margins of the labour market. Books, websites and a broader class prejudice become mobilised around perceptions of danger, sexual deviance (lone and teen parenthood) and crude attempts at trying to emulate conventional symbols of success in the form of expensive designer clothing elements (Burberry clothing, gold jewellery).

On the other hand the term chav, a term of denigration, has been used as a symbol of resistance, social difference and perhaps also a celebration of having a reputation for being dangerous or violent. Ultimately something we might deem to be a chav culture is a reaction to the difficulties of contemporary white working class identity, community change and consumer capitalism. The incorporation of brands such as Burberry, in an act of bricolage, is an endeavour to resolve their problems of occupying the margins of society and appropriate a more aspirant lifestyle. Whilst chavs have inhabited the space of the streets and won real cultural space in their neighbourhoods, in Gramscian terms they have achieved little, since their behaviour offers no real solution to the problems of long term unemployment, educational disadvantage, dead-end jobs and neighbourhood decline. Excluded from formal spaces of consumption they create their own culture of resistance by hanging out on street corners and playing up to stereotypes.

Subculture remains an important concept for thinking about class structure, cultural forms of domination and the importance of style and taste in demarcating social boundaries and inequalities. Yet the notion that subcultures are simply underground or resistant social formations is naive since their attempts to appropriate and resist often end up being co-opted or reincorporated into mainstream social conventions and values. Nevertheless, by observing subcultures it is possible to discover the dynamics of social power and the periodic challenges to it.

References

Ferrell, J. (1999) Cultural Criminology, *Annual Review of Sociology*, 25, pp. 395–418.

Hebdige, D. (1979) *Subculture: The Meaning of Style*, London: Methuen.

Martin, G. (2009) Subculture, Style, Chavs and Consumer Capitalism: Towards a Critical Cultural Criminology of Youth, *Crime, Media, Culture*, 5, (2), pp. 123–45.

Massey, J. (2011) Commodification, Control and Civic Space: Findings from Manchester, UK, *Crime Prevention and Community Safety: An International Journal*, 13, (3), pp. 187–204.

Willis, P. (1978) *Learning to Labour: How Working Class Kids Get Working Class Jobs*, Farnham, UK: Ashgate.

Watch:

The Virgin Suicides (1999), film, directed by Sofia Coppola. USA: Paramount.

13

FASHION

Katherine Harrison

When we talk about deviance, we frequently and, perhaps, unconsciously use language that recalls clothing and body modification. For instance, the word 'loose', used to describe prostitutes and the sexually promiscuous, refers to the loosened stays that produced the uncorseted silhouette which differentiated disreputable from respectable women in the nineteenth century. More recently, social groups considered to be dangerous have acquired names that refer explicitly to dress or hairstyles, like 'skinheads', 'casuals' and 'hoodies'. Current debates about youth crime and delinquency are peppered with references to 'prison white' trainers, 'tramp stamps' and 'stripper shoes', all of which are used to denote a harmful, not to mention distasteful, deviation from the norm in terms of appearance and socially acceptable behaviour. Understanding deviance on the basis of attire cannot be regarded as dispassionate, however. For nearly forty years, sociologists have argued that ascribing deviance through fashion is tied up with subjective and misleading judgements linked to broader power relations between social classes, age groups, genders and ethnicities.

The study of fashion and deviance is influenced by research conducted by Stanley Cohen and Dick Hebdige during the 1970s. Both sociologists focused on the roles of rebellious white working-class male youth subcultures, recognisable by their distinctive styles, in revealing social differences. Cohen (2011) argues that the media's exaggerated representation of violence between Mods and Rockers at English seaside resorts in the 1960s established these groups as modern-day 'folk devils'. Although the trouble was limited and largely contained within the youth groups themselves, newspapers produced a disproportionate sense of threat, so that any young person adopting the same spectacular raiment as the Mods or Rockers came to be stereotyped and, subsequently, vilified. This process is known as 'deviance amplification' and may result in a more widespread 'moral panic' in which others imagine themselves as potential victims, despite the unlikelihood of ever experiencing harm (Cohen, 2011).

Hebdige's (1987) research concluded that young, working-class punks and teddy boys contrived subversive fashions to signify a refusal of the values of their parents' generation: what they saw as an oppressive establishment. Though an apparently superficial protest, it revealed defiant differences of opinion within a society that had prided itself on consensus during the post-war years. This drew down the hostility of the dominant middle class, consolidating working-class subcultures as dangerous. The youth subcultures of the 1960s, 1970s and successive decades disrupted the illusion of social harmony that was essential for maintaining the status quo after the great societal shifts that occurred in the first half of the twentieth century. The price paid for this challenge to the social order was the conflation of difference with deviance. Recent research into fashion and deviance has, more often than not, maintained this focus on youth groups.

The demonisation of certain fashions raises questions about who has the power to confer judgements of deviance upon others. The matter of 'taste' – what reflects 'good' and 'bad' taste – is not natural but socially constructed. Taste makers are usually from the dominant class in society as they require economic and cultural power (such as control of the cultural industries) to determine what constitutes tastefulness. Bourdieu (1984) claims that middle-class domination of taste disbars the style of the working class from ever being in 'good taste'. For example, when copies of the signature print fabric of the exclusive fashion house Burberry became popular with working-class 'chavs' during the 2000s, the brand suffered a crisis as affluent consumers fled from association with the same style as a group considered to be vulgar. From the distinctive trousers of the eighteenth-century 'sans-culottes' in Revolutionary France to the leisurewear of twenty-first-century British 'hoodies', the styles seen to exemplify deviance have been working-class. That said, the many cases of ironic middle-class appropriations of deviant 'looks' complicate this picture, as does the victimisation of members of more middle-class subcultures, like goths and emos.

While an understanding of class is essential to any discussion of fashion and deviance, gender and ethnicity also play significant roles. Subcultural theory has traditionally concentrated on male youth groups, but public debates about deviance are played out, predominantly, over female bodies and their adornment. The contemporary cultural dilemma over the place of Muslim women's veils in European societies exemplifies this. On the one hand, Muslim women who cover their heads and bodies are held to be, simultaneously, symbols and victims of an oppressive gender politics that is seen as central to Islam and detrimental to modern, open societies. The comparatively exposed bodies of non-Muslim European women are considered to embody progressiveness and equality with men. Yet, on the other hand, women of any religion or ethnicity who dress scantily are castigated as sexually 'loose' and indicative of declining moral standards in society. Contests over the meaning of women's dress have little to do with choices made by women as individuals, but reflect the broader values of the patriarchal societies in which they live. While men's bodies are judged to be unremarkable, stable entities, women's bodies, and the clothing that conceals and reveals them, are sites of ferocious struggles for propriety and social control.

Sartorial choices are often conflated with morality within a 'vestimentary vocabulary' (Wrigley, 2002: 19) that is used to establish and police the boundaries between normalcy and deviancy in society. These boundaries are not merely conceptual, however, because they have the power to produce material effects. Despite moral panics, the harms generated by deviant fashions are less to society in general, perhaps, than to the wearers of the offensive garments. There are detrimental effects for groups viewed as deviant that go beyond simple stereotyping or derision. In twenty-first-century Britain, 'hoodies' are barred from entering shopping centres and pubs, while those who dress in a way considered to be indicative of moral degeneracy are more likely to be treated as figures of suspicion by the authorities or to experience other forms of victimisation.

References

Bourdieu, P. (1984) *Distinction: A Social Critique of the Judgement of Taste*, London: Routledge and Kegan Paul.

Cohen, S. (2011) *Folk Devils and Moral Panics: The Creation of the Mods and Rockers*, Abingdon and New York: Routledge.

Hebdige, D. (1987) *Subculture: The Meaning of Style*, London and New York: Routledge.

Wrigley, R. (2002) The Formation and Currency of a Vestimentary Stereotype: The *Sans-culotte* in Revolutionary France, in W. Parkins (ed.), *Fashioning the Body Politic: Dress, Gender, Citizenship*, Oxford and New York: Berg.

Watch:

Quadrophenia (1979), film, directed by Franc Roddam. UK: Universal Pictures.

14

TATTOOS

James Treadwell

Tattooing is a form of body modification, made by inserting indelible ink into the dermis layer of the skin to change the pigment, and hence resulting (for the most part) in a permanent marking or scarring. Such modifications of the body appearance have been practised for centuries in various cultures since Neolithic times, yet it has also been the concern of some of the earliest and most recent investigations of criminologists and those working around the sociology of deviance.

Western tattooing has its origins in sixteenth- and eighteenth-century maritime expeditions, particularly when Polynesian tattooing practices became popular among European sailors exposed to these cultures, who then took the Samoan word *tatau* to describe the process. From the eighteenth century tattooing was seen as medically important, and choosing to decorate the body in this way was thought to reveal 'primitive' urges and tendencies. It was also held to demonstrate insensibility to pain, which was widely believed to be a sign of an underlying physical defect. The Italian biological positivist criminologist Cesare Lombroso (2006) famously considered tattoos in his attempt to measure and indicate the presence of particular characteristics in the body of a criminal. His book *L'Uomo Delinquente* contained a full chapter on the significance of tattoos to criminality, suggesting they were a sign of failure of the individual fully to evolve (Morrison, 2004). Similarly French criminologist Alexandre

Lacassagne, a contemporary of Lombroso's, associated criminality with the presence of tattoos.

Since the early work of Lombroso and others, the topic of tattooing has been a periodic interest within criminology, with discussions continuing around the possible relationship between the marking of the body and criminality. Historically criminologists sought to use anthropometric measurements of the body to identify repeat offenders and build up a profile of the physical characteristics of 'born' criminals (Horn, 2003) but more recently the association between tattoos and criminal behaviour has tended to consider tattoos as a more general indication of inclinations toward risk taking and rule violating behaviour. Yet typical of much of this 'research' are unsound methodological practices and the personal biases of writers. For example, numerous earlier studies focused exclusively on those tattooed individuals already institutionalised in psychiatric establishments and prisons. This group of individuals is typically described as being more likely to exhibit personality disorders than those found within the general population, hence the tattooed individuals under study were already diagnosed and labelled as psychopathological, or were already convicted of committing a crime (often rendering much of the literature ultimately tautological).

While the prevalence of tattooing in offender populations remains an infrequent yet recurrent theme in the wider criminological literature, the relevance of tattooing to discussions of deviance and criminality is arguably much broader (DeMello, 1993). Tattooing carries several medical risks, including the transmission of infectious diseases, and this might help to explain long-entrenched prejudices towards bearers of tattoos but also makes it a potential concern in the management of prison health. Perhaps more importantly tattoos are used among some criminal subcultures, such as the Yakuza in Japan and white supremacist gangs in the USA, to show gang affiliation; they record an individual's personal history, accomplishments and convictions much in the way that Lombroso observed. In some cases, notably that of the Russian penal system, elaborate tattoo designs have developed which feature widely recognised subcultural yet coded meanings reflecting the socio-economic and political conditions of the state. Discussion of tattoos has therefore featured prominently in ethnographic and subcultural studies of crime and deviance, particularly for example in the stylistic concerns of cultural criminology (Morrison, 2004).

In addition to voluntary tattooing, tattoos can be used to stigmatise and punish individuals. In the Russian penal system, the tattoo can also be applied as a sanction, with blatant sexual images forcibly applied to the forehead as a means of humiliating the bearer and as a warning to others. Similarly the use of tattoos by the Nazi regime, famously on Jewish prisoners in Auschwitz, demonstrates the power to confer stigma and control through indelible markings (though the practice first came about in 1941, for Soviet prisoners of war). We can also find examples of the control of the bodies of those with tattoos, such as prohibitions that exclude individuals from occupational roles. Here employers, including criminal justice agencies, may exclude or prohibit some forms of tattoos (those that are on the hands, wrists or ankles, or on the neck above the collar), while geographical injunctions have also been applied, as with some public places in Tokyo that have a 'no body tattoos' policy as part of an attempt to exclude Yakuza.

There is some suggestion that the stigma associated with visible tattoos has eroded as social conventions and norms shift, with the practice becoming increasingly normalised. Tattooing has attained a degree of aesthetic–cultural legitimacy in recent years, and with this shift from marginal and outsider status different issues come to the fore. Yet such practices bring with them their own sense of prestige, shame or embarrassment in relation to prevailing tastes and class distinctions. This can take the form of lampooning celebrities with 'bad' tattoos or the deriding more generally of those carrying such marks. For example, Australian website Gizmodo recently lampooned 'twelve idiots' with 'hideous' Apple brand tattoos, and there was much public debate about the footballer David Beckham deciding to be tattooed. In another example Kari Smith, a 30-year-old mother in the USA, had a GoldenPalace.com tattoo on her forehead after being paid $10,000 by the online casino company to use it as advertising space on an auction website on the Internet. Although she claimed this was a freely made choice, such cases raise important questions about the relationship between the body, social conventions and corporate logics. Tattoos also raise interesting questions about what constitutes exploitation and harm and whether governments should regulate such activities or indeed whether individuals are capable of offering full consent to practices where lasting physical 'harm' may result (Lehane, 2005).

References

DeMello, M. (1993) The Convict Body: Tattooing among Male American Prisoners, *Anthropology Today*, 9, (6), pp. 10–13.

Horn, D. (2003) *The Criminal Body: Lombroso and the Anatomy of Deviance*, London: Routledge.

Lehane, P. (2005) Assault, Consent and Body Art: A Review of the Law Relating to Assault and Consent in the UK and the Practice of Body Art, *Journal of Environmental Health Research*, 4, (1), pp. 41–9.

Lombroso, C. (2006) *Criminal Man*, Durham, NC: Duke University Press.

Morrison, W. (2004) Lombroso and the Birth of Criminological Positivism: Scientific Mastery or Cultural Artifice?, in J. Ferrell, K. Hayward, W. Morrison and M. Presdee (eds), *Cultural Criminology Unleashed*, London: GlassHouse, pp. 67–80.

Watch:

The Mark of Cain (2000), documentary film, directed by Alix Lambert. Russia: Go East Productions.

15

DRUG DEALING

Craig Ancrum

The drug dealer has become one of our foremost contemporary 'folk devils'. Those who trade in substances prohibited by law are the subject of an astonishing array of inaccurate myths and spurious urban legends. From the 'evil' pusher lurking at the school gates to tales of children's stick-on tattoos being laced with LSD, the drug dealer is demonised and dehumanised. Amoral and totally unconcerned with the misery and death he brings, he epitomises the ills of modern times (Coomber, 2006).

From the earliest societies we can find records of people altering and tempering their state of consciousness through the ingesting of psychoactive substances. Evidence of cannabis, opium and other substance use dates back to at least 6,000 BC – often for religious purposes but clearly used for pleasure and recreation too; numerous examples exist throughout history. Early Sami tribesmen in northern Sweden would drink the urine of their reindeer herds after allowing them to graze on hallucinogenic fungi. The ancient Greek poet Homer waxes lyrical on the effects of the opium poppy in the *Odyssey*. English gentlemen would find solace in the opium dens of Victorian London rather than face the stigma of being seen to imbibe 'the demon drink', which the temperance movement had declared immoral. As many commentators argue, drugs have been used in all cultures at all periods in history.

Uneasiness over drug use arose not through concern over harm but from the association of certain drugs with detested and vulnerable racial groups. Opium, for example, was inextricably linked with the Chinese, whilst in the United States marijuana was used as a political stick to beat Mexican immigrants and became associated with the corruption of innocent American youth. In Britain, although drug laws had been introduced following the First World War, which saw thousands of servicemen return home addicted to opiates, it wasn't really until the 1960s and 1970s that the drug dealer's fate was sealed. The 'war on drugs', which began in the USA under Nixon, was soon adopted in the UK, despite the absence of a significant 'drug problem' at that time. The dealer reflected the ills of the new permissive age and the folly of the burgeoning counter culture and served to re-draw the blurred lines of morality.

Criminology has tended either to shoehorn drug dealers into neat typologies (Pearson, 2007) or to portray them as 'victims' of an uncaring, predatory post-modern society (Williams, 1989). In reality we know relatively little about the complex and diverse world of drug markets and our concentration inevitably falls on low-end 'retail' dealers who operate in the most visible sectors of the illegal economy. The accounts we hear are usually those of the dealer/addict and are often bound up with biographies of social exclusion and poverty. We may still be drawn into making the moral assumptions that those involved would prefer not to be and that they can be 'saved' by means of coerced rehabilitation. Our knowledge of upper- or even middle-level transactions is more limited. Pearson argues that because of this, massive public expenditure on drug prohibition is underpinned by an embarrassingly thin evidence base.

There is still a tendency within society at large to see drug dealers in terms of otherness. They are people 'not like us', and yet many people, in their youth or middle age, will be supplied cannabis, cocaine and other illicit substances by friends or friends of friends; such drug usage is either denied or defended as being unproblematic. Similarly the source of drugs is exoticised in discussions of 'foreign' drug rings and mafia style organisations: our drugs are supplied by 'Yardies', 'the Russian Mafia', 'Turkish heroin gangs'; any British involvement is secondary and we are still seduced and corrupted into involvement. This despite the fact that as a nation we are one of the largest consumers of illegal drugs in the world and more than 90 per cent of cannabis used in Britain is grown there.

Myths about drug dealers abound. They are often seen as ruthless predators who sell products adulterated with highly dangerous substances while preying on our children, offering free samples to get them hooked. In truth, drug dealers are rational economic actors and thus selling products laced with toxic adulterants such as bleach and strychnine would be counterproductive. In addition to the huge police attention any resulting deaths would bring, they would be unable to trade again once their products had hit the market. Dealers thus rely on reputation and any negative 'reviews' severely damage business. Similarly, the notion that drug markets are fraught with danger is not always true. Clearly there are staggeringly high levels of violence in *some* markets but there is huge diversity, and there are regional and national variations in how such 'business' is managed. There is a huge amount of trust involved in some cases, especially in high-end deals which often involve receiving large amounts of drugs on 'bail' or credit. Again, if a dealer rips off either a customer or supplier, he not only instantly loses that avenue of trade but also faces the threat of informal 'sanctions', not just the possibility of violence but also the lack of being a 'name' in the market, which can be extremely damaging both financially and socially.

Our image of drug dealers then is at best sketchy. The anonymous and sinister stranger handing out free drugs, if he exists at all, is the exception, not the rule. Most people who use drugs will be supplied by a friend or relative – such avenues involve little 'pushing'! Whilst acknowledging that in some contested and crowded markets, such as 'corner dealing' in the USA, free samples are used as part of an inverted brand loyalty mechanism, our own research tells us that those involved in drug supply have no difficulty selling their wares (see Hall *et al.*, 2008). The illicit drug markets in the USA and UK are worth billions and this demand is clearly not driven by supply. Unsurprisingly, many drug traders see themselves not as pushers of unwanted and corrosive poisons but as service providers, simply meeting the requirements of eager consumers who do not see their pastimes as deviant; we need to acknowledge that for millions of ordinary people illegal substance use is part of everyday leisure and recreation. In a society in which hedonism and pleasure are at the forefront of our culture it seems paradoxical that we should seek to prosecute those who facilitate this.

References

Coomber, R. (2006) *Pusher Myths: Re-situating the Drug Dealer*, London: Free Association Books.

Hall, S., Winlow, S. and Ancrum, C. (2008) *Criminal Identities and Consumer Culture: Crime, Exclusion and the New Culture of Narcissism*, Cullompton, UK: Willan.

Pearson, G. (2007) Drug Markets and Dealing: From Street Dealer to Mr. Big, in M. Simpson, T. Shildrick and R. MacDonald (eds) *Drugs in Britain: Supply, Consumption and Control*, Basingstoke, UK: Palgrave Macmillan.

Williams, T. (1989) *The Cocaine Kids: The Inside Story of a Teenage Drug Ring*, London: Bloomsbury.

Watch:

Layer Cake (2004), film, directed by Matthew Vaughn. UK/USA: Columbia TriStar.

16

GRAFFITI

Tara Lai Quinlan

Graffiti refers to a broad spectrum of words or images placed on fixed or movable physical spaces, and is not usually permitted by law. Although graffiti has existed for centuries (examples can be found in ancient Roman ruins, among others), contemporary graffiti first appeared in American urban areas in the late 1960s, and has since spread globally. Varieties of modern graffiti include 'tagging' names or nicknames, gang signs or codes and elaborate, multi-coloured murals displaying words, images or a combination thereof. Graffiti is applied with pen, marker, spray paint or acrylic paint, or a mixture of media. It is written on extremely varied physical surfaces, although most commonly on public and private buses, subway cars, bus shelters, building walls, tunnels, building pipes and, more recently, canvases.

Graffiti in all its forms has always tended to be criminalised by authorities. Authorities react oppressively to graffiti writers' appropriation of public and private space, targeting them with criminal sanctions and trying to erase graffiti immediately after it is made. Authorities regard graffiti writers as criminals. Authorities argue that they will often commit more serious crimes and graffiti writing is just the beginning of their criminal activities. Authorities use this rationale to punish graffiti writers harshly. They not only fine, arrest and jail graffiti writers, but also require them to paint over graffiti and attend youth education and job training programmes.

They also seek to reduce graffiti by restricting access to graffiti-making materials, including markers and spray paint, and use technologies to create graffiti-resistant paints and surfaces in public and private spaces.

Beyond simply treating the creation of graffiti as a criminal act, police and city authorities assert that graffiti has negative social impacts, often arguing that the presence of graffiti in neighbourhoods makes residents feel unsafe. Authorities will also often argue that where there is graffiti this signals neighbourhood decline and invites more serious criminal activities, ushering in neighbourhood decay and more serious forms of social deviance. Thus graffiti has tended to be used to help justify harsh policies, like zero-tolerance policing, to control the socially deviant behaviour that it is deemed to represent.

Attempts to control graffiti also serve an important legitimising function. To the extent that residents see neighbourhood graffiti as a proxy for decay and invitation to social deviance, the authorities' ability to control graffiti signifies a government's effectiveness in controlling decay and social deviance. Where authorities can control graffiti, they appear more effective and thus more legitimate in the eyes of neighbourhood residents. Thus local authorities' desire to control graffiti is closely tied to their self-interest in preserving the semblance of control over social problems in the eyes of their citizens.

Despite being criminally sanctioned, graffiti serves important social, cultural and political functions. It has come to be seen by some as a form of artistic and communicative expression for the graffiti writer. Graffiti is also grounded in subcultures that are often in an oppositional relationship to mainstream society and authority. Graffiti's defiant nature is linked to its emergence in the 1960s and 1970s amidst an anti-authoritarian youth culture, and racial identity and counterculture movements. Yet beyond simply serving as an expression of political resistance graffiti can also be seen as an expression of the frustrations of marginalised communities.

Contemporary graffiti first emerged in American inner cities in the 1960s and 1970s as a means for disempowered communities to respond to their marginalised status. With few other outlets for social and political expression, marginalised communities used graffiti to express social and political angst. Graffiti facilitated political expression to re-appropriate public and private space for these city residents on their own terms. It thus allowed marginalised populations literally and figuratively to add colourful political expression to a bland or run-down urban environment Norman Mailer once described as a 'monotonous iron-grey and dull brown brick environment, surrounded by asphalt, concrete, and clangor'

(Mailer, 1974). Graffiti was but one political expression of urban angst for marginalised communities that was closely tied to the break-dancing and hip-hop music that emerged in the mid-seventies.

Finally, contemporary graffiti also serves an important cultural function as an antithesis to corporate advertising and product placement in public and private spaces (Baudrillard, 1984). Graffiti represents a re-appropriation of public or private spaces from corporate-driven advertising and government-approved marketing projects. It functions to jar a complacent public accustomed to corporate advertising into remembering alternative uses for public and private space, sometimes subverting corporate messages, for example. Recognising this important cultural power of graffiti, some corporations have now even appropriated graffiti's counter-cultural ethos for corporate marketing purposes.

Graffiti now appears on clothing, in advertisements, as the subject of films and documentaries (Banksy, 2010), and is even displayed on art gallery walls, but city authorities remain opposed to it and continue to brand it as a form of social disorder. For example, while the 2011 Los Angeles Museum of Contemporary Art exhibition 'Art in the Streets' was the first showcase of graffiti in a major American museum and was wildly popular, authorities blamed it for an uptick in graffiti in downtown Los Angeles during the exhibition, and discouraged it from being exhibited at New York's Brooklyn Museum. Thus while graffiti now has a wider audience than ever before, it remains a criminalised form of political and cultural expression of opposition and defiance, particularly within more marginalised communities.

References

Baudrillard, J. (1984) *Simulacra and Simulation*, Ann Arbor, MI: University of Michigan Press.

Mailer, N. (1974) The Faith of Graffiti, *Esquire*, May, available online at http://testpressing.org/2012/06/esquire-the-faith-of-graffiti-norman-mailer/ (accessed 10 December 2012).

Watch:

Exit through the Gift Shop (2010), film, directed by Banksy. UK/USA: Paranoid Pictures.

17

ARSON AND FIRE-STARTING

Nicoletta Policek

Arson can be defined as the act of intentionally and maliciously setting fire to buildings, private or public properties, woodland areas or vehicles, with the intent to cause damage. Sanctions against arsonists take the problem extremely seriously given the risk to life as well as damage to property. Arson is prosecuted with attention to the degree of severity of the alleged offence. In the United States, first-degree arson generally occurs when individuals are harmed or killed in the course of the fire, and second-degree arson when significant destruction of property occurs. Usually a felony (serious crime), arson may also be prosecuted as a misdemeanour, criminal mischief or the destruction of property.

In England, arson, defined as the malicious burning of the dwelling of another, was a common law offence dealing with the criminal destruction of buildings by fire. The offence was abolished by the Criminal Damage Act 1971, which made no general distinction as to the mode of destruction except that if the destruction is by fire then the offence will be charged as arson. The Act also provides a maximum penalty of life imprisonment for convictions, whether or not the offence is charged as arson. Scotland has no offence of arson as such. Here events constituting arson elsewhere may be dealt with as one or more of a variety of offences, such as wilful fire-raising, culpable and reckless conduct, vandalism or other offences that will depend on the circumstances of the event, though more serious offences can incur a sentence of life imprisonment. However, in thinking about the problem of arson we also need to think about the differing motivations for what may otherwise seem like a dangerously reckless act.

Arson is often considered the archetype of social rebellion, often involving symbolic locations, like schools or youth centres. These are sometimes targeted for thrill and status-seeking motivations or because such sites represent places of authority or personal humiliation to those involved. 'Firestarter', the song released by the English band The Prodigy in 1996, has become the imagined anthem of any self-respecting arsonist, playing with fire, setting fire to public properties as a way of enacting dissent towards the establishment. In the USA, Detroit hip-hop group D12's 2001 debut album, entitled *Devil's Night*, is associated with one of the most notorious urban sites of arsonist activity. Taking place once a year before and during Hallowe'en, 'Devil's Nights' in the USA, in particular in Detroit, date from as early as the 1940s. Traditionally, city youths engaged in acts of petty vandalism, causing little to no property damage. However, in the early 1970s, vandalism escalated to more destructive acts that included arson. These acts took place primarily in the inner city where there was an abundance of derelict homes. They reached a peak in the late 1980s, prompting a community response: the 'Angels' Night' in which volunteer teams of two or more people would be assigned to patrol a specific neighbourhood by car from six p.m. to midnight during the three-day Hallowe'en period, often adopting a vacant house or commercial building in their neighbourhood to help prevent arson.

Arson can also often be motivated by the desire to collect insurance compensation by setting fires deliberately to the property of another, or to one's own property. Because insurance usually covers fire damage, the incentive for home owners to set fires intentionally, or be neglectful in maintenance, may be raised where the market value of a property is lower than its insured value (Corrigan and Siegfried, 2011). Owners may also deliberately set fire to their businesses to avoid losses during recessions, or to collect insurance payments when the cost of continuing the business exceeds its expected revenue. By the same token, home owners whose properties' values have plummeted due to a recent severe downturn in the housing market may find it more attractive to collect insurance than to sell, repair or continue to live in their homes. For example, in the USA the devastation caused by Hurricane Katrina in 2005 was blamed for increased arson in the Gulf Coast area following the disaster. Yet arson for profit is not limited to commercial or private buildings: for example, the City of Science in Naples, the first Italian scientific interactive museum, was destroyed by an arson attack in March 2013 by property developers allegedly linked to the local mafia (Margottini, 2013).

There are significant pressures on government and public agencies to be seen to be responding assertively to the issue of arson. In the current political environment, where governments tend to promote the idea that increasingly punitive and authoritarian measures are the most effective way to reduce crime, such pressure is producing policies that favour monitoring and longer periods of incarceration. Current arson prevention policies tend to operate through both formal and informal control measures, often aimed at monitoring and managing individuals deemed to be at risk of committing arson. In the juvenile setting this might justify establishing a specialised assessment and treatment capacity within child and adolescent mental health, juvenile justice or adolescent mental health services. For juveniles who are not involved in the criminal justice system, referrals to mental health services are often made through existing fire education and awareness programmes. However, if there is a genuine wish to reduce long-term risks to the community from deliberate fire-setting, attention and funding must be given to methods that have demonstrated effcacy in reducing the overall incidence of repeat fire-setting and which seek to engage closely with the diverse motivations that underlie the actions of arsonists.

Bibliography

Corrigan, F. E. and Siegfried, J. J. (2011) Arson and the Business Cycle, *The American Economist*, 57, (1), pp. 1–6.

Hurley, W. and Monahan, T. M. (1969) Arson: The Criminal and the Crime, *British Journal of Criminology*, 9, (1), pp. 4–21.

Margottini, L. (2013) Fire Destroys the City of Science in Naples, Italy, *New Scientist*, March.

Watch:

Point of Origin (2002), film, directed by Newton Thomas Sigel. USA: HBO.

PART III

Technological change and new opportunities for harm

In some branches of criminological theory great emphasis is placed, not on the choices people make or their social circumstances, but on the opportunities to commit crimes. These have become important frameworks from which to view and challenge certain forms of criminal and harmful behaviour that may be prevented through design or environmental modifications (such as chip and pin credit cards, better locks on windows or locked cabinets in shops). In many ways these ideas have helped to improve security but also raise questions about the adequacy of explanations that reduce the scope for thinking about the social influences (such as social inequality, gender, family environment, education and opportunities) that underpin certain crimes, as well as being less helpful in explaining other forms of criminal behaviour (such as violence, rape or hate crime) that tend to be better explained by reference to other factors.

Some criminologists now argue that technological change has generated new opportunities for a range of types of criminal and socially harmful conduct. These changes are multiple: new forms of social networking that allow cyberbullying; anti-social behaviour that becomes possible via online anonymity; Internet websites that allow communities of hackers and new counter-cultures to emerge that challenge corporate providers and government agencies through attacks on websites or attempts at defrauding customers and companies. Yet even in this emerging landscape of apparently random, disorganised networks and anarchic spaces we can trace codes of conduct among new communities of networked users and criminal groupings.

This section contains cutting-edge treatments of issues like hacking and video-gaming. In each case we find a series of complex and thorny issues; some might claim that they have few victims, yet we know that profound damage is inflicted by bullying, and that proliferating and increasingly violent sexual images on the Internet are not simply virtual phenomena but result from real encounters with and violence towards women and children across the globe. Many such harms are not currently codified in law, and do not see concerted or effective responses from governments or other crime control agencies, despite growing social anxiety about these issues. In other activities, like video-gaming, the low-level deviance of teenage bedroom gamers can now be seen in more complex and open social contexts alongside on-going debates about the possibility that such games influence behaviour. Finally we have corporate/government projects in arms manufacture and attempts to develop effective weapons that stop short of lethality to populations deemed to be problematic. These issues arguably represent some of the most interesting and challenging areas for criminology today.

18

SPEEDING AND JOY RIDING

Karen Lumsden

Speeding refers to driving a motorised vehicle (such as a car or motorbike) above the speed limit prescribed by the state. Like other forms of crime, definitions of speeding are dependent upon the historical context, situational factors and societal norms and laws. Joy riding involves the theft of a vehicle, its use in various driving performances (including speeding) and often its subsequent destruction through setting fire to it (or 'torching' it).

Since the invention of the car, issues of road safety and in particular the regulation of speeding have been matters of contestation for governments, police, road safety organisations, the media and concerned citizens alike. The car has historically been viewed as both a means of increasing mobility and freedom, and as a socially harmful technology. In the wrong hands the car is a deadly weapon which has the potential to kill and/or injure innocent city dwellers such as pedestrians, cyclists and drivers or passengers in other vehicles. Over 90 per cent of the world's fatalities on the roads occur in low- and middle-income countries, which have only 48 per cent of the world's vehicles (World Health Organization, 2009). The maxim 'speed kills' is reflected in the number of road traffic fatalities in high-income countries, with the recurring claim that young male drivers are generally more likely to partake in risky driving behaviours, such as speeding. Factors behind the elevated risk are said to include mobility patterns and vehicle characteristics (for instance the vehicle is often borrowed); psychological characteristics, such as thrill-seeking and over-confidence; lower tolerance of alcohol compared with older people; and excessive or inappropriate speed, the most common error among young drivers and motorbike riders (Peden *et al.*, 2004: 79).

In various countries, speed limits have long been the subject of political and public contestation and debate. The vast majority of motorists have at some point exceeded the speed limit, and in some countries there has, for instance, been reluctance from those in positions of power (such as magistrates, politicians and the authorities), and many motorists themselves, to view car crime (including speeding) as 'real crime' (Corbett, 2003). Thus, licensed motorists found guilty of speeding have tended to receive minimal sentences and/or punishments. In terms of the detection of speeding (and other road traffic offences), police and the authorities have come to utilise a range of surveillance technologies such as speed cameras, radar guns and automatic number-plate recognition (ANPR), in addition to regular police patrols. Speed is also legitimised by agents of the state when used in the context of high-speed police pursuits and by other emergency services such as the fire and ambulance services. This again highlights the contextual nature of definitions of deviance, as driving at speed is deemed acceptable in emergency situations involving the authorities.

In contrast to legally licensed motorists who may speed during their daily car journeys, and state agents authorised to drive at speed for the purposes of public protection and safety, joy riders can be seen directly to challenge and transgress boundaries of legality and illegality in relation to the car. Joy riding and similar forms of car theft such as 'taking without the owner's consent' (TWOC-ing) and 'taking and driving away a vehicle' (TDA), shed light on the relationship between car culture, social class and gender. The term 'joy riding' highlights the pleasurable, thrilling and transgressive nature of the act for its participants. For young working-class males, joy riding allows for participation in car culture which is otherwise prevented due to their stagnated social and economic positions. Thus, many criminological studies of joy riding recognise that the popularity of the practice is indicative of, and related to, the car's totemic status as a (desirable) consumer item. Classic criminological studies of joy riders also highlight the importance of spectators who gather to watch the performances of the joy riders.

Boy racers (as they are known in the United Kingdom, New Zealand and Australia) also highlight the blurry boundaries between the deviance engaged in by the legal motorist and that of the joy rider. As legally licensed motorists, boy racers challenge and invert the norms of mainstream car culture via their engagement in speeding, illegal street racing and other risky driving manoeuvres (such as 'wheel-spins', 'doughnuts' and 'handbrake turns') and also via their customisation of technical, mechanical and aesthetic aspects of the car (Lumsden, 2013). Young male drivers are seen to threaten the vast majority of respectable motorists. Importantly, however, for both joy riders and boy racers, participation in car culture (albeit via deviant means) is crucial for the formation of individual and peer identity and provides a rite of passage into adult life.

Speeding, joy riding and illegal street racing are common forms of entertainment in the media and popular culture, which reinforce the image of the 'dangerous' young male driver. Examples include the classic film *Rebel without a Cause* (Ray, 1955), starring James Dean, and the illegal street racing scene found in the *Fast and the Furious* films. The high-speed police pursuit and images of the joy rider and boy racer also regularly feature in reality television exposés and 'live' news reports on television. These examples highlight the criminalisation process which occurs in terms of the individuals' engagement in the act of speeding, joy riding or boy racing; the response of the police, government and other criminal justice agencies; and the representation of the act in media and popular discourses. This process brings the image of the deviant driver to the public's attention.

A criminological analysis of speeding and joy riding draws attention to the historical labelling and stereotyping of certain groups and individuals as dangerous drivers by those in positions of power, in contrast to the mass of respectable motorists. These activities each have in common the quest for participation in car culture, whether through legal or deviant means. In short, there is a clear tension inherent in these car cultures wherein the freedom of the open road (and unrestricted automobility) is purveyed widely while we seek to instil a need for regulation, self-control and the governing of deviant driving behaviours.

References

Corbett, C. (2003) *Car Crime*, Cullompton, UK: Willan.

Lumsden, K. (2013) *Boy Racer Culture: Youth, Masculinity and Deviance*, Abingdon: Routledge.

Peden, M., Scurfield, R., Sleet, D., Mohan, D., Hyder, A., Jarawan, E. and Mathers, C. (eds) (2004) *World Report on Road Traffic Injury Prevention*, Geneva: World Health Organization.

World Health Organization (2009) *Global Status Report on Road Safety: Time for Action*, Geneva: World Health Organization.

Watch:

Rebel without a Cause (1955), film, directed by Nicholas Ray. USA: Warner Bros.

19

VIDEO-GAMING

Thomas Rodgers

Over the last three decades video-gaming has developed into one of the largest sectors of commercial popular culture. In the USA, recent demographic figures indicate that over 63 per cent of the population are 'video-game players' of one form or another, and that around 49 per cent of US households own a dedicated games console (ESA, 2012). European figures paint a similar picture, with recent data suggesting that around 68 per cent of people aged between 16 and 19, 57 per cent between 20 and 24, 49 per cent between 25 and 29, and 30 per cent of people aged between 30 and 49 are 'gamers' of some form or another (ISFE, 2010).

Today, 'video-gaming' refers to a wide array of interactive experiences made possible through computing technologies. Although contested by some as a non-technical or 'platform specific' term (Kerr, 2006), video-gaming is widely used to denote the various ways in which computing technologies are used as a means to simulate game-based scenarios and environments. These can range from simple puzzles, akin to those practised with pen-and-paper, to immersive three-dimensional environments in which scenarios as varied as warfare, dancing or Tolkienesque fantasy can be played out.

Playable scenarios based around real and perceived forms of social harm and deviance are noticeably prevalent throughout video-gaming culture. Themes of interpersonal violence, destruction, warfare and anti-social conduct have repeatedly served as the foundations for hugely successful franchises throughout the course of video-gaming history – widely known examples being Rockstar's *Grand Theft Auto*, Activision's *Call of Duty* and Square Enix's *Hitman* series. Video-games such as these – and others founded upon the simulation of deviant and/or harm-inflicting scenarios – have become renowned for generating both record-breaking sales figures and intense public debate. For example, the 2010 instalment of *Call of Duty* (entitled *Black Ops*) generated around one billion US dollars in revenue within six weeks of its release, reportedly surpassing all previous sales records for commercial entertainment of *any* type. At the same time, video-games premised upon strong motifs of visceral violence and interpersonal harm continue to attract prolonged public criticism and debate, particularly in relation to whether or not violence in video-games influences or cultivates real violent impulses. In response to a recent shooting at a primary school in Newtown, Connecticut – resulting in the deaths of twenty children and six adults – a community group set up a local return programme in order to collect and destroy violent video-games, stating that media portraying violence and killing have contributed to increasing aggressiveness and a mass desensitisation to acts of violence.

Questions concerning whether or not violent video-games cultivate or 'effect' real-world violence have a protracted history of public and academic debate that, for the most part, have been characterised by a mixture of outspoken moralising about perceived negative 'effects' on the one hand, and methodologically problematic laboratory research on the links between media violence and observed aggressive behaviour on the other. Experiments deprived of real-world context aiming to determine whether short-term exposure to violent video-games increases aggressive behaviour, whilst raising issues of importance on their own terms, provide little understanding of the status deviance, violence and destruction hold within video-gaming culture as core themes of mass entertainment. Whilst it is important to be aware of such issues and the questions they give rise to, perhaps a more pertinent issue is one of the *cultural status* of themes of violence, destruction and deviance, and the ways in which these find expression in video-game entertainment as a newly dominant aspect of popular culture.

To begin to come to grips with such questions and issues requires an in-depth look into the products of an industry that, in its darker and less widely available catalogues, makes available the interactive experience of stalking and raping a Japanese family – a game known as *RapeLay* by Illusion Soft – or the means to take on the role of participating in snuff movies in Rockstar's *Manhunt* series, in which the player-controlled character murders victims in extreme ways, using tools and weapons found within the virtual gaming environment. On the more popular and well-known side of video-gaming are the 'big sellers' based around the simulation of intense theatres of warfare and special operations in which players must train themselves to be capable of shooting for the head, tactically positioning themselves in order to eliminate the other without pause, and learning technical details about how modern warfare is conducted. These are but a few examples of the more general way in which video-game themes based around violence, deviance and extreme forms of conduct are normalised as staple reference points for playful engagement. What is striking throughout, however, is the overt encouragement to *play at* human harm and social deviance that is programmed into these virtual game-spaces that require the mere push of a button to 'make the kill' – spaces where notions of 'head shots', 'frags' and 'kill points' are at the heart of this playful, often accomplished engagement.

Sociological research into such questions is currently under-developed in contrast to the research, largely psychology-informed, into effects of video-game violence on individual behaviour. Nevertheless, what might attention to the themes of violence, interactive killing or criminality in video-games yield in terms of an understanding of the status and position these hold – not just for audiences, but for commercially driven companies – as sources of popular (and profitable) entertainment? Moreover, what might such a focus tell us about the enmeshing of norms and the interpretative dispositions of gamers with social problems like violence, criminality and murder? In short, the rise of a video-gaming culture of playful, *ludic* engagement in diverse forms of violence, if nothing else, tells us something about the status and importance of, and fixation on, violent themes within commercially driven aspects of our popular media culture more generally (see Hayward and Presdee, 2010). The increasing interplay between video-game franchises and Hollywood film production, multi-million dollar investment into the creation of 'blockbuster' games and the continued acceleration of computing power all point towards a further growth in the significance of video-gaming within our culture. The challenge for future research will be to maintain a sustained critique of the dominant themes and commercial imperatives upon which this popularity is founded and sold to us.

References

Entertainment Software Association (2012) Essential Facts about the Computer and Video Game Industry: 2012 Sales, Demographic, and Usage Data, ESA, available online at www.theesa.com/facts/pdfs/ESA_EF_2012.pdf (accessed 19 December 2012).

Hayward, K. J. and Presdee, M. (eds) (2010) *Framing Crime: Cultural Criminology and the Image*, Abingdon: Routledge.

Interactive Software Federation of Europe (2010) Video Gamers in Europe 2010, ISFE, available online at www.isfe.eu/content/video-gamers-europe-2010-gamevision-study (accessed 20 December 2012).

Kerr, A. (2006) *The Business and Culture of Digital Games: Gamework/Gameplay*, London: SAGE.

Play:

Hitman: Absolution (2012), video-game, developed by IO Interactive. UK/USA: Square Enix.

20

'HARMLESS' WEAPONS AND CROWD CONTROL

Steve Wright

Sub-lethal weapons for law enforcement are now a lucrative business. They have gone from relatively cheap rubber bullets to directed energy devices such as the Silent Guardian, costing several million pounds. Much of the accelerated interest in using such technology has come from the US military's take-up of 'non-lethal doctrines', particularly where they have been forced to fight mixed populations of civilians and combatants. Current variants include systems based on optical, microwave, electrostun, kinetic energy, micromillimetre wave, malodorant and bio-chemical effects, and on flight stabilised capture nets.

Colonel John Alexander, a Vietnam War Special Forces veteran, was the key mover behind persuading the US Department of Defense (DoD) to fund seriously new research into sub-lethal weapons (Alexander, 1999). The grants subsequently spawned new generations of incapacitating and paralysing weapons like VMAD pain weapons, XREP Taser shotguns and laser dazzlers. Such weapons now form a core capability set for militaries facing new threats from terrorism, and can also aid in stemming migration caused by climate change.

The summer riots of 2011 saw renewed calls for police to have access to more powerful crowd control weapons such as CS gas, water cannon and plastic bullets. Within the terms of the ACPO Public Order Manual of Tactical Operations, a case could easily have been made by chief constables for deploying such crowd control weapons when their officers were facing fire bombs. Indeed, since the 1980s, all UK police forces have been trained in new public order tactics using so-called 'baton rounds'. They have their own stocks and access to Home Office regional stores. Outside Northern Ireland, British police have appeared reluctant to control crowds with new weapons. Part of that stance relates to the management of public relations: maintaining the mythology of the unarmed British Bobby policing by consent; part is both strategic and pragmatic (Rappert and Wright, 2000). In certain parts of London, officers attempting to 'up the ante' with riot weapons might have been seen as fair game for an armed response by local gangs. But how will the undercurrents of police–public perceptions change in the twenty-first century as social and political divisions deepen and new weapons capacities emerge? Will this lead to new decisions about what is legitimate use of violence by agents of the state?

Ever since new crowd control technologies were deployed in Northern Ireland in 1969, their use has been divisive. Government attempts to present them as humane alternatives to guns were challenged by NGOs such as the British Society For Social Responsibility in Science (BSSRS), who argued that the science to defend such a stance didn't add up: they were designed to *appear* rather than *be* safe. For example, research on the safety of CS gas was woefully inadequate and led to the Himsworth Committee concluding that in future all chemical agents for riot control should be seen as drugs rather than weapons, and that all relevant research should be published in full prior to deployment. Similarly BSSRS said that the technical characteristics of plastic bullets made them extremely dangerous across their entire flight path, and reported the work of Belfast surgeons who found scalpings, eye loss, severe damage to internal organs and deaths resulting from them.

The British Council for Science and Society warned in 1978 of the dangers that once such weapons had been deployed they would be likely to proliferate and would exacerbate ethnic divisions and fuel future conflict – a reality focused on by the Patten Report on Policing in Northern Ireland. Some writers naively argue that, compared to lethal weapons, these weapons are relatively humane. However, such weapons represent technologies that enable political control, with new rules emerging around what can now constitute acceptable force against political opponents or unruly citizens. The Omega Research Foundation has found convincing evidence that, when replaced, these new weapons can be more dangerous than conventional weapons.

All of this raises the question of why these weapons are becoming increasingly evolved and deployed when they do not increase public safety. Yet it was never a case of choosing between lethal or sub-lethal, since lethal weapons are always co-deployed as backup by policing agencies. Even the nomenclature is political since such weapons cannot be 'non-lethal' if they occasionally kill; this has resulted in 'less-lethal' becoming the favoured term. Studies undertaken for the European Parliament by the Omega Research Foundation found extensive evidence that, even though such weapons could offer a reduced force option, far too often they were capable of being used for serious human rights abuses if deployed in abusive or illegitimate operations.

Such concerns have led human rights NGOs such as Amnesty International (2003) to refocus their mandate on the role and function of such weapons and the merchants that sell, broker, supply and manufacture them. They have tracked the role of such tools as neuromuscular incapacitation devices in implementing deviant state crimes such as torture, and Amnesty has also gathered evidence to challenge weapons such as Tasers, which they found to be associated with 330 deaths in the USA between 2001 and 2008 (90 per cent of victims were unarmed). Worrying evidence also emerged of stun weapons used to exert dominance and compliance through pain. Similar concerns were raised by the UK charity Rethink Mental Illness over excessive use of Taser weapons by British police forces against those suffering mental health issues, where an ambulance call might have been more appropriate.

University projects such as the Bradford Non-lethal Weapons Research Project (BNLWRP) and NGOs such as Pugwash Conferences on Science and World Affairs and the International Committee for Robot Arms Control (ICRAC), which looks at autonomous robotic formats like those featured in the video game *Metal Gear Solid 4*, are monitoring the future evolution of non-lethal weapons. Yet it does not seem possible to discount the possibility that further waves of European social turbulence may generate more militarised versions of law enforcement for crowd control. Even in a time of austerity, tooling up police with the latest gizmos may prove a seductive techno-fix that has the investment of major corporations and politicians (Davison, 2009).

References

Alexander, J. (1999) *Future War: Non-lethal Weapons in Twenty-first Century Warfare*, New York: Thomas Dunne.

Amnesty International (2003) *Pain Merchants: Security Equipment and Its Use in Torture and Other Ill-treatment*, London: International Secretariat. Available online at www.amnesty.org/en/library/info/ACT40/008/2003 (accessed 2 October 2013).

Davison, N. (2009) *'Non-lethal' Weapons*, Basingstoke, UK: Palgrave Macmillan.

Rappert, B. and Wright, S. (2000) A Flexible Response? Assessing Non-lethal Weapons, *Technology Analysis & Strategic Management*, 12, (4), pp. 477–92.

Watch:

No More Killing (2009), documentary film, directed by Wolfgang Bergmann. Germany: Lichtfilm, available online at http://wn.com/No_More_Killing_07_von_09 (accessed 2 October 2013).

21

HACKERS AND CYBERCRIME

Craig Webber

'Now pay attention, 007'. This famous line delivered by James Bond's quartermaster was often followed by a diametrically opposed response. Bond, impatient with Q's tedious instructions on the correct way to use the gadget, would roar off into the field, masterfully controlling the device and sometimes skilfully and creatively circumventing the gadget's original purpose. This is not what most people would recognise as the epitome of the definition of the term 'hacker'. But this is what many hackers would recognise as their key skill. Controlling a device through technical mastery and making it do things the inventor never intended is the hallmark of the hacker. One could argue that the apps created for smartphones are a prime example of this. The proliferation of apps that utilise the internal sensory apparatus (GPS, camera, gyroscope, microphone and audio output amongst others) has allowed for the huge evolution of such instruments. Smartphones can be used as a torch or a spirit level, a compass and GPS locator, handheld computer, music library and television; sometimes they are even used to telephone friends. Such examples highlight ostensibly positive uses of the creative impulse to innovate and become a master of technological constructions. Moreover, many people who were caught and prosecuted for hacking have since been employed as security advisers for technology companies. The problem is that the term hacker has come to embody a far more negative connotation, that of the deviant who lurks unseen on the Internet and infiltrates computers, spying on us, stealing from us and infecting our computer systems (Webber and Vass, 2010).

So hackers occupy an ambivalent position in our culture. A 'geek' culture has arisen around the proliferation of information technologies since the early 1980s and the skills of young producers of code, software and technology have become central to the information-driven economy of the West. It is from within these cohorts that a range of hacking activities has arisen. Some of this is related to general objectives (the targeting of corporate and government websites by the Anonymous network for closing down the availability of information) or indeed the showing off of hackers who set out to impress others in this loose community as to their computing skills. Even within the body of individuals who would see themselves as hackers there is variability in the codes and norms adopted around what is and is not acceptable. This suggests that hackers are not a monolithic grouping. Similarly it is clear that where the objectives of hackers align with public concerns and interests hackers have enjoyed tacit support despite raising anxieties about their possible power.

Where did this image of the deviant hacker come from? Certainly, the problem has been shaped by military, political and media concerns. The UK coalition government suggested in 2010 that the threat from cyber-attacks was one the most important and dangerous developments, necessitating immediate and substantial investment. According to the latest UK National Security Strategy in 2010, cybercrime has been assigned as a Tier One threat to the United Kingdom, alongside international terrorism. Similar concerns have also been raised in the US and Australia. Recent cyber-security statistics (Yip, Webber and Shadbolt, 2013) conclude that cybercrime remains as the primary threat facing nations, corporations and people in 2013. In response, new government-recognised centres of excellence have been set up at universities to engage in cutting-edge research on cyber-security, and law enforcement agencies have become far more aware of the need to take cyber-security seriously.

In order to understand the massive range of activities that can be included under the term cybercrime, it is necessary to differentiate between its various forms (Wall, 2008). This can include the distribution of illegal images such as child pornography, defacing websites for fun or to make a political point (hacktivism), trolling and cyberbullying. There is also a fear over state-sponsored hacking of essential infrastructure, or the stealing of data from the state or from business, essentially cyber-espionage.

Hacking can be a solitary activity, but many cybercrimes require cooperation from many specialist people. For example, 'carding' is the buying and selling of stolen credit cards. The network of people can include pickpockets, those who skim cards in shops and restaurants, the makers of the device that skims the card, the maker of fake cards, the seller of the credit card numbers and other identity details, the online forum administrators where the trading takes place and the person who takes money out of an ATM machine. In addition, this is a global enterprise where a card could be stolen or skimmed in London, but 'cashed out' in New York. In other words, hacking is too simple a description for just this one form of crime (Yip, Webber and Shadbolt, 2013). Indeed, much that we regard as cybercrime takes place offline as much as it does online (Webber and Yip, 2012). The massive variation in the forms that cybercrime can take is rarely at the forefront of our thinking. This means that the security response tends to focus on the technology and not the people. Making more secure systems ignores the fact that cybercrime is based on trust, as in any criminal (and non-criminal) enterprise. Human intelligence of cybercrime networks and the ability to disrupt trust is just as important as the continual need to improve technological security.

This trend towards greater investment in security systems and fear of hacking threats is not without its critics. It could be argued that this problem is largely manufactured through flawed evidence and questionable statistics. Wall (2008) further notes that the systems set up to counter the perceived problem are themselves doing significant harm to our civil liberties. It is important that we do not drift further into a surveillance culture where our every move is subject to monitoring. Already we leave a digital trail that follows us and can never be deleted or forgotten; a 'sticky identity' that is built up from our social media trails and Google searches. Our contemporary identities are more open to control, policing and theft because of our significant online presence and often a naive belief in our safety and ignorance of the harvesting of such data by governments and corporations.

References

Wall, D. (2008) *Cybercrime: The Transformation of Crime in the Information Age.* Malden, UK: Polity Press.

Webber, C. and Vass, J. (2010) Crime, Film and the Cybernetic Imagination, in Y. Jewkes and M. Yar (eds), *Handbook of Internet Crime*, Cullompton, UK: Willan, pp. 120–44.

Webber, C. and Yip, M. (2012) Drifting On and Off-line: Humanising the Cyber Criminal, in S. Winlow and R. Atkinson (eds), *New Directions in Crime and Deviancy*, pp. 191–205.

Yip, M., Webber, C. and Shadbolt, N. (2013) Trust among Cybercriminals? Carding Forums, Uncertainty and Implications for Policing, in *Policing and Society*.

Watch:

The Girl with the Dragon Tattoo (2009), film, directed by Niels Arden Oplev. Sweden: Yellow Bird.

22

SEXTING AND CYBERBULLYING

Anne-Marie McAlinden

While 'sexting' and 'cyberbullying' are beginning to come out of the shadows and be investigated by academics as forms of deviance, little attention has been afforded to these issues at public policy level. The most publicly prominent forms of harms to children which occur through online methods relate to 'grooming' by predatory sex offenders (McAlinden, 2012). Legislation to cover online grooming, for example, has been put in place in an array of jurisdictions including the United States, Australia, Norway, Sweden and throughout the United Kingdom. Media campaigns also abound on the safe use of the Internet and the need to protect children from predatory adult offenders in the virtual environment. Such public and official responses to online risks are, however, based on distorted notions of 'deviance', in particular on stereotypical and culturally entrenched images of victims and offenders in such cases – that is, that the offenders are usually adult male strangers ready to prey on unsuspecting, much younger victims.

More recently, several studies have emerged which have directly challenged such paradigms of deviance and the notion that children and young people, as 'innocents', may be the victims but not the perpetrators of such offences. Finkelhor *et al.* (2000), for example, found that 48 per cent of online offenders in their study were under 18. The phenomena of cyberbullying (Kofoed and Ringrose, 2011) and sexting (Ringrose *et al.*, 2012) in particular, however, demonstrate the existence of 'peer-to-peer grooming' and exploitative and abusive behaviours *by* and *among* as well as *of* young people. Such forms of deviance are among the fastest growing forms of harm experienced by children and young people (McAlinden, 2012).

Cyberbullying, broadly defined, is the use of the Internet and other mobile technologies to harass, threaten or harm other people, usually in a deliberate and sustained manner. Recent NSPCC figures show that 38 per cent of young people have been affected by cyberbullying (NSPCC, 2013). Sexting, on the other hand, is the act of sending sexually explicit messages and/or photographs, primarily between mobile phones, via text messages, e-mail, instant messaging or social networking sites. Typical examples include a young boy forwarding a sexually explicit image of a girl, with whom he had a prior relationship, to his friends, and perhaps threatening to show her parents or teachers if more images were not forthcoming. The latter instance also denotes a potential cross-over with cyberbullying. Findings from a range of studies have revealed that rates of between 15 and 40 per cent among young people have received sexting messages, depending on age parameters and how 'sexting' is defined and measured (Ringrose *et al.*, 2012). Such studies demonstrate collectively that the onset, prevalence and range of sexual, exploitative and abusive behaviours by children and young people is an area of growing concern and one that must be taken seriously by policy makers in formulating future legal and social policies on child protection.

To date, such forms of deviance by children and young people have largely remained in the dark area of unknown crime. The notion that children and young people may be offenders as well as victims is a difficult one for policy makers, as well as society, to countenance. Such difficulties stem in large part from the fact that academic as well as professional understandings of sexual or exploitative behaviours committed by young people are largely split between whether they represent innocent exploration and an experimental transitory phase or early indicators of the onset of something more sinister. Moreover, as noted above, they also directly conflict with deep-seated notions of the innocence of children and the need to protect them at all costs.

There are a number of challenges inherent for both policy makers and wider society in recognising the existence of sexting and cyberbullying as significant social problems in need of specific action. In particular, there is a fundamental tension between the need to protect children from harm and the many forms of contemporary popular culture which tend to sexualise children or to treat them as mini adults. Further, online forms of communication are pivotal to our contemporary daily lives and to the leisure and social activities of most young people. There may be considerable difficulties, therefore, in getting children and young people to view such behaviours as exploitative or harmful and in encouraging them to report behaviours which they do not particularly regard as unwelcome, especially at the early stages of the process. Moreover, there are also burgeoning difficulties relating to technological advances, particularly in relation to the use of smart phone and related technologies (Martellozzo, 2012). This presents challenges not only for the police and law enforcement in keeping abreast of such advances but also for parents and carers in their understanding and awareness of how young people communicate with each other or spend their leisure time.

It would seem that any solution, however, does not lie in extending regulatory frameworks to create an even greater range of possible offences involving sexualised harms or exploitative behaviours towards children. Such actions would only tend to alienate children and young people from such debates and lead to significant net-widening of official definitions of deviant behaviour. The answer may then lie in engaging with parents and carers, and with children and young people themselves via their peer groups as well as traditional authority figures and policing interventions. This would include education and information, not only about safe use of the Internet and so-called 'stranger danger', but about a wider range of issues beyond child protection per se – related, for example, to consent, sexual health, respect, privacy and healthy inter-personal relationships. It also lies in the greater involvement of the providers of social media platforms to get them to take increased ownership of and responsibility for the problem. Such companies need to move beyond apathy and the pursuit of profit and embrace the mantra that 'child protection is everyone's responsibility'.

Child abuse in general has only been recognised as a specific social problem within the last few decades. Even then the focus has been on 'stranger danger' rather than the majority of abuse that occurs within intra-familial or inter-personal contexts. In short, in defining how we perceive and respond to new and emerging forms of deviance involving children, there is a very real danger of repeating these same mistakes of narrowing the definitions and the scope of the problem. 'Sexting' and 'cyberbullying' broaden our traditional understandings of harm to children and challenge us to accept that children and young people can be both the perpetrators and the victims of exploitation or abuse.

References

Finkelhor, D., Mitchell, K. J. and Wolak, J. (2000) *Online Vicimization: A Report on the Nation's Youth*, Alexandria, VA: National Center for Missing and Exploited Children.

Kofoed, J. and Ringrose, J. (2011) Travelling and Sticky Affects: Exploring Teens and Sexualized Cyberbullying through a Butlerian-Deleuzian-Guattarian Lens, *Discourse*, 33, (1), pp. 5–20.

McAlinden, A. (2012) *'Grooming' and the Sexual Abuse of Children: Internet, Institutional and Familial Dimensions,* Oxford: Oxford University Press, Clarendon Studies in Criminology.

Martellozzo, E. (2012) *Online Child Sexual Abuse: Grooming, Policing and Child Protection in a Multi-media World*, Abingdon and New York: Routledge.

National Society for the Prevention of Cruelty to Children (2013) 'Statistics on Bullying', March 2013, available online at www.nspcc.org.uk (accessed 9 October 2013).

Ringrose, J., Gill, R., Livingstone, S. and Harvey, L. (2012) A Qualitative Study of Children, Young People and 'Sexting': A Report Prepared for the NSPCC, available online at www.nspcc.org.uk (accessed 9 October 2013).

Watch:

Cyberbully (2011), TV film, directed by Charles Binamé. USA: ABC Family.

PART IV

Changing social attitudes and perceptions of social problems

Social change is a critical ingredient in explorations of crime and deviancy. Societies change in complex and sometimes dramatic ways, involving related shifts in social attitudes and conventions that may become more tolerant or punitive over time. These factors are incredibly important in understanding how attitudes towards deviant behaviour change. Take the example of homosexuality, which was illegal in many countries (and indeed still is in some today), but which now sees a much more tolerated and indeed positive social position, to the extent that homophobia is itself seen as deviant behaviour. On the other hand, while some forms of drug taking are now widespread in many Western countries, large parts of the population continue to see such activities as major problems, even where their own health or well-being is unaffected. Such shifts and continuities highlight the importance of social contexts and forces as major determinants of how particular behaviours may come to be defined as problematic or as something more acceptable, with different directions of travel to be found on issues in different national contexts over time.

The chapters in this section focus on questions of crime and social rule-breaking that have seen significant changes in public attitudes and legal positions over time, as well as contested perspectives on issues that arise between different social groups (such as the aggressive vilification of welfare recipients or the castigation of newly deviant groups like smokers). Focusing on these issues helps us to understand more about the societies we live in and the kinds of social divisions that continue to drive negative perceptions towards identifiable social groups. The study of deviation and crime requires us to locate groups and actions in social contexts and to offer careful analyses of why it is that particular behaviours may see censure or celebration at different social moments.

23

DRUGS

Emma Wincup

Drug use for many is synonymous with the use of substances which are prohibited through criminal law, whilst for others a broader and more effective understanding of a 'drug' recognises that a wide range of everyday legal substances can be as harmful, if not more so, than those subject to strict legal controls. This includes alcohol, tobacco, glues and solvents, over-the-counter medication and caffeine. The role of drug legislation is to outlaw the consumption of drugs in unregulated contexts whilst permitting their legitimate use for medicinal purposes; for example, for pain relief or to treat depression. Yet such legislation is based upon official perceptions of harmfulness which may not be shared by all.

Recently the growing availability of 'legal highs' has blurred the boundaries between legal and illegal substances. These new substances are designed to mimic the effects of illegal drugs but can be purchased with ease from websites and 'head shops'. In an attempt to bypass current legislation, they are labelled 'unfit for human consumption' and/or use a careful combination of legal and banned substances. Criminalisation has been the typical response to the proliferation of legal highs although there are real concerns about the ability of formal controls to keep pace with the rate at which they enter the drug market. For example, in the UK (since March 2012), legal highs which are judged to be harmful have been banned on a temporary basis in the first instance whilst the harm they might cause is investigated further. It remains to be seen – and it seems unlikely – whether substances that were once viewed as potentially harmful can later be deemed sufficiently 'safe' to warrant a lifting of the ban.

Despite the criminalisation of many forms of drug use, the taking of illicit drugs is widespread. For example, the 2011–12 Crime Survey for England and Wales (Home Office, 2012) estimated that 37 per cent of 16- to 59-year-olds have used one or more illicit drugs in their lifetime, and similarly high figures are found across the globe. For many drug use is short-lived, confined to experimentation when young people are making the transition to adulthood, and restricted largely to so-called 'recreational' drugs (most commonly cannabis). In recognition of this, it has been argued that recreational drug use has become 'normalised' and is no longer viewed as a deviant activity engaged in by atypical sub-cultural groups. Instead it forms part of growing up in contemporary society.

Recreational drug use is often contrasted with problem drug use, characterised by dependency, regular excessive use or use which exposes users to serious health (for example, through injecting) or other risks (social, psychological, physical or legal). There are links between problem drug use and other social problems such as homelessness, offending and unemployment, but it is important to appreciate the complexities of such linkages and note that drug use often exacerbates problems which already existed. Whilst recreational use is widespread and cuts across the social spectrum, problem drug use appears to be most heavily concentrated in particular groups and is, in many respects, a product of wider social inequalities. Responses to drug use play a pivotal role in reproducing such inequality by excluding further already marginalised groups. This is especially pronounced when problem drug use is defined in terms of a threat to law and order rather than to individual health and well-being.

Debates about the most effective policy response to tackle the drug 'problem' are often heated. It has been variously defined as a crime, a medical issue and a public health problem, with consequently differing implications for the policy solutions offered. In particular, it is worth noting the diametrically opposed views that often exist, with some calling for tougher laws and others for decriminalisation or legalisation. Advocates of the former argue that further prohibition is necessary to protect individuals from harm, partly through taking action against those who supply drugs but also to deter individuals from drug-taking. The position rests upon assumptions made about the role of law in regulating behaviour, which widespread illegal drug use has brought into question. Conversely, proponents of legalisation have argued that, rather than preventing harm, this approach exacerbates it by removing the opportunity to regulate such substances through imposing tight controls on their composition and distribution. Less controversially, some jurisdictions have opted for decriminalisation. For example, since 2001 Portugal has treated drug possession as a civil, rather than criminal, offence. Even the USA, which has been heavily criticised for pursuing a 'war on drugs', has recently experimented with this approach. In 2012, the states of Colorado and Washington made steps towards making it legal to buy and sell cannabis.

In many respects drug use in contemporary societies provides a vivid illustration of the contested nature of what constitutes deviant behaviour. It demonstrates the plurality of views on behaviours that some perceive as 'normal' and others 'deviant', and exposes the gap between 'official' definitions and those held within wider society. It is therefore perhaps unsurprising that some of the classic studies in the sociology of deviance (Becker, 1963; Young, 1971) have used empirical research with drug users to develop theoretical concepts such as deviancy amplification. Although dated, they continue to provide some insights into societal responses to drug use and especially in relation to the stigmatisation of drug users. Now largely focused on 'problem' drug users, powerful interests, such as politicians and the media, continue to portray such individuals as irresponsible, undeserving non-citizens with little attempt to understand the socio-economic context in which their drug use occurs. Upon closer analysis we can see the contradictions within the state's attempts to censure particular forms of drug use, often by the most marginalised individuals in society, whilst condoning (and perhaps even promoting) other forms of substance use.

References

Becker, H. (1963) *Outsiders: Studies in the Sociology of Deviance*, New York: Free Press.
Home Office (2012) *Drug Misuse Declared: Findings from the 2011/12 Crime Survey for England and Wales*, London: Home Office.
Young, J. (1971) *The Drugtakers*, London: Paladin.

Watch:

Human Traffic (1999), film, directed by Justin Kerrigan. UK: Miramax Films.

24

SADOMASOCHISM

Andrea Beckmann

Common stereotypes of consensual sadomasochism (SM) tend to associate these practices with violence, often generating a sense of otherness and danger around such acts. Such inaccurate constructs generate a sense of consensual sadomasochism as 'deviance', 'perversion' or 'crime' (selectively criminalised and enforced) and reflect attempts to instil and delimit the scope of 'natural sexuality' (often represented as heterosexuality), which is thus cast as normality. Concepts of truth in the sexual realm constitute the limits of legitimate human sexual expression and discredit certain forms of experience, thereby establishing conditions that dominate our everyday existence. These broader socio-political and cultural conditions and relations of non-consensual power are appropriated in the context of consensual 'SM' practice for the generation of mutual pleasures. Consensual SM is a conscious and closely negotiated bodily practice that is based upon agreed limits by those involved (Beckmann, 2009).

For the wider community consensual SM appears to destabilise conventional societal power relationships, interfering with monopolies of power and of professional expertise, for example by challenging expert authority over what constitutes a happy or fulfilling sexual relationship. This is partly because what is known as consensual SM 'play' frequently breaks down the public/private administration of the body, its pleasures and its sensations. As consensual SM is fundamentally based on communication and negotiation, a more fluid understanding of power in contrast to fixed and strictly hierarchical sets of 'normal' power relations is required. This alters the meaning and interpretation of the dynamics of personal/political struggle for individuals as well as for groups of practitioners because they become dynamic and do not remain fixed, as is frequently true in 'normalised' societal situations (for example, living up to gender expectations and those around age, sexuality and national identity).

The crucial point of difference between consensual SM and violence is that all acts are negotiated. The contemporary popularity of the *Fifty Shades* trilogy and others of a similar genre can be seen as representative of the way that on various levels of our consumer culture (literature, fashion, sex-toys and advertisements, for example) decontextualised elements of SM and of fetish culture have become integrated for profit. However, while this development on the one hand opens up possibilities of engagement and transgression of the realm of normatively imposed ideas about what constitutes normal sexuality, it is crucial to reflect on capitalism's tendency to facilitate the commodification of apparently 'kinky' sex (Beckmann, 2001). Put simply this means that representations of SM sex, related goods and services can be made into products that can be bought and sold. Thus such experiences become integrated into forms of capitalist exchange which thereby reduce the authenticity of power transformations through such experiences. Representations of consumer-kink do not totally determine behaviour and inferred meaning but they do impact on the ways in which practices are interpreted and lived out. While this trend might be seen to imply a greater understanding of or openness to a wide variety of bodily practices, the simultaneous selective criminalisation of such behaviour might suggest otherwise (Beckmann, 2009; Langdridge and Barker, 2007).

Consensual SM aims at the production of pleasure through the empathetic play with the body, not limited to sexual pleasure and more fittingly described as a bodily practice. Mainstream understandings of SM only partially acknowledge that many practices of consensual SM are not genitally focused and that even the involvement of the body is often more crucially focused on the inner experience and important existential, inter-relational and political dimensions of consensual SM play that are frequently absent from public representations.

Consensual SM involves the appropriation of, and resistance to, traditional modes of social and sexual power, traditionally established to subject human beings. It is through the transformation of such forms of authority into games that they become tools and toys in a game that aims for the achievement of consensual pleasures. Rigid socio-political structures and roles become part of a consensual game that, via negotiation, ensures safety through continuous reflexive observation by the 'dominant' and the possibility of the use of a safety-word or gesture by the 'submissive', as well as through the practice of switching of roles, which are thus dynamic and not fixed. Representations of commodified kink, on the other hand, predominantly embrace a capitalist logic and value-system that foster the consumption of objects and people rather than their respect or acknowledgement.

In contrast to the conditions of domination that pervade Western, patriarchal and capitalist consumer cultures, the more reflexive and empathetic ethic of consensual SM practitioners offers the possibility of the creation of counter-narratives and bodily practices that re-constitute and shake up concepts of individuality. In this explorative space the inter-dependence of self and environment, the lived body and its potentiality for change and fluidity can be experienced. It is at this level of interde-pendency, so often totally suppressed in commodified representations of the body and sex, that the possibilities of more ethical relations can be explored. On a philosophical level consensual SM can facilitate unique insights into the inter-relationships between the political and the corpo-real as practitioners are engaged with the learning of a contextual taking care of the self in the scenes played out in consensual SM. Rigid catego-ries of separation (of 'gender', of 'sexuality', and so on) are broken down, and communication and exchange (verbal and non-verbal) are made possible (Beckmann, 2009).

In the current context in which the global, corporate and governmen-tal grip on 'bodies' is becoming more and more relentless, the potential for the criminalisation of 'bodies' engaged in consensual SM needs to be challenged. 'Bodies' are more than corporate future investments, items of commodity value to picture-takers or bearers of patentable genetic mate-rial. They should be allowed to explore philosophical and spiritual levels of their embodiment, instead of being expected to be forever consuming or submissive to these forms of authority. It is a telling hypocrisy that we value elective cosmetic surgery procedures and contact sports while con-sensual SM practices are reduced to simple impressions of criminality or dangerous perversion.

References

Beckmann, A. (2001) Deconstructing Myths: The Social Construction of 'Sadomasochism' versus 'Subjugated Knowledges' of Practitioners of Consensual 'SM', *Journal of Criminal Justice and Popular Culture*, 8, (2), pp. 66–95.

Beckmann, A. (2009) *The Social Construction of Sexuality and Perversion: Deconstructing Sadomasochism*, Basingstoke, UK: Palgrave Macmillan.

Langdridge, D. and Barker, M. (eds) (2007) *Safe, Sane and Consensual: Contemporary Perspectives on Sadomasochism*, Basingstoke, UK: Palgrave Macmillan.

Watch:

Safe, Sane, Consensual SM: A Documentary (1992), documentary film, co-produced by Bob Dern and Anne Soucy-West. USA: Rigid Video Incorporated, clip available online at www.youtube.com/watch?v=Uvrr0L4QMNw (accessed 3 October 2013).

25

EUTHANASIA

Mike Brogden

Euthanasia has been used colloquially to describe an easing of the pains of life to ensure that an older or severely disabled person is enabled to die with some dignity, as a means of curtailing their suffering. Such acts can be viewed from a range of perspectives and thus remain contested, viewed by some as deviant and by others as desirable, or legitimate under certain circumstances. These competing views rely on the particular social and legal context and the perspective of those receiving such treatment to give them meaning. Early labels implied a positive process, with the term 'euthanasia' deriving from two Greek words, *eu* (good) and *thanatos* (death). That is only one contextual perception. In the twentieth century, the concept absorbed more brutal, self-interested dimensions. Euthanasia encompasses the intentional killing of those in a subordinate position. It no longer automatically assumes the practice of killing for the latter's own alleged benefit. Euthanasia can be diverse in form, including requiring the involvement of a second person. It includes the deliberate killing of a subordinate group such as 'mental defectives' under the Nazis (especially in the killing camp of Hadamar). But it also covers the action of a hospital doctor who places a 'DNR' (Do Not Resuscitate) sign on a patient's door. It includes therefore both sins of commission – deliberate disposal of the 'Other' – and sins of omission – speeding up the dying process by not maintaining a patient's survival, for example by not providing necessary sustenance. Confusingly, in the latter example, the primary actor may also conduct acts of commission by furnishing, for example, an excessive amount of a pain-killing drug.

Being in a position of dependency is a further criterion and can vary between the extremes of a coercive relationship and one of physical or mental dependence. Euthanasia has a dual position: voluntary euthanasia (when the person who is killed has requested that action, or inaction) and homicide (when the person who is killed made no request and gives no consent). Sometimes it may be that an individual is provided with the information, guidance and means to take his or her own life so that more direct assistance is not required in the final stages.

When it is a doctor who helps another person to kill themselves this is called 'physician assisted suicide', and can take active or passive forms. 'Active euthanasia' refers to a situation when the doctor's (or another person's) direct action causes the patient's death, such as giving the patient a lethal injection of drugs. 'Passive euthanasia', on the other hand, is when doctors do not do something which will keep the patient alive or stop doing something which is keeping the patient alive. This includes turning off life-support equipment, removing a feeding tube and not carrying out a life-extending operation. Euthanasia is also categorised by the patient's consent or non-consent as voluntary and involuntary. Voluntary euthanasia is when the patient asks another person to end his or her life with full knowledge that this will lead to death; involuntary euthanasia takes place when the patient does not wish to die. Voluntarism – allowing people to do what they choose – is both a confused and enabling concept, with little legal precision. The recent acceptance in the UK of a 'Living Will' allows medical staff to respect a patient's wish to die through a process of omission, but the majority of historical cases are less clear-cut. Voluntarism and coercion overlap in complex ways. It is difficult to deal with such imprecision in legal statutes. Resistance by powerful groups with different motives ensures that arguments will continue.

Geronticide (Brogden, 2001) shows that many societies practised euthanasia for both the elderly and the physically infirm. The procedure was especially evident in hunter-gatherer societies where inability to hunt for game or the fruits of the forest required disposal of the unfit. Inuit people might cast the elderly adrift on an ice floe; certain Siberian tribes would guide the elderly over a rock face; amongst aboriginal Australians, the practice was common. Tradition, rather than coercion or voluntarism, ruled. The Greeks were divided on the subject: Hippocrates rejected coercion but accepted euthanasia by omission, while Socrates rejected both.

Examples can also be found in literature. The Grimms' Fairy Tales include examples of coercion in Sorbian society, while also noting the resistance of the elderly. Sir Thomas More wrote, disapprovingly, of the inevitability of euthanasia in Utopian society. Novelist Anthony Trollope (Trollope, 1993) depicted it in *The Fixed Period* (1882) as necessary for colonial survival. The 'period' of the title refers to the age (67 years old) at which a citizen of Britannula, a fictional island, must begin preparations for death by euthanasia the following year. Kurt Vonnegut's short story '2BR02B' (Vonnegut, 1962) describes resistance to the process, and Martin Amis envisaged euthanasia booths on every street (Davies, 2010).

In Britain, the nineteenth-century Poor Laws pushed the elderly into the slow-motion euthanasia of the workhouse, in which conditions were so harsh that premature death almost inevitably followed. These places of forced labour in return for a meagre existence might also be seen as the predecessors of some of the less benign care homes today ('Granddad, it's time to go'). Yet criminologists have rarely been concerned with such potential victims, the handicapped and the elderly on the margins of society whose rights may be abused behind closed doors, with more or less coercion involved.

The arguments against euthanasia

1   Euthanasia may be used for persons who are not terminally ill – for example, those suffering from depression.
2   Euthanasia may be conducted for economic reasons: the 'bed-blocking' terminally ill may be seen as using scarce resources in a cost-centred health service; the liminal are occupying capacity that could be used for those with a future. Similarly an heir of the dependant may seek the other's death for financial purposes (though there are few documented cases). Economic considerations are especially important for candidates whose continual support requires resources furnished by others. In turn, that situation may result in the patient feeling implicitly pressed to reduce the burden on others.
3   The 'slippery slope' argument: once a society allows euthanasia for serious cases of physical illness, may it then, having set the precedent, eventually extend that practice to less serious cases? This has been the case with regard to the limited legalisation of abortion.

4   While the Living Will is promoted by pro-euthanasia NGOs such as Dignity in Dying, who makes the decision in relation to a person who is comatose and has left no instructions?

5   As with infanticide, euthanasia may be determined by gender and socio-economic class as well as by age. Poverty-stricken rural societies may see particular population segments as a burden, irrespective of human rights.

As with arguments over abortion, there is no public consensus over the sanctity of human life; different moralities influence approaches to practice and so deviance in relation to the question of euthanasia may be hard to assess, even by determined, impartial commentators. Internationally, there are no common legal standards. For example, Belgium accepts euthanasia with relevant caveats (in practice, it is mainly used in the case of home-bound younger male cancer victims), yet in Ireland, commission of an act to assist a person to die is illegal. However, the state also permits omission as justifiable in law. Canadian legislation is currently confused, with formal punishment for those who assist, but, as in Britain, rarely imposes more than a token penalty. Statute and legal practice vary. In the UK, though euthanasia is illegal, no second party has been given a custodial penalty for it in the last decade. While nearly one hundred Britons have utilised relatively lax Swiss legislation, no assisting relative has been charged. Such variations highlight the difficulty of understanding the ways in which euthanasia is interpreted as being a transgression of legal or social codes across different communities.

Bibliography

Brogden, M. (2001) *Geronticide*, Cullompton, UK: Willan.

Davies, C. (2010) Martin Amis in New Row over Euthanasia Booths, *The Guardian*, 24 January, available online at www.theguardian.com/books/2010/jan/24/martin-amis-euthanasia-booths-alzheimers (accessed 2 October 2013).

Gormally, L. (1992) The BMA Report on Euthanasia and the Case against Legalization, available online at www.linacre.org/bma.html (accessed 2 October 2013).

Keown, J. (2002) *Euthanasia, Ethics and Public Policy: An Argument Against Legalisation*, Cambridge: Cambridge University Press.

Trollope, A. (1993) *The Fixed Period*, Harmondsworth: Penguin.
Vonnegut, K. (1962) 2BR02B, *Worlds of If Science Fiction*, January.

Watch:

Amour (2012), film, directed by Michael Haneke. Austria: Canal+.

26

BINGE DRINKING

Oliver Smith

Described as a 'new culture of intoxication' (Measham and Brain, 2005) binge drinking emerged, as identified by many tabloid newspapers, as a new moral disease in the early 1990s. Differing from previous incarnations of social concern around alcohol consumption, such as the 'gin craze' so memorably depicted by Hogarth in the eighteenth century, or the lager louts of the 1980s, binge drinking is a distinctly consumerist phenomenon. The term resists clear definition and is often used in a pejorative sense, a semantic tool with which to denigrate the leisure choices of the young and those who would traditionally have been described as 'working class'. It describes excessive forms of alcohol consumption and drunkenness, usually focused on weekends.

The definition of binge drinking favoured by the government and UK National Health Service suggests that a binge drinker is anyone who consumes double the daily guidelines of 2–4 units of alcohol for men, and 2–3 units of alcohol for women. While this definition easily encompasses the middle-class couple in their fifties enjoying a bottle of wine with a meal at the end of a long day, the public image of binge drinking is primarily the night-time high street, where corporate-run zones of excess and social freedom facilitate purposeful and expressive alcohol consumption, and drunken revellers frequently come into conflict with guardians of this night-time space as well as each other.

The night-time alcohol-based leisure economy (hereafter NTE) entered a period of prolonged and rapid growth as a result of clear and distinct government policy that prioritised the need to fill the gap left by the death of industrial modes of production in many towns and cities. Initial success in luring young consumers away from the largely alcohol-free, unregulated, untaxable rave culture and back into pubs, bars and clubs was celebrated, ushering in a new dawn of collaboration between the drinks industry and government. This culminated in the Licensing Act 2003, which, despite vociferous warnings from experts in fields such as health, economics and criminology, resulted in the market-led liberalisation of the NTE. The lure of profit from retail sales and excise duties within this burgeoning market was impossible to resist. However, while city centres may have been financially rejuvenated, violence and disorder rose in line with profits, suggesting a clear link with these liminal and hedonistic spaces. Faced with a raft of evidence suggesting that the cosy relationship between the drinks industry and the government was linked to a number of problems around public order and health, the government embarked on a project of responsibilisation, vociferously blaming those failing to consume in a socially acceptable, prescribed manner.

Excessive public drinking was soon demonised and identified within popular discourse as 'binge drinking'. The antics and occasional violence of drinkers were roundly condemned by politicians, even as government itself continued to liberalise licensing laws and cut funding to policing agencies. This standpoint led some commentators to see the response to binge drinking as a kind of excessive moral panic, yet this explanation appears insufficient given the real consequences of massive drinking in the form of health impacts, the clear association of the NTE with casual and often brutal violence and the wider exclusion of people from many town and city centres because of the unpredictability of such spaces.

Critical scholars of alcohol consumption need to recognise that such binge drinking is widely accepted in our society. Far from being a form of social deviance, drinking is the mark of transitions from youth to adulthood, the source of much humour in daily life and a major part of the cultural history of British society in particular. The normative undercurrents that drive the acceptability of this social excess are at odds then with government attempts to import continental attitudes towards drinking in city centres, in tandem with the regeneration of many British cities. Instead the liberalisation of drinking has attached itself to social demands built upon cultural values that celebrate, rather than condemn, drunkenness and unchecked social behaviour.

The attraction of hedonistic excess within the NTE appears to be a complex amalgam of both 'push' and 'pull' factors. Such spaces undoubtedly have the potential to help individuals momentarily escape social pressures. They promise the benefits of collective inebriation in a world characterised by frail bonds and weakened personal ties, and hold the potential to fulfil (vicariously for most) needs for sex and violence. Yet for all the criticism of the NTE, and in spite of the artificiality of these consumer experiences, it can provide an involving and gratifying consumer spectacle that allows issues such as debt, relationships, work, careers and housing to fade into the background. The consumption of alcohol that forms the background of binge drinking may be viewed as a more or less unconscious but undeniable commitment to the excess and hedonism that appear to be key elements of consumer identity. Drunken comportment fulfils a desperate desire on the part of these revellers to punctuate the dull normality of work and consumerism (Presdee, 2000). However, the true essence of the experience is largely commodified and devoid of real transgression. Excessive alcohol consumption within the NTE provides the most simple, legal and accessible route to where those characterised as binge drinkers want to be, even though they know, in a barely conscious way, that real 'liberation' is illusory.

Our understanding of binge drinking is necessarily changing in the light of the current financial crisis. With the young and the urban poor being disproportionately singled out by the government and austerity policies, the NTE appears to be shrinking at a pace not seen before. With several major corporations even entering administration, and the reported closure of pubs at the rate of 18 a week, the landscape has shifted. Despite the impending introduction of minimum unit prices for alcohol, supermarket-bought drinks are relatively inexpensive and present consumers with opportunities to pre-load, drinking before going out, thus reducing their financial outlay without affecting consumption levels. Similarly, the much-publicised proliferation of 'legal highs' provides a facet to the NTE that offers cheaper routes to intoxication. This is then a complex landscape of cultural values that celebrate excess, corporate imperatives for profit and political actions that often bridge these forces in hypocritical ways.

Bibliography

Measham, F. and Brain, K. (2005) 'Binge' Drinking, British Alcohol Policy and the New Culture of Intoxication, *Crime, Media, Culture*, 1, (3), pp. 262–83.
Presdee, M. (2000) *Cultural Criminology and the Carnival of Crime*, London: Routledge.
Žižek, S. (2002) *Welcome to the Desert of the Real*, London: Verso.

Watch:

Saturday Night and Sunday Morning (1960), film, directed by Karel Reisz. UK: Bryanston Films.

27

SQUATTING

Keith Jacobs

Squatting is generally understood to mean the occupation of land or property without the consent of the owner or those legally entitled to occupy it. Governments will always condemn squatters, because the act of moving into a property without prior consent not only evokes the ire of owners but also serves as a signifier that government housing policies are ineffectual. For this reason, politicians frequently castigate squatters as lawbreakers and free-riders. Since squatting is such a visible sign of housing policy failure and emblem of entrenched inequality, governments have striven to frame it as both an illegal and unjustified activity. In the UK, the coalition government passed legislation in 2012 to make squatting in a residential building a criminal offence. Whilst condemnation of squatters is commonplace, it is helpful in any discussion to distinguish three forms of contemporary practice. First, squatting to secure shelter; second, squatting as a campaigning tactic to advance political protest; and third, mass squatting in neighbourhoods within the developing world. Each practice is considered in turn.

The most appropriate lens for understanding squatting for the purposes of accessing accommodation is to view it as a manifestation of underlying inequalities within the social structure. Simply put, such an apparent deviance from the contemporary norms of ownership or renting in fact takes place because secure affordable accommodation is not available to large numbers of households. Whilst squatters are usually condemned in the popular press, there have been periods when more sympathetic portrayals were aired. In fact, societal attitudes towards those who squat to access shelter can shift over a short period of time. A clear example is the period following the end of the Second World War when the UK experienced a housing crisis, primarily because of the damage inflicted by German aerial bombardment. Many returning servicemen were homeless and had little alternative but to squat in properties that were unoccupied. There was very widespread sympathy amongst the public and even traditional right-wing newspapers such as the *Daily Mail* were supportive of 'homeless' servicemen who had resorted to squatting.

Whilst squatting is largely viewed in relation to housing, it is increasingly used as a form of protest; for example, squatting on land to prevent new airport runways or road development and as a way to protest against government spending cuts. A recent example took place in the north London suburb of Finchley, when local residents established a squat in a local library branch to protest at draconian spending cuts imposed by the Conservative-led local authority. Squatting as an instrument of political protest is likely to persist as activists seek to make their voices heard in a disparate media context. For many engaged in political campaigning, squatting is seen as an effective way to generate coverage in the media and to delay enactment of policy. This political form of squatting is widely condemned by government agencies and the media, not only because it serves as a threat to bureaucratic modes of governance but also because it subverts conventional channels of political protest.

Yet while squatting of this kind usually evokes a critical reaction from authorities, it can be highly effective in shifting attitudes and the understanding of social problems. An example of the impact of squatting in reframing a social problem is the issue of homelessness. In the 1970s squatting took on a highly political character, with activist groups occupying buildings to protest against government policy. Squatter groups played a major role in highlighting the plight of the homeless and the large number of properties that were unoccupied in high demand areas such as London. In the last 20 years squatting has been undertaken to promote alternative ways of living and an explicit environmental agenda, to critique consumer materialism. Opponents of new airport runways and road schemes have used squatting as a campaign tactic to great effect.

Up to this point, the discussion has been focused on the UK, but some mention should be made of squatting in the developing world. In many nations in Asia, South America and Africa, neighbourhood squats are a feature of most large conurbations. UN-HABITAT has estimated that over one billion people across the globe live in slums, which are a de facto form of squatting. These squatter settlements are often referred to colloquially as shanty towns, favelas or geçekondus. For example, in Rio de Janeiro as many as 25 per cent of the population live in squatter settlements. Increasingly, these communities perform, in spite of their illegal status, a key role in the economic life of the city, providing cheap labour and a space for newly arrived households. Over time, community leaders within these informal squatter settlements lobby government for resources to boost sanitation and basic infrastructure. As long as cities expand in size and social inequality persists, squatting will remain a feature of the contemporary world, both as a form of political protest and as a tactic to avoid rooflessness.

Two key conclusions can be drawn from the above discussion. First, for those who have no direct experience of squatting, their understanding is usually reliant upon and framed through the outlets of the popular media. The dominant media categorisation that endures is that squatters successfully exploit loopholes in the legal system at the expense of others. Media stories that circulate on squatting generally reinforce the view that the disadvantaged and excluded are largely responsible for their predicament. However, this popular categorisation is now being challenged as a consequence of increased social inequalities and the imposition of welfare cuts on basic public services. Second, the rights and wrongs of squatting will remain deeply contested. Government agencies, landlords and private homeowners vehemently oppose squatting and have successfully criminalised this response to housing stress and poverty. Such groups have persisted in portraying squatting as a form of deviance that should be legally prohibited, as an infringement of the rights of a property owner and as a means by which individuals can avoid paying their accommodation costs or in a surreptitious way engage in political protest. However, for the homeless and dispossessed, squatting is increasingly regarded as a necessary act when other options remain closed off.

Watch:

Mouth to Mouth (2005), film, directed by Alison Murray. UK: Artistic License Films.

28

SMOKING

Georgios Papanicolaou

True to Howard Becker's well-known aphorism that 'deviant behaviour is behaviour that people so label', it is becoming rapidly plausible today to approach the habit of inhaling and exhaling the smoke of tobacco as a form of deviancy. Across the globe, particularly in developed countries, smoking bans of various types are firmly in place and public, often publicly funded, campaigns hard-press the message that 'smoking seriously harms you and others around you'. Smokers are not merely segregated and banished, but increasingly stigmatised and vilified as anti-social, irresponsible and dangerous.

In a recent advertisement screened in the UK, a country where by law tobacco products in large stores are hidden from public view, the smoke exhaled by two adult women sitting in the front seats of a car assumes the form of a snake constricting the neck of an infant sleeping in the back seat of the car. Such hard-hitting ads, when they do not feature diseased smokers explaining their condition, typically depict young children as victims of passive smoking. Young people are equally likely to fill the pages of publications intended to report more soberly on smoking, such as World Health Organization reports. Beyond freedom of lifestyle choice, respect of others or even health, thinking about smoking is increasingly cast along the lines of good versus evil.

The frenetic advance of tobacco control today relies on strong emotions and expediency as much as the earlier wars between the anti-smoking campaigns and the tobacco industry did. For centuries, social, religious, scientific and fiscal controversy has surrounded tobacco and its use. The rapid rise of tobacco production, trade and consumption ultimately meant that governments came to view it more as a handy source of revenue to be exploited boldly as fiscal needs dictated than a satanic influence to be purged through persecution and prohibition. By doing so, they laid the firm foundations of the underground economy of tobacco smuggling that continues to thrive to date.

In more recent times the controversy seemed to have settled in favour of a growing industry that successfully turned cigarettes into a mass commodity. Capitalising on developments in the cultivation and curing of tobacco as well as the mechanisation of the rolling process, the US tobacco industry began to offer a more appealing and affordable product, in volume that was high-end enough to cater for the mass markets of the burgeoning turn-of-the-twentieth-century American cities. Portability and ease of use on one hand and successful marketing techniques on the other quickly turned cigarettes into products of choice, particularly among the men and women of the working class.

Offering a visceral hatred of smoking and laments about the moral decay of society, anti-smoking campaigns gained a foothold in the public domain by anchoring their message around the figure of the child smoker condemned to a life of failure, alcoholism, crime and immorality. While the temperance movement in the USA ultimately succeeded in achieving its goal of a complete ban on the production and sale of alcohol in 1920, progress in tobacco control was stalled by the cigarette becoming the indispensable companion of soldiers experiencing the terror of the trenches during the First World War. Having achieved a status equal to the necessities of bullets, first aid and moral support of the troops, cigarettes gained enormous popularity and symbolic ascendancy. In the era following the Second World War, the tobacco industry's carefully targeted marketing techniques consolidated this state of affairs, with later generations not failing to notice that many memories of the mid-twentieth century appear surrounded by a thick veil of tobacco smoke. But the tides turned.

What explains the persistence of tobacco is what it does *for* smokers; what explains the persistence of the controversy about smoking is what it does *to* smokers, and to others around them. Beyond cultural uses, tobacco chemicals – nicotine in particular, which acts either as a stimulant or a sedative depending on dosage – induce a mild and generally pleasing experience. Many people, however, find the experience irritating and disgusting, since burning tobacco has a distinctive smell and the passive inhaling of smoke is also involved. These experiences of and emotions towards smoking preclude a resolution of the issue on scientific grounds alone. Medical evidence on the harmful effects of smoking on smokers began to emerge as early as the 1930s and links between smoking and lung, throat and other cancers, heart disease and emphysema have been documented. On the other hand, epidemiological evidence on the effects of environmental tobacco smoke ('second hand' or 'passive' smoke) appears less conclusive. Yet it is on the basis of this latter issue that current campaigns for environments completely free of tobacco smoke have gained momentum.

It appears that wider social forces beyond individual preferences decide the question of smoking. For a long period, the success of the tobacco industry allowed it to maintain the positive, symbolic status of its products, and also actively and effectively to employ techniques to misinform about the risks of smoking and to block litigation and legislative intervention. But in the emerging long war over smoking, determined and organised anti-smoking lobbies have been able to ignite a process of discrediting opponents, gaining critical footholds within the circuits of public health provision and consolidating wider public support by appealing to sensibilities aroused by the issue of second hand smoke. The ascendancy of the anti-smoking lobby is today secured by the backing of big pharmaceutical companies that appear to be already positioned to claim parts of the nicotine-thirsty US$600 billion tobacco market: the developing market for smoking cessation drugs was estimated to have reached US$2.4 billion in 2012.

Trapped in a web of exploitation by the tobacco industry and vilification due to contemporary health sensibilities, smokers rapidly sink to the bottom – to return to Becker – of twenty-first-century 'hierarchies of credibility'. It thus seems rather unlikely that smokers huddled outside offices and bars globally will shake their positions as modern-day deviants.

Bibliography

Brandt, A. (2007) *The Cigarette Century: The Rise, Fall and Deadly Persistence of the Product that Defined America*, New York: Basic Books.

Snowdon, C. (2009) *Velvet Glove, Iron Fist: A History of Anti-smoking*, Ripon, UK: Little Dice.

WHO (2011) *WHO Report on the Global Tobacco Epidemic, 2011: Warning about the Dangers of Tobacco*, Geneva: World Health Organization.

Watch:

Coffee and Cigarettes (2003), film, directed by Jim Jarmusch. USA: United Artists.

29

'WELFARE DEPENDENCY'

Robert MacDonald

This chapter considers how ordinary social practices, in this case claiming state welfare benefits because of worklessness and financial necessity, have come to be seen as a form of deviance, particularly within the popular media and by some politicians. As a consequence large swaths of the working class have become demonised. Some might look to welfare claimants for signs of resistance to contemporary capitalism's degrading forms of work, or might think to find examples of canny 'ducking and diving' that outwits the state benefits bureaucracy. Yet what many sociologists, social policy researchers and psychologists will tell them is that, in fact, unemployed people tend to have deeply conventional views about the moral, social and financial value of working.

We can say with some authority that it is benefit systems that tend to bamboozle claimants, rather than claimants managing to abuse or confuse those systems. Occasionally criminologists will interview 'career criminals', dismissive of 'mugs' who follow the daily grind of wage labour. Similarly sociologists in their studies will sometimes meet highly educated young adults who reject low-quality employment. Nevertheless, these encounters can be seen as exceptions to a general conformity within which the majority of people across all classes view paid work and conventional lifestyles as the much preferred way of getting by.

The modern parade of the 'undeserving poor', notoriously presented in the tabloid press on an almost daily basis, is largely absent from the findings of social surveys and determined, community-based ethnographies. 'Work-shy welfare scroungers' may exist but they are the few, overshadowed by the invisible mass that, still, would prefer to have a job and not be on benefits. Take the idea popular with politicians and the press that there are 'three generations of families where no-one has ever worked'; this has become a widely asserted, taken-for-granted shorthand for the idea that worklessness is sub-cultural and deviant, learned in families and passed down the generations in the form of values and practices that deplete the work ethic and foster 'welfare dependency'. Arguably, this idea has become the cause célèbre of the UK government's agenda to fix 'Broken Britain' with a drive to create policies for welfare reform and, more counter-intuitively, the pursuit of social justice. Yet there is no evidence that such families exist. Shildrick *et al.* (2012) determinedly sought them out in the most likely, severely deprived neighbourhoods but failed to find 'them', while surveys show that less than *half of one per cent* of all workless households *might* hold '*two* generations where no-one has ever worked', let alone three.

How do we explain this lack of fit between the facts and political and public views of welfare and worklessness? Golding and Middleton's classic 1980s work showed how scroungerphobia – 'shrill and mounting antagonism to the welfare system and its clients' (1982: 59) – is mobilised by the dominant class at moments of economic crisis. This analysis is timely since, from 2010, the newly elected Conservative-led coalition has prioritised cuts to welfare spending (£18 billion to date) to reduce government deficits. This process has been justified by painting claimants as pursuing 'a lifestyle choice' and being 'just not entitled to it' (in the words of the Chancellor of the Exchequer and Prime Minister, respectively). The tabloid press are willing cheerleaders, running regular features on 'dole scroungers' and 'benefit cheats'. Indeed, in August 2010, *The Sun*, Britain's biggest selling daily newspaper, even 'declared war' on the 'hundreds of thousands of scroungers in the UK' and those who 'claim to be sick when they are perfectly capable of work' but 'prefer to sit at home watching widescreen TVs'.

These ideas appear to be absorbed by the general public, with benefit recipients becoming a new kind of folk devil within the community at large – seen as being deviant via a moral failure that arises through 'choosing' not to work. Support for extra spending on welfare benefits is at a historically low ebb; two-thirds think that welfare benefits are too high and discourage people from finding jobs. These ideas permeate our culture and fuel more vicious forms of predatory behaviour, with data showing that hate-crime targeted at people with disabilities is soaring, fuelled by tabloid tales of welfare fraud.

At the same time that poor and vulnerable people are being made poorer and more vulnerable, private companies that implement 'welfare reform' make increasingly healthy profits. Two examples can be given from many. First, Emma Harrison, former chairwoman of the private 'welfare to work' company A4e (and formerly the government's 'back-to-work tsar') was reported to have enjoyed, in addition to her salary, a £1.3 million dividend windfall from A4e's multi-million pound government funding. This was despite the company's pitiful record in 2012, with their 'success rate' of placing less than 4 per cent of its 'clients' into jobs – a *lower* rate than might be expected if unemployed people had just been left to their own devices. Similarly, Atos has received multi-million pound government contracts, primarily to assess whether claims for disability benefits are warranted. Its 'work capability assessments' have been heavily criticised as inaccurate, unfair and inhumane; some passed fit for work then died from their illnesses or committed suicide (Shildrick *et al.*, 2012). Most rulings are overturned if the claimant is accompanied at the appeal by a welfare rights advisor. Stretching irony to its limits, Atos was a sponsor of the 2012 Paralympic Games.

These examples highlight the fact that attacks on the payment of social insurance to those who lose their jobs, and those on wages so low that such payments are needed, are not simply about cost-cutting, but ideological attacks on the welfare state more broadly. In the case of Atos, given the real cost of contracts, it could only offer 'value for money' by reducing claims way beyond the estimate of those who wrongly receive benefits. There is little fraud in the welfare system (DWP, 2012). Statistics show a rate of only 2 per cent 'fraud/error' in respect of all welfare payments (with *underpayment* being a substantial chunk) – and losses are dwarfed by those incurred through tax avoidance. One middle-range estimate puts this at £17 billion per annum, and benefit fraud at £5 billion (see Chapter 30).

A time of economic crisis has fuelled the abandonment of evidence in favour of attacks based on myths and anecdotes that feed on crude media images of a feckless and work-shy underclass. Yet research highlights how inaccurate such images are. Despite this, the public and politicians continue to attack and vilify those in need of the assistance of the state.

These views help to justify the attack on these forms of state expenditure, rather than targeting more progressive methods of taxation to help fund state expenditures. All of this has served to foment significant symbolic violence against some of society's most vulnerable people. People who are unemployed, sick or disabled have been cast as deviant pariahs in a new and particularly vicious round of scroungerphobia, and subject to material harm through drastic cuts to their welfare benefits.

References

Department for Work and Pensions (2012) Fraud and Error in the Benefit System: 2011/12 Estimates, revised edition, available online at www.gov.uk/government/uploads/system/uploads/attachment_data/file/222892/fem_1112.pdf (accessed 2 October 2013).

Golding, P. and Middleton, S. (1982) *Images of Welfare*, Oxford: Martin Robinson.

Shildrick, T., MacDonald, R., Furlong, A., Roden, J. and Crow, R. (2012) *Are 'Cultures of Worklessness' Passed down the Generations?* York: Joseph Rowntree Foundation.

Watch:

Boys from the Blackstuff (1982), TV series, directed by Philip Saville. UK: BBC.

PART V

Invisible and contested harms

Public orientations towards crime and criminality often tend to focus on violence, street crime and acts of abuse. Yet criminologists have become increasingly observant of crimes of the powerful and more hidden forms of social harm that may be concealed from public view. Criminal and deviant behaviour always generates intense debate and reflection about how harmful, prevalent and problematic particular crimes may be. This section contains chapters that focus on issues which are less well reported but which also represent major forms of damage and violence to people and communities (such as harassment and family violence).

Many crimes and harmful behaviours may be less well monitored, or their harms less well documented, because those who are deviant are also devious, pursuing measures to remain concealed (notably paedophiles and white collar criminals). When dealing with such problems we may also find complex and contested readings of what the harms of such actions are. For example, it is increasingly clear that corporate culture has normalised practices of tax evasion and other forms of malpractice to increase profitability, while ignoring or circumventing legal rules. Perhaps more importantly the rising profile of such crime has been advanced in no small way by pressure groups keen to shame these organisations and put pressure on governments to reduce tax losses that lead to social harms in other areas of society (the inability to pay for adequate education and other social services, for example). In the cases of human experimentation and elder abuse it is only in relatively recent times that the extent and depth of such harms has been revealed, and yet national governments have historically done little to challenge these problems. It is critical that criminologists are able to track and assist in challenging those acts that may not always be considered criminal in the eyes of the state but which may impact dramatically on individuals and families.

30

TAX AVOIDANCE AND EVASION

Prem Sikka

'The difference between tax avoidance and tax evasion is the thickness of a prison wall': an explanation once offered by former UK Chancellor Denis Healey. However, the difference in reality is often more complex, with numerous shades of grey in between these legal and illegal practices. These complexities are exploited by a tax avoidance industry dominated by accountants, lawyers and financial experts. This industry and those who both evade and avoid tax are now increasingly subjected to public 'outing', shame and avoidance by consumers – they are seen as being deviant organisations and individuals in a way that was not even thinkable until quite recently.

The amounts lost due to tax avoidance and evasion are not known precisely, but the European Union has estimated them to be around €1 trillion each year, equivalent to £830 billion or US$1.25 trillion.[1] The UK's tax authority, Her Majesty's Revenue and Customs (HMRC), has acknowledged a 'tax gap' (the difference between the amount that should be collected and that actually collected; this consists of tax arrears, tax avoidance and tax evasion) of £35 billion, though others estimate it to be more than £100 billion each year (Mitchell and Sikka, 2011). Major multinationals such as Google, Starbucks, eBay and Microsoft have all received negative publicity for shifting profits to their subsidiaries in tax havens through contrived charges for the use of trademarks, logos and management expertise (Sikka and Willmott, 2010).

HMRC is scrutinising some 41,000 avoidance schemes, which threaten some £10.2 billion of tax revenues. The identity of the designers of the schemes is rarely revealed, but an unpublished 2005 HMRC internal study concluded that the 'Big Four' accounting firms were behind almost half of all known avoidance schemes. The Big Four accounting firms are PricewaterhouseCoopers (PwC), Deloitte, KPMG and Ernst & Young. These global mammoths operate from hundreds of cities, including offshore tax havens that do not levy income and corporate taxes, or require companies to file audited financial statements. An inquiry by a UK Parliamentary Committee noted that PwC will sell a tax product if there is a 25 per cent chance that it will withstand a legal challenge by the tax authorities. In the words of Committee chairman, 'you are offering schemes to your clients – knowingly marketing these schemes – where you have judged there is a 75 per cent risk of it then being deemed unlawful' (UK House of Commons Public Accounts Committee, 2013, p. Ev 4). Other firms said that they used a threshold of 50 per cent.

The US authorities have accused PricewaterhouseCoopers, KPMG and Ernst & Young of selling abusive and potentially illegal tax avoidance schemes (US Senate Permanent Subcommittee on Investigations, 2005). In 2005, KPMG admitted 'criminal wrongdoing' and paid a fine of $456 million while a number of its former personnel were sent to prison. Prison sentences were also handed out to a number of former Ernst & Young personnel for facilitating tax evasion, and in March 2013 the firm paid a fine of $123 million to avoid prosecution. PwC settled the cases by making a $10 million payment and handing over certain client lists to the US tax authorities; Deloitte designed tax avoidance schemes for US energy giant Enron and are still under scrutiny (Mitchell and Sikka, 2011).

Fines and prison sentences are often considered to be just another business cost for those corporations associated with the lucrative tax avoidance trade. The firms are still active players in the tax avoidance industry. Here are some examples of the tax avoidance schemes marketed by them in the UK.

Ernst & Young designed schemes to enable directors of Phones 4u to avoid UK National Insurance Contributions (NIC) by paying themselves in gold bars, fine wine and platinum sponge.[2] As soon as the government plugged this loophole, the firm designed another to enable the same clients to avoid NIC and income taxes by securing payments through an offshore employee benefit trust in Jersey. It was outlawed by the case of *HM Inspector of Taxes* v. *Dextra Accessories Ltd* (2005).

Deloitte devised a scheme to enable bankers at Deutsche Bank to avoid income tax and National Insurance Contributions (NIC) on bonuses adding up to £92 million. The scheme operated through a Cayman Islands-registered investment vehicle. The presiding judge in the case of *Deutsche Bank Group Services (UK) Ltd* v. *Revenue and Customs* (2011) said that 'the Scheme as a whole, and each aspect of it, was created and coordinated purely for tax avoidance purposes', and threw it out.

KPMG sold a tax avoidance scheme to 64 millionaires who sought to shield £156 million from taxes. The test case of *John Astall and Graham Edwards* v. *Revenue and Customs Commissioners* (2007) heard that a series of self-cancelling complex transactions were designed to generate paper losses. The presiding judge threw out the scheme because it was 'entirely artificial…had no commercial purposes … other than generating an artificial loss to set against taxable income'.

All of the above schemes masqueraded as lawful but when challenged through the courts at considerable public expense, they turned out to be illegal. In the tax cat-and-mouse games, governments continue to revise legislation to counter avoidance schemes, but little progress is made in preventing the sale of highly contrived tax avoidance schemes to a large number of taxpayers. The tax avoidance industry provides a window for studying trajectories of capitalism and its challenges to the state and society. It also draws attention to the role of professionals who create little of any social value, yet who deprive elected governments of much needed public revenues which could enable them to provide public goods, alleviate poverty and meet public aspirations. Nevertheless these forms of deviance are increasingly facing media scrutiny, public accountability and a greater sense of anger and condemnation within the community at large.

Notes

1 European Commission press release, 'Tackling tax fraud and evasion in the EU – frequently asked questions', 27 June 2012; available at http://europa.eu/rapid/press-release_MEMO-12-492_en.htm (accessed 9 October 2013).
2 The *Mail on Sunday*, '£6m tax threat to Phones4U founder', 15 February 2004; www.thisismoney.co.uk/money/news/article-1514887/1636m-tax-threat-to-Phones4U-founder.html (accessed 27 August 2012).

References

Deutsche Bank Group Services (UK) Ltd v. *Revenue and Customs* [2011] UKFTT 66 (TC).

HM Inspector of Taxes v. *Dextra Accessories Ltd* [2005] UKHL 47.

John Astall and Graham Edwards v. *Revenue and Customs Commissioners* [2007] SpC00628.

Mitchell, A. and Sikka, P. (2011) *The Pinstripe Mafia: How Accountancy Firms Destroy Societies*, Basildon, UK: Association for Accountancy and Business Affairs.

Sikka, P. and Willmott, H. (2010) The Dark Side of Transfer Pricing: Its Role in Tax Avoidance and Wealth Retentiveness, *Critical Perspectives on Accounting*, 21, (4), pp. 342–56.

UK House of Commons Public Accounts Committee (2013) *Tax Avoidance: The Role of Large Accountancy Firms*, London: The Stationery Office.

US Senate Permanent Subcommittee on Investigations (2005) *The Role of Professional Firms in the US Tax Shelter Industry*, Washington, DC: USGPO.

Watch:

The Producers (1968), film, directed by Mel Brooks. USA: MGM.

31

WHITE-COLLAR CRIME

Mark Horsley

The concept of white-collar crime remains an area of intense debate within criminology. There is little agreement over the range of malpractices a discriminating definition should cover, or over its relationship to other kinds of 'economic', 'occupational' or 'corporate' criminality. Nevertheless, definitions of white-collar crime generally boil down to a recognition of an offender's elevated occupational status and the possibility of their exploiting power, trust, responsibility and respect for personal financial gain resulting from immediate monetary rewards or long-term professional advancement. White-collar crime, in other words, is a label generally applied to the crimes of businesspersons, managers, administrators and other professionals – crimes that appear to be generated by the kinds of privileged access derived under certain occupational conditions. It is, for example, all but impossible to defraud consumers without, at the very least, being deemed to be in a position of relative trust, often generated by having some kind of specialist knowledge.

White-collar crime is generated within the context of the workplace, in which a range of offence opportunities may be presented to professional people that would be absent beyond the bounds of their working lives. Such crime covers an extensive range of offences including tax fraud, consumer fraud, misrepresenting items for sale (everything from food quality offences up to mortgages, pensions and insurance), insider trading, trading in fraudulent investments, money laundering and manufacture and sale of counterfeit goods, along with copyright and intellectual property infringement. It can also take the form of embezzlement, illegally appropriating employers' resources or obtaining financial recompense in excess of basic salary through bribery or blackmail. We might also point to the untold possibilities of corrupt payments, illegally awarded contracts, health and safety violations and the dangers of management negligence that sit between white-collar and corporate forms of criminality (Croall, 2001).

The real difficulty with white-collar crime, however, comes with any attempt to offer an assessment of its relative frequency. It is notoriously difficult to put a reliable figure on many types of criminality, but such difficulties count twofold for white-collar crime because such offences are rarely reported, processed or recorded in the same way as interpersonal violence and property crime, nor do they generally have immediately apparent effects on victims. While it is usually obvious that a burglary has taken place, for instance, the same cannot be said for something like a mortgage loan made on false pretences or biased financial advice. Many forms of white-collar criminality have what is often called a 'long tail', in which it can take many years of sifting through highly specialised evidence, luck on the part of enforcement agencies and vigilant victims to realise that a crime has occurred.

While it is all but impossible to gauge the full incidence of such criminality, there is evidence to suggest that the upsurge in consumer borrowing since the mid-nineties may have triggered an escalation of white-collar criminality within the financial services industry. Between 1994 and 2007, outstanding consumer credit – money owed by the British public for property, goods and services – more than tripled, which necessarily entailed an expansion of the lending industry, more loans being made, more brokers and more advisors, all of which presented companies and their employees with a range of opportunities centred on encouraging their customers' borrowing habits. In response, the industry created a set of practices, particularly in the UK and USA, designed to encourage an unchecked escalation of consumer lending. This included self-certified loans, performance-related bonuses for mortgage brokers, the proliferation of arcane, opaque products and the growth of 'sub-prime' mortgages (loans made to people with low or unpredictable incomes who would not previously have qualified). In huge numbers of cases, loans well in excess of property values were made and special offers – easier but time-limited repayment conditions – were offered to lure customers (Lanchester, 2010).

The result of the expansion of the consumer credit industry and this range of lending practices was the proliferation of white-collar and corporate criminality (see Chapter 50) on the part of lenders and their employees. Increased scope for consumer lending led, according to a recent US government report (FCIC, 2011), to pervasive mortgage fraud in which borrowers were encouraged to take out loans that they had no realistic prospect of repaying by a subset of mortgage brokers who routinely misrepresented their products or payment conditions, or otherwise promoted unsustainable lending. The same mortgage brokers benefited personally from increased sales, potentially qualifying for greater year-end bonuses and promotions, while some of their customers were left struggling with an unsuitable mortgage, having to skip meals in order to be able to continue to service their loans or, in many cases, putting mortgage payments on to credit cards in order to maintain their obligations, never realising that they had been victims of a form of mis-selling that many now see as a form of white-collar criminality.

While such practices belong to just one type of many possible mortgage-related frauds, and constitute an even smaller proportion of overall white-collar criminality, they are indicative of the way that such crimes are enabled by the occupational freedoms afforded professional employees. Nevertheless, the expansion of the credit industry since the early nineties, along with an emphasis on lending volume and the growth of the lending professions, perhaps accounts for many of the criminal opportunities associated with a twenty-fold increase in cases of mortgage fraud between 1996 and 2005. In this way white-collar criminality in the consumer credit industry intersects with some of the most significant political and economic events of the last few decades. With what appears to have been a growing incidence of illegal lending, some of which produced debts that were defaulted on only months after the initial loan, it seems likely that many of the unpaid debts which fed into the global economic crisis resulted from white-collar criminality on the part of some financial professionals. All in all, white-collar crime appears to merge with broader questions of corporate criminality and with it individual forms of professional deviance bleed into industrially organised forms of commonplace corporate malpractice (Ferguson, 2012).

References

Croall, H. (2001) *Understanding White Collar Crime*, Buckingham, UK: Open University Press.

Ferguson, C. (2012) *Inside Job: The Financiers who Pulled Off the Heist of the Century*, Oxford: Oneworld.

Lanchester, J. (2010) *Whoops! Why Everyone Owes Everyone and No One Can Pay*, London: Penguin.

United States. Financial Crisis Inquiry Commission (2011) *The Financial Crisis Inquiry Report*, New York: Public Affairs. Available online at: http://fcic-static. law.stanford.edu/cdn_media/fcic-reports/fcic_final_report_full.pdf (accessed 22 November 2012).

Watch:

Inside Job (2010), documentary film, directed by Charles Ferguson. USA: Sony Pictures.

32

PAEDOPHILIA

Maggie Wykes

There is probably no identity deemed *shadier* or more *deviant* in popular discourse than the paedophile. The archetypal figure haunts parks and playgrounds in his dirty raincoat or lingers invisibly, anonymously or pseudonymously in children's cyber chat rooms. He is the dangerous stranger who inhabits parents' worst nightmares and renders modern childhood a 'behind closed doors' experience. Except it is precisely behind the closed doors of the institutions in which children are supposed to be safe that sexual abuse happens: in families; in homes; in closed communities; in schools; and in leisure contexts. Such abuse is primarily perpetrated by someone known to the child, often someone related to the child, and it is a crime most usually perpetrated against girls by a male relative, father or stepfather in 51.6 per cent of cases (Richards, 2011), despite claims – from sources including the Vatican, defending celibacy – that homosexuality is to blame.

'Paedophilia' tends to be applied as a blanket term to all types of attraction to children under the age of consent, whether acted upon or not. Goode (2013) writes that one in five men can be aroused by children but only 4 per cent of this group would act on that desire. Paedophilia may simply be an aspect of the chaotic continuum of human sexuality. Many experience it but manage that passively, whilst some actively sexually abuse children. Such acts are considered to be violations, internationally, but definitions and laws vary greatly. In English law, 16 is the age of consent to sex. Any sexual act involving a child under 13 is unequivocally abuse, and a rape charge requires penile penetration. Under the Sexual Offences Act 2003 any person over 18 who has sex with a child under 16 can be prosecuted, even if the victim has consented. Much sexual offending against children is also incestuous, involving biological or step-parents or siblings; incest is illegal in the UK even between consenting adults. Variations can be found in other legal jurisdictions. In South Africa coercive penetration of any orifice with any part of the body or object can lead to a rape prosecution; in Mexico 12 is the age of consent, in Vietnam it is 18 and in Saudi Arabia only marriage makes sex legal. Consensual adult incest is legal in the Netherlands and Australia. Despite these legal-cultural variations child sexual abuse is consistently present internationally. Pereda *et al.* (2009) calculate that 7.9 per cent of men and 19.7 per cent of women, globally, experience sexual abuse prior to the age of 18, most pre-pubescently. Although this data shows highest rates in Africa, countries such as Australia and the USA show 37 per cent and 25 per cent of girls abused, despite nearly 50 years of feminist campaigning in the West.

In 2010 just '309 people in England and Wales were cautioned or found guilty of sexual activity with a child under 13, and 1,184 of sexual activity with a child under 16' (NSPCC, 2012) despite crime records showing '17,727 sexual crimes against children under 16 were recorded in England and Wales in 2010/11' (Chaplin *et al.*, 2011: 4). It is hard to begin to understand how or why this attrition happens but adult victims of abuse very often retract under pressure, or out of fear or love (Stanko, 1990). Sexual abuse is prevalent but often hidden and secret; prosecutions are remarkably low and few children report it.

One explanation for this is the power of the father, within the institution of the family, to abuse, control and conceal, and the lack of critique of that power. In 2006, Timothy Cox was arrested in Britain for trading child pornography online. It depicted men abusing 31 children on live webcams. But there had been no outcry about child abductions because the children were filmed in their homes being assaulted by fathers and other male relatives, with no means to resist or reveal the violations. However, so revered is the *family* myth and so powerful is the *stranger-paedophile* myth that journalists focused on the paedophile pornography rather than the men depicted raping their own children (Wykes and Welsh, 2009).

Many other institutions also shield men from exposure. After disc jockey Jimmy Savile died in 2011 women revealed his sexual abuse of them as girls. Some of this allegedly happened during filming of his popular television shows at the BBC over decades. Civil law suits are being brought against the BBC for compensation because Savile was given access to hundreds of young people, despite rumours and gossip within the institution. Male power within many institutions often serves to make perpetrators unassailable, making victims reluctant to come forward. Often appalling treatment by the criminal justice institution, if they do complain, is also a disincentive. For example, violinist and mother Frances Andrade claimed she was sexually abused from the age of 14 by her teacher, Michael Brewer, at a music school in Manchester. He was found guilty, but not before she killed herself after being accused in court of being a liar and fantasist. Since then, other women have brought complaints against male staff dating back to the 1980s and the school has been accused of ignoring and even promoting their abusers. Numerous such cases highlight the fact that abuse is often denied and thrives within institutional contexts in which a culture of male dominance, exploitative norms and appalling standards become engrained.

In each context it is male power and authority, protected by institutional norms and values, that enables child sexual abuse. The sexualisation of little girls and infantilisation of women riddles our culture and is highly gendered, indicative of the cultural dominance of male heterosexuality. The power and interest behind this is patriarchal but the product is paedophiliac and it touches us all when we buy products eroticised by young bodies or emulate the waiflike women who inhabit celebrity, or the men who desire them. Paedophilia is not a crime but the rape and sexual abuse of girls and women is. Blaming paedophiles does nothing to prevent child sexual abuse but it does symbolically protect the heterosexual and often paternal men who sexually violate; they are securely concealed by our institutions and constantly reassured that they are not *deviant* by the validating prevalence of eroticised, pubescent representations of femininity in our culture.

References

Chaplin, R., Flatley, J. and Smith, K. (eds) (2011) Crime in England and Wales 2010/11: Findings from the British Crime Survey and Police Recorded Crime (PDF), London: National Statistics.

Goode, S. (2013) How Can we Prevent Child Abuse if we Don't Understand Paedophilia? *The Independent*, 7 January.

National Society for the Prevention of Cruelty to Children (September 2012) Child Abuse Cases: Deciding to Prosecute, available online at www.nspcc.org.uk (accessed 9 October 2013).

Pereda, N., Guilera, G., Forns, N. and Gomez-Benito, J. (2009) The Prevalence of Child Sexual Abuse in Community and Student Samples: A Meta-analysis, *Clinical Psychology Review*, 29, (4), pp. 328–38.

Richards, K. (September 2011) Misperceptions about Child Sex Offenders, *Trends & Issues in Crime and Criminal Justice*, 429.

Stanko, B. (1990) *Everyday Violence,* London: Pandora.

Wykes, M. and Welsh, K. (2009) *Violence, Gender and Justice,* London: SAGE.

Watch:

Capturing the Friedmans (2003), documentary film, directed by Andrew Jarecki. USA: Magnolia Pictures.

33

POLICE DEVIANCE

Bob Jeffery and Waqas Tufail

Concerns about rule-breaking within the police force have existed since the early days of the creation of an institutionalised force. Maurice Punch defines police corruption, or police deviance, as:

> the abuse of authority, of the oath of office, of trust (of fellow officers, the police organisation and the public) and of the rights of colleagues, suspects and citizens. It involves the misuse of police power and authority, utilising organisational position and resources largely to avoid preventing crime, to encourage crime by others, to engage in crime, to combat crime by illegal means or simply to exercise power for illicit ends.
>
> *(2009: 30)*

Yet in keeping with the wider aims of this collection, this entry seeks to destabilise dominant and taken-for-granted notions regarding exactly what constitutes deviance. In doing so we can differentiate between police deviance on its own terms, violations of the laws, codes and regulations that govern police practice, and police practices that are considered deviant with reference to the norms and values of the community within which the police operate.

Significantly, it is the special status of the police that converts 'ordinary crime' into corruption, given that law-breaking is being committed by an individual whose *raison d'être* is to uphold those laws. A recent example of this involved a police officer being dismissed and imprisoned for having sex with a vulnerable woman after responding to a welfare call.

Taking police corruption on its own terms, there is a number of competing analytical definitions of the forms this might take. A key line of demarcation relates to whether the failure to uphold the law can be seen primarily as an individual failure, or an institutional one, relating to the organisational situation or networks of individuals within which officers are embedded. It is clear from studies of police deviance that the institutional features of policing are of considerable importance in understanding the existence and extent of this phenomenon. These in turn have 'organisational' and 'occupational' components. The former refers to the features inherent to policing that might promote deviant practices and includes issues relating to organisational oversight and individual autonomy. Numerous studies have revealed the extent to which policing is contingent upon the discretion of individual officers, acting as 'street-level bureaucrats', which considerably widens the possibility of corrupt behaviour. Occupational deviance refers to the culture of the police and the ways in which this might promote deviance (both 'on its own terms' and by external criteria). Critical issues in this culture relate to the officers' 'sense of purpose', which may act as a justification for law-breaking, and the expectation of 'solidarity' and a 'code of silence' amongst fellow officers, as well as a deeper cynicism accumulated from repeated exposure to the darker aspects of the human character.

The structural components of the police officer's role in society can be seen to promote deviance in a variety of ways, as measured by official standards, regulations and laws. But police deviance can also be considered from a much more general perspective, as a component of deviant political cultures that promote inequality, restrict democratic processes and unfairly target particular groups. This relates to the 'dual purpose' of policing in class-dominated, hierarchical societies, what Marenin (1983) referred to as 'parking tickets' and 'class repression', which is to say the police are mandated not only to preserve general social order, but also to act as agents of class-control. Such class-control is most evident in the designation of 'police property', those people who occupy a marginal social position with little power – the poor, ethnic minorities, young people and those with non-conventional identities. Such individuals are 'disproportionately likely to be treated as suspects at each stage of the criminal justice process: stop–search, arrest, detention, charge and prosecution' (Reiner, 2010: 25).

It is also the case that the class repression function of the police becomes more overt with the transition to market-oriented societies. The social hurricane of un- and under-employment, rising inequalities and rolling back of welfare protections has necessitated a shift to a 'law and order' society, now explicitly endorsed in the UK by both major political parties. Largely unaccountable and partisan policing has characterised this period, evident in the policing of Northern Ireland and in the 1984 Miners' Strike. However, such methods of policing are not unique to the UK and are mirrored internationally. For instance, in South Africa a recent video revealed police officers handcuffing a foreign national to the rear of a police van, dragging him along as they drove away. The man later died of his injuries. In Brazil, police officers have been accused by human rights organisations and the United Nations of summarily executing thousands of people a year over the last decade.

Finally, it is worth noting some of the problems that exist in relation to measuring police deviance and holding the police to account. Reiner (2010) has noted that historically, journalists have been more likely to probe police malpractice than academics, and it might be suggested that this is strongly connected to the sheer prevalence of 'embedded' police studies and the growing patronage of criminological research by the state and its agencies in terms of research funding.

We know that in the last thirty years, the numbers of those who have died in police custody have increased; however, no police officer has ever been successfully prosecuted for these deaths, despite the existence of official investigative bodies such as the UK's Independent Police Complaints Commission (IPCC) (Pemberton, 2005). We also know that legal reforms (such as the Police and Criminal Evidence Act 1984), an attempt to regulate police behaviour, have failed and resulted in less accountability. A radical alternative would be the establishment of independent police monitoring groups to track instances of police deviance and hold up contemporary policing practices to democratic scrutiny. The recent creation of the Northern Police Monitoring Project and Tottenham Defence Campaign (the latter set up in the immediate aftermath of the English 2011 riots), allied with the existence of much longer standing groups such as the Newham Monitoring Project, indicate that spaces of resistance to police deviance can be found.

References

Marenin, O. (1983) Parking Tickets and Class Repression: The Concept of Policing in Critical Theories of Criminal Justice, *Contemporary Crises*, 6, (2), pp. 241–66.

Pemberton, S. (2005) Deaths in Police Custody: The 'Acceptable' Consequences of a 'Law and Order' Society?, *Outlines*, 7, (2), pp. 23–42.

Punch, M. (2009) *Police Corruption: Deviance, Accountability and Reform in Policing*, Abingdon and New York: Routledge.

Reiner, R. (2010) *The Politics of the Police* (4th edition), Oxford: Oxford University Press.

Watch:

Training Day (2001), film, directed by Antoine Fuqua. USA: Village Roadshow Pictures.

34

HUMAN EXPERIMENTATION

Paddy Rawlinson

Unethical human experimentation describes the practice of using human subjects for research, usually intended for medical or social scientific purposes, without due regard for their well-being. This kind of abuse can include a number of actions and impacts such as deliberately distorting or withholding information about the aim and form of the experiment(s), pressurising individuals into participation and inflicting injury as a result of the research, sometimes even causing death. While the range of acts and their consequences linked to unethical behaviour are broad and diverse, the profile of victims tends to be narrowly predictable: those marginalised by race, ethnicity, gender, disability, socio-economic class and so on. It is the exploitation of the vulnerable by the powerful triumvirate of the state, medical science and the pharmaceutical industry that draws unethical human experimentation into the field of critical criminology.

Unethical human experimentation first became a focus of international concern during the Nuremberg (Nazi) Doctors' Trial (1946–47). In response to the appalling suffering and death caused by the medical experiments conducted largely on Jews and the Roma in the concentration camps of the Third Reich, the resulting Nuremberg Code was drawn up to provide a framework for the protection of human subjects in medical research. Its ten guidelines include the requirement of the voluntary consent of the subject, who should have 'sufficient knowledge and comprehension of the length, nature and purpose' of the experiment, and the avoidance of any situation that might inflict injury on the subject by those conducting the experiments. Subsequent ethical principles and guidelines have been articulated by the World Medical Association's Declaration of Helsinki and the US Belmont Report. Yet, despite the establishment of these protections on paper, there continues to be a litany of abuses in medical research beyond Nuremberg. Most worryingly, many of these have taken place in the very countries which position themselves as prime adherents of individual freedom and human rights (LaFleur *et al.*, 2008).

The infamous Tuskegee Syphilis Experiment, which duped almost four hundred black Americans into placebo treatments they believed were actually curing the condition disingenuously referred to by the researchers as 'bad blood', the medically futile trials of a herpes vaccine on infants in Australian orphanages, the testing of toxins for biological warfare on unsuspecting groups in the UK, the widespread high-risk trials using prisoners in the USA and, more recently, inmates in Guantanamo Bay, comprise just some of the abuses that stand in defiance of the Nuremberg Code and its legacy. With the progressive medicalisation of advanced market economies, the increasing commodification of public health and more stringent regulatory frameworks for clinical trials (despite their continuing transgression), human experimentation is being constantly outsourced to foreign jurisdictions where rule of law is weak, poverty extensive and corruption endemic. The benefits accrued invariably stack on the side of the developed countries, as the marginalised 'volunteers' in the so-called developing world (India is a particular favourite) become little more than lab rats (Rawlinson, 2013).

The resounding injustices that permeate this type of abuse have barely caught the eye of academics, and even in the field of bioethics, a more obvious discipline for the study of unethical human experimentation, the literature is relatively limited. If we consider some of the reasons for this it becomes apparent that critical criminology can play an important role in advancing the discussion into the area of state and corporate crime, and harms, especially in relation to the latter category.

While unethical experimentation does include criminal acts, as was evident *retrospectively* in Nazi Germany, the very label 'unethical' reinforces the perception of a lesser transgression than, say, that of homicide, even though the outcome might be the death of a human subject. A further dilution of the seriousness of these abuses is the fact that they involve a complex chain of actors connected to public and private medical research, including the state and the pharmaceutical industry, whose stated purpose is to advance the health of citizens. This benign motivation from the state's perspective (though in the case of the pharma-industry, profitability is the main driver) can distract attention away from those inequities arising from the nature of certain clinical trials necessary for the provision of health care.

The burgeoning of human experimentation per se is part of a wider picture in which health is increasingly becoming a political, economic and security issue. Pandemics, such as swine flu and HIV/AIDS, have allowed governments to impose compulsory vaccination schemes and introduce quarantine restrictions which, although well-intentioned, often come at a high price to individual freedom. The veracity of these declared pandemics has also come into question, exposing the close links between international governmental organisations, such as the World Health Organization, and the pharma-industry. The proximity between the state and drug companies is also evident in the problems many victims of unethical experimentation face when seeking legal redress. Legislation is often complex, favouring corporate bodies, and punitive responses to their transgressions usually amount to inadequate payments to the plaintiffs and relatively small fines for the offenders. The focus on preventive medicines has provided the opportunity for high-profit margins in the pharma-industry, which is becoming an ever more powerful voice in lobbying political support for its services and products. As with much of the literature on state–corporate crime and harm, it is money that plays the most active role in decision-making and the ability to make and break the law.

In this typical 'David and Goliath' scenario, critical scholarship plays an important role in redirecting the criminological gaze away from those with less social status – often blamed for society's ills – to the powerful structures that, in this case, purport to heal but ultimately play a significant part in creating these ills. While much good ensues from public and private health initiatives, there is an increasing price to pay. Unethical human experimentation, which invariably targets the vulnerable, demands continued and rigorous study.

Bibliography

Godlee, F. (2010) Conflicts of Interest and Pandemic Flu, *British Journal of Medicine*, 340:c2947 doi:10.1136/bmj.c2947.

LaFleur, W., Böhme, G. and Shimazono, S. (eds) (2008) *Dark Medicine: Rationalizing Unethical Medical Research*, Bloomington, IN: Indiana University Press.

Rawlinson, P. (2013) Of Mice and Men: Violence and Human Experimentation, *State Crime*, 2, (1), pp. 72–90.

Watch:

Syphilis Laboratory: Guatemala (2011), short documentary film, directed by David O'Shea. Australia: Journeyman Pictures.

35

ELDER ABUSE

Nicole Asquith

Elder abuse is an umbrella term used to capture a myriad of victimisation processes that focus on the mistreatment of older people. This mistreatment may variously involve what is known as a structural artefact (violation of human rights, discrimination), intentional acts of commission (physical assault, fraud) or unintentional acts of omission (neglect, social exclusion). Elder abuse occurs to both men and women, and occurs across all classes and income levels and in all educational, religious and ethnic backgrounds. Conventionally, elder abuse is managed by governments as a health or welfare problem, or treated by them as would be comparable crimes committed against victims under the age of 65. The first approach has the same problems as traditional responses to family violence: elder abuse is often hidden, and rarely considered as a criminal justice issue. The second approach pays little attention to unique victimisation processes, or unique offender behaviours and motivations.

Elder abuse is expected to increase over the next thirty years as many countries shift from the population 'pyramid', with sustainable distributions of older and younger people, to the population 'high-rise', with more equal numbers of older and younger people (structural ageing). By 2050, in most developed nations, more than a quarter of the population will be over 65, and close to 10 per cent over 80. Greater numbers of older people and declining fertility and morbidity rates may create intergenerational discord, especially in relation to health and welfare costs, taxation and intergenerational sharing of the family home. Ideally, the last of these may lead to stronger families, but it may also lead to intergenerational conflict and elder abuse.

In line with its early construction as a non-criminal issue, elder abuse was first identified in medical journals in the 1970s. Since then, research has expanded beyond medical analyses to include a range of academic disciplines, often employing their own definitions of elder abuse. Across these approaches, several factors have been identified as important in the experience and prevalence of elder abuse, including:

- living arrangements, especially the victim's dependence upon others
- biological issues relating to the older person
- interpersonal conflict, including histories of family dysfunction
- psychosocial issues, including an offender's inability to deal with anger
- informal carer issues (such as burden and stress) and formal carer issues (such as limited expertise and inappropriate attitudes and practices)
- insufficient resources to provide appropriate, safe and necessary care
- malice or hatred of older people on the part of the offender
- ageism and discrimination.

(Wolf, 2000)

Victims of elder abuse tend to be frail, vulnerable and dependent, and are more likely to be 'old, old' (over 75), female and poor. However, the World Health Organization cautions against resorting to stereotypes of ageing when it comes to elder abuse. For example, wealthy elderly people with property and valuables are more likely to be targeted in cases of fraud and financial abuse. Older men are more vulnerable to abuse because they can be more dependent on others for daily routines. Across all research into elder abuse, older people with meagre social networks are identified as more at risk than those with dense networks.

Biggs and Goergen (2010: 56) suggest that a lack of conceptual clarity and an inadequate defining of the issue have made it difficult to 'determine incidence, prevalence, antecedents, and costs' of elder abuse. Despite increased surveillance of elder abuse in institutions (such as nursing homes), there continues to be little or no reliable data on the prevalence of elder abuse. In a small number of US studies, 17 per cent of nursing home staff used excessive physical restraints and 10 per cent admitted pushing, grabbing or shoving (Bachman and Meloy, 2008). The data on rates of victimisation outside aged-care facilities is even more limited, with prevalence rates ranging between 2 per cent and 28 per cent, depending on the population being studied and the measures and definitions used. One study found that 20 per cent of older people had been abused over an 18-month period up to June 1999, and that 56 per cent of those victims lived with the offender. The victim's adult child is the most common perpetrator of elder abuse (Cripps, 2001).

While physical abuse is more likely to be reported if the older person lives with an abuser, financial abuse is less likely to be reported. This is because the victim's income is often merged with the family income, making financial abuse harder to detect. Victims of elder abuse are also reluctant to report abuse inflicted by another person, especially when there is an intimate or familial relationship with the offender. There may be shame associated with being abused by people they trust, as well as the fear of jeopardising relationships with family and friends. Additionally, older people may fear that a complaint of elder abuse may result in their placement in a residential facility and a consequent loss of independence.

Most cases of elder abuse are not reported to anyone and only the most obvious cases come to the attention of criminal justice agencies. When elder abuse is reported, police and other investigators face challenges in making a criminal investigation. Payne and Gainey (2006) found that senior police officers in the United States believed that some older complainants were not good witnesses for reasons of frailty, senility, poor memory or lack of understanding of the legal system. Many factors reduce the likelihood of elder abuse victims reporting to a criminal justice agency. These factors have led some advocates to call for the introduction of mandatory reporting mechanisms for elder abuse. However, unlike child abuse, such measures are not supported due to the loss of victims' autonomy. Meanwhile elder abuse is not given significant social attention despite notable cases in the media and the fact that our existence in an ageing society makes us more likely to be victimised in our own lifetimes.

References

Bachman, R. and Meloy, M. L. (2008) The Epidemiology of Violence against the Elderly: Implications for Primary and Secondary Prevention, *Journal of Contemporary Criminal Justice*, 24, (2), pp. 186–97.

Biggs, S. and Goergen, T. (2010) Theoretical Development in Elder Abuse and Neglect, *Ageing International*, 35, (3), pp. 167–70.

Cripps, D. (2001) Rights Focused Advocacy and Elder Abuse, *Australasian Journal on Ageing*, 20, (1), pp. 17–22.

Payne, B. and Gainey, R. (2006) The Criminal Justice Response to Elder Abuse in Nursing Homes: A Routine Activities Perspective, *Western Criminology Review*, 7, (3), pp. 67–81.

Wolf, R. S. (2000) The Nature and Scope of Elder Abuse, *Generations*, 24, (2), pp. 6–12.

Watch:

Dad (2005), TV film, directed by Sarah Harding. UK: BBC Wales.

36

DOMESTIC AND FAMILY VIOLENCE

Molly Dragiewicz

Stereotypes of crime and deviance are focused on violence perpetrated by strangers in public spaces. However, women and girls face their greatest risk of victimisation from known men. The domestic home and private family life are two primary contexts for such victimisation. *Domestic violence* refers to violence and abuse by current or former intimate partners. It includes physical violence, sexual violence, emotional or psychological abuse and economic abuse. Domestic violence is generally understood to describe the type of ongoing abusive, controlling and violent behaviour that was originally called 'wife beating'. While the shift to de-gendered terminology reflects the recognition that violence and abuse extends beyond heterosexual men's violence against women, domestic violence remains a highly gendered phenomenon.

Many more women and girls are victims of domestic violence than men and boys, who face their greatest risk from other men who are strangers or acquaintances. Accordingly, while violence and abuse in same sex couples and by women against men in heterosexual couples does occur, men's violence against women is prioritised as an international human rights problem because it is widespread, has serious implications for public health and perpetuates gender inequality.

Men's violence against female intimate partners has not always been considered deviant. Instead, a man's violence against his wife has historically been understood as chastisement. Today, condemnation of domestic violence is uneven and often predicated upon the victim's adherence to gender norms. Despite forty years of antiviolence advocacy, blaming the victim is common, whether for provoking the violence or for failing to leave the abuser.

Family violence incorporates violence and abuse against children, elders, siblings, parents and other family members, as well as intimate partners; it also includes neglect. Child abuse and family violence are significantly under-reported and many countries do not have a mechanism for collecting data on them. To a great extent, violence against children is not considered to be deviant. Corporal punishment is seen by many as an appropriate form of discipline. More than twenty countries have outlawed all physical violence against children, but normalisation of spanking co-exists alongside laws prohibiting child abuse in many locations, illustrating the contested boundaries of this form of deviance.

While female perpetrators are more common in family violence than non-family violence, this type of abuse is also highly gendered. The majority of victims of family violence are female and the majority of perpetrators are male, despite women's disproportionate role in child and elder care. While women are most likely to perpetrate neglect, men are more likely to commit physical and sexual abuse. These sex differences reflect persistent patriarchal family realities, from social norms prescribing hierarchies within the family to labour patterns in which mothers are disproportionately responsible for family care.

While crime studies in the United States indicate that family and domestic violence account for about a tenth of all violent victimisations, about a third of calls to police are related to family and domestic violence (Durose et al., 2005). This disproportionate demand for police intervention points to the seriousness of family and domestic violence, as well as the need to craft police practices that meet the needs of family and domestic violence victims.

Domestic and family violence differ from other crimes in a number of ways. Arresting a perpetrator has different implications when the perpetrator is also a victim's primary caregiver or family breadwinner. Furthermore, familial attachments, both legal and emotional, mean that simply avoiding the perpetrator of violence may not be a viable option, increasing the risk of repeat victimisation. In addition, the ongoing, repetitive, cyclical, and often escalating nature of family and domestic violence means that incident-based interventions, such as arrest based on one assault, are insufficient and often inappropriate, especially in the absence of adequate support for income, housing and medical care for dependent family members.

The complexity of domestic and family violence requires careful attention to research methods. Crude quantitative approaches to studying violence, especially those that rely on counting decontextualised acts, are ill-suited to increasing our understanding. Best practices for the study of domestic and family violence include: utilising broad measures of violence that span the wide range of abusive, violent and controlling behaviours reported by survivors; ascertaining the context in which the violence took place (including the history of violence and whether it was defensive); assessing the consequences or outcomes of the violence; and incorporating violence in intact couples as well as by former partners. In order to be comprehensive, a review of the research should include studies conducted using multiple methodologies, including qualitative and quantitative studies; consider lethal and non-lethal violence; and include studies of those who have reported violence or sought help as well as those who have not.

Critical criminologists have made significant contributions to the growing body of research, but there is still more to be done. Significantly, violence prevention continues to lag behind other areas of research. Since most people are not violent, despite the sometime glamorisation of violence, there is much to be learned about why people choose not to use violence. Likewise, variation in rates of violence across countries and by sex may hold clues to the cultural factors which produce and inhibit violence.

Reference

Durose, M. R., Harlow, C. W., Langan, P. A., Motivans, M., Rantala, R. R. and Smith, E. L. (2005) *Family Violence Statistics: Including Statistics on Strangers and Acquaintances*, Washington, DC: United States Department of Justice, Office of Justice Programs, Bureau of Justice Statistics.

Watch:

No Way Out but One (2012), documentary film, directed by Garland Waller and Barry Nolan. USA: Passion River Films.

37

STALKING AND HARASSMENT

Rowland Atkinson

In the UK stalking refers to repeated and unwanted behaviour creates alarm or distress in a victim, while in the USA it is similarly defined as 'a course of conduct directed at a specific person that would cause a reasonable person to feel fear' (Catalano, 2012: 1). Self-identifying victims of stalking are considered to be harassed – in other words, they feel a sense of deep anxiety and are put in fear of violence. Stalking has become a more widely acknowledged form of deviance that generates fear and distress but is frequently unreported to the police or other agencies. Around 20 per cent of women and 10 per cent of men have been stalked on at least one occasion since the age of 16 (between 8 per cent of women and 6 per cent of men in the past year, around 1.2 million women and 900,000 men) (Walby and Allen, 2004), though this conceals the fact that many women in particular are victimised many times by current or former partners. Like domestic violence, stalking is another undercurrent of social violence that remains partly concealed – the regular transition of stalking into physical violence makes it considerable cause for concern, though many victims do not report it to the police, either thinking it might be seen as trivial or fearing an escalation of such behaviour.

Stalking includes making unwanted phone calls, sending unwanted letters or e-mails, following or spying, waiting at places for the victim or posting information and spreading rumours on the Internet or by word of mouth. While such acts on their own may not appear particularly serious it is clear that they are intended to have a destabilising impact on the victim. In many cases such behaviour is intended to appear as though violence is clearly possible and this is why researchers include stalking within broader definitions of interpersonal violence. The perception that violence may occur is often the primary motivation of an offender since it offers a sense of power over a victim. Other motivations can be identified including feelings of personal rejection, revenge for real or perceived slights, a desire for reconciliation in a relationship (which often slips over into resentment or anger at the loss of the relationship) and attempts at controlling behaviour.

A better understanding of the problem by the police now means that such threats are treated more seriously than in the past and a range of support groups now exists, including the Suzy Lamplugh Trust and digital-stalking.com, while the National Stalking Helpline was created in the UK in 2010. Research suggests that around 10 per cent of stalkers are strangers, the overwhelming majority being current or former partners or people known to the victim (for example, through work), and so stalking is often linked to problems of domestic violence. Yet in discussing practices of predatory surveillance, following and threatening behaviour it is essential that we critically examine many of the features of our society and new media culture that appear to be supportive of such behaviour.

Cyberstalking involves the use of social media and other networking technologies (mobile phones, Internet, and so on) to communicate with or locate personal information about a victim. Such behaviour can be particularly worrying because victims may have little idea about who is pursuing them in this way and this can generate profound anxiety. It is important to consider the links between cyberstalking and the growing number of acts of cyber bullying, Internet 'trolls' and other aggressive forms of behaviour that arise because of the interpenetration of new media into our lives and the possibilities for anonymity that such media enable. Texting sexually explicit images and cajoling girls into having pictures taken of them, with subsequent shaming in public and online, generate major anxieties for parents and traumatic experiences for young people. Navigating a social world of predatory, unformed male sexuality and new networked technologies is likely to continue to present major risks of stalking, harassment and gendered bullying into the future.

Our new media landscape facilitates a culture of voyeurism, spite and guilty pleasures which have lured many people into arguably more aggressive and predatory mindsets. Presdee's (2000) account of an impulsive and sadistic culture has now been more emphatically realised, with stalking and harassment part of how we live today. Presdee would perhaps be keen to locate the double standards by which we decry pornography, the pursuit of celebrities and the bullying of wives, partners and children while privately taking delight in the 'fails', pictures and explicit images of those caught in videos on YouTube, reality TV programmes or paparazzi shots of celebrities. Multiple websites and networked media systems like Twitter have facilitated and perhaps legitimised the real-time surveillance and monitoring of celebrities and bullying of others. Similarly an obsession with celebrities and newsworthy individuals has generated cultures of illicit monitoring and phone-tapping by major newspapers in the UK, ultimately revealed during the Leveson Inquiry.

These developments feed a predatory relationship to women, with female celebrities and others singled out because they have become fat, thin or pregnant. An amateur paparazzi culture has grown up around taking pictures of celebrities and sending them to news media or posting them on websites. Similarly the massive proliferation of former partner 'revenge porn' websites and encouragement of privately photographing women in public spaces are notable developments to which we appear to have few responses as yet. This voyeurism is supportive of norms that denigrate and devalue women. New media technologies have facilitated hyper-masculine norms and make more people vulnerable to stalking and harassment.

It is possible to locate the gendered nature of stalking victimisation within broader cultural values that serve to normalise and legitimise women as victims. For example, the belief of many men that women are, or should be, sexually available. This culture of wolf-whistles, asides to colleagues and unwanted overt attention can be seen in action in the video of the sexual harassment of a woman walking around Brussels, highlighting the daily abuse of women by men and deeper problematic attitudes that generate threatening and intrusive behaviour that can be connected to stalking as a much broader phenomenon (see www.stop-streetharassment.org/2012/08/brussels/). Yet this kind of low-level harassment of women is so engrained in our culture that it often goes without mention and we do not see a fundamental conflict between condemning predatory sexual behaviour such as stalking and the persistence of such conduct norms in society.

References

Catalano, S. (2012) *Stalking Victims in the United States*, Washington, DC: US Department of Justice.

Presdee, M. (2000) *Cultural Criminology and the Carnival of Crime*, London: Routledge.

Walby, S. and Allen, J. (2004) *Domestic Violence, Sexual Assault and Stalking: Findings from the British Crime Survey*, London: Home Office.

Watch:

In the Company of Men (1997), film, directed by Neil LaBute. Canada: Alliance Atlantis.

38

PORNOGRAPHY

Simon Winlow

Pornography is now a global business. Like it or not, it represents a significant portion of global Internet traffic. As many academics have acknowledged, pornography has seeped into mainstream culture and this, I will argue, has a powerful corrosive effect upon our shared lives together.

It is now commonplace to argue that Western culture has been polluted by crass sexualisation. This is not simply a matter of using sex to sell an array of consumer items, and nor is it simply a matter of the ubiquity of porn, especially in an age in which a growing proportion of the population carry with them mobile Internet devices. The most worrying aspect of this is the apparent sexualisation of children and young people, but my focus lies elsewhere. In this section I will argue that an often underappreciated harm of pornography is its ability to intrude upon and refashion the intimacies of sexual fantasy. Perhaps counter-intuitively, I will also argue that the ubiquity of porn does not lead to a growth in promiscuous sexual activity. Instead, porn erodes interest in a sexual encounter with another and in its place develops a new sexualised virtual reality. This process, I will argue, essentially turns Western culture into one increasingly oriented to the base solipsism of sexual pleasure. The 'two scene' (Badiou, 2012) of sexual intimacy becomes only a solipsistic exploration of one's own fantasy space. This means that we become an increasingly sexualised culture, but one that is essentially masturbatory in nature, that eschews a genuine intersubjective encounter in favour of an anxious and selfish individualism. In order to pursue this argument I will draw principally on the psychoanalytic theory of Jacques Lacan.

'There is no sexual relationship' is one of Lacan's most oft-cited phrases. Not only does it appear counter-intuitive, in that one tends to assume that sexual intimacy must be based upon a relationship of one sort or another, but it also acts as a useful conduit to Lacan's model of subjectivity as such: a subjectivity understood in relation to a fundamental and irreducible loss. Here Lacan is claiming that there is no guarantee that one can find a harmonious sexual relationship with one's partner. Rather, with human sexual activity, one is, always, on one's own. Human sexual activity is always structured in relation to fantasy. During the sex act, even when interlinked with the body of another, one is entirely dependent upon fantasy. One must fantasise and sexualise the act and the body of the other in some way in order for sexual activity to possess the energy it needs to be operative. If our internal fantasy space is not engaged in mediating the body of the other, and in sexualising our own bodily activity, the sex act becomes merely a series of bizarre repetitive movements, entirely devoid of pleasurable sensation. One gets some sense of this on those occasions when, during the sex act, the spell is broken and we lose connection with fantasy. The sex act can then appear rather comedic or alien, as if we have been suddenly awakened to the absurdity of it all. Lacan's proposition is essentially that, despite the close proximity of bodies, sex takes us quite far away from each other, and our pleasure remains tied to a base narcissism that cannot be adequately 'socialised' or overcome. Using Lacan's lexicon, those things that appear to unite the couple in sexual union are placed firmly in the realm of the Imaginary. In sex, one is actually engaged in a relationship with oneself rather than the other. For Lacan, love is what fills the absence of the sexual relationship.

What has this to do with pornography? Here it's instructive to turn to Slavoj Žižek's interpretation of Lacan's theory of sexual difference. Žižek suggests that, with sexual activity, one is always forced to use the body of the other as a masturbatory device to secure one's own sexual fulfilment. We are, according to Žižek, engaged in an essentially solipsistic activity. And furthermore, the desire that structures our fantasy is never our own desire. It is always the desire of the other, structured in relation to those around us. At this stage we start to get some sense of how, in an age of ubiquitous media and consumerised porn, culture itself infiltrates, informs and re-patterns those intimate aspects of our internal life we believe to be fundamentally of our own making.

The staggering rise of the porn industry therefore acts to extend the marked individualism of sexual activity as such. It rapidly speeds up the reduction of the other to a mere body to be used for one's own sexual pleasure, and the irreducible gap that exists between the two involved in the sex act can no longer be filled in with love. Pornography disposes of the need for a really existing other and encourages the stupid, solipsistic pleasure of masturbatory enjoyment. My central claim here is that these stupid individualistic pleasures reflect a historic drive towards an *atonal* world (Badiou, 2009) that lacks the structuring logic of a master signifier capable of imposing meaning upon a world of perpetual flux and imponderable diversity. In the sociological sense, it functions as an outcome of selfish individualism: a withdrawal into the cocoon of subjectivity, free from the threats and obligations that pertain to a genuine intersubjective encounter. Contemporary postmodern sexuality is then an increasingly selfish and solitary activity.

Notwithstanding the painful exploitation of damaged subjectivities and the obscene sexualisation of children, the principal harm of pornography relates to its ability to shape postmodern sexual practice. Of course, even before the rise of porn, our internal fantasy space always reflected the desire of the other. This continues with the rise of the global porn industry. Porn patterns the sexual fantasies of an increased proportion of the population, but it also reinforces and exemplifies the collapse of the symbolic order and the withdrawal of that which makes social life real. Our sexual lives are increasingly reflective of asocial sexual egotism, and little shame accrues for the sexual egotist. As Badiou suggests, we must overcome our cultural obsession with stupid selfish pleasures and instead embrace an account of love that goes beyond absurd masturbatory enjoyment and creates the space in which we can begin to appreciate and engage with the other in mutually beneficial ways.

References

Badiou, A. (2009) *Logic of Worlds*, London: Continuum.
Badiou, A. (2012) *In Praise of Love*, London: Verso.

Watch:

The Pervert's Guide to Cinema (2006), documentary film, directed by Sophie Fiennes. UK: Mischief Films.

PART VI

Attacks on social difference

Hate and culture

This section focuses on crimes towards, and the victimisation of, those who deviate from social norms, positions and conventions. Social difference, in the form of variations in religious practices, being homeless or having a different ethnic background from most others in society, can generate powerful reactions from majority groups or those with countervailing beliefs and ideas. The problem of what is known as hate crime – acts of violence, discrimination and abuse motivated by hatred because of the actual or perceived position of an individual or group – forms a significant theme of the chapters to be found in this section. The groups identified here are not criminal; rather it is the reaction to the perceived deviance or difference of these groups that forms the basis of attacks on them. Much hate crime is the stuff of everyday life: hard stares, passengers on public transport who refuse to move, verbal abuse or mocking humour. The absolute bulk of such acts go unrecorded and the experience is chalked up by victims as something that needs to be braved, rather than reported to policing agencies. More extreme forms of hate crime, including serious assaults and murders, are reported but victims and their families may find negative and institutional attitudes that hinder investigations and justice.

Attacks of any kind that are motivated by hate and repulsion tend to be directed through asymmetric power relations, that is from those who feel more powerful and bolder than those they victimise. Critical in understanding this dynamic are the feelings that perpetrators tend to experience – they see their acts as being supported, tacitly or publicly, by others in the community. This means that newspaper editorials and politicians that give voice to stereotypes or demeaning attitudes enable assailants to feel that their acts are supported by a morally and numerically superior community. The chapters here deal with familiar territory, international migrants and homophobic hate crime, but also include important chapters on homelessness and emotional deviance that highlight the need for on-going and vigilant monitoring of such worrisome acts.

39

DISABILITY

Cassandra A. Ogden

When we think of disability we might picture a person in a wheelchair, feel pity or, more 'positively', conjure up the image of the 'super cripple', epitomised in events such as the Paralympics. To regard disability as a form of 'deviance' appears erroneous even from the most uninitiated position, and yet this social position appears confirmed by the treatment of governments who seek to defund support for vulnerable disabled people and by prevailing community attitudes that support attacks, abuse and the ill-treatment of disabled people more broadly. While many people would believe that attacks on disabled people, simply because of their condition, are a major social taboo, Home Office data reported that 1,744 disability hate crimes were recorded by the police in 2011–12. The increasing problem of hate crime is linked to a perception of disability as conferring the position of being 'other', less than human, or different in ways that justify abusive or violent behaviour.

The idea that disability is a form of deviance in its own right can be located within earlier work in sociology itself. For example, the work of US functionalists in the 1950s contributed to the construction of disability as deviant. Talcott Parsons classified disease, illness and disability as manifestations of social deviance, and in doing so suggested that such forms of impairment are undesirable within society (cited in Thomas, 2007).

This perspective further suggested that those with long-term illness or disability cause dysfunction within society, as disability disrupts 'usual' or normal social practice. These beliefs underlie a longer history of social discrimination against this group and unpleasant beliefs about what to do with or about disabled people. Attacks against disabled people are deeply linked to these historical constructs of disability as deviance.

Discussions of 'deviant' or criminal behaviour within the Criminal Justice System (CJS) and the media often encourage us to forget about the kinds of structural inequality, inequitable educational experiences and reduced choices that many groups within societies face. Instead we are encouraged to concentrate on individual criminal psyches, mental health and past (individual) histories that result in our locating criminality and sickness in individuals rather than within the broader causal mechanisms that generate such problems. Similarly, disabled people's problems are seen as stemming from individual physical or mental biological differences as the 'causes' behind their life experiences and difficulties. This medical model of disability can be contrasted against a social model that positions the problems of disabled people more firmly within the disabling environments and social attitudes that confront them throughout their lives (Oliver and Barnes, 2012). Yet such perspectives have largely failed to make an impact on 'commonsense' social understandings of disability.

When disabled people are regarded as 'deviant', processes for punishing are more subtle because they are variously portrayed as pitiable and vulnerable or as welfare 'scroungers', or are ostracised because of their difference. These latter attitudes within communities underpin physical attacks, abuse and the neglect of those who are disabled. Yet we can also argue that those measures that serve to undermine the experiences of the disabled, taking away essential government funding for care and support, are criminal and regressive to the extent that they harm and limit the social lives of vulnerable people. Such approaches to the problems of disability are rationalised by public understandings of disability as an individual problem that people need to deal with by themselves. The more that governments and communities take on such ideological beliefs, the more disabled people are likely to be neglected, and indeed attacked more directly in acts of disability hate crime.

The portrayal of disabled athletes in the UK Paralympic Games 2012 helps us to understand the construction of the 'deviant' disabled. While the perception and treatment of disabled athletes was positive, this may have been because these disabled people could 'do' things, were productive, efficient and functional. Much of the media reporting on the Paralympic athletes and events was heavily punctuated with 'inspirational' stories of people who have achieved highly 'despite' individual adversity. These disabled people did not have to rely on welfare, so the UK government was able to produce the narrative that disabled people are 'able', and that those who do not behave in this way are deviant 'others', particularly disabled people on benefits. By appropriating the Paralympics in such a way, the government and well-intentioned sports fans have in many ways perpetuated the need for disabled bodies to be seen as productive, resilient, wealth creating, neo-liberal subjects, as opposed to bodies of difference.

Awareness of hate-motivated crime towards disabled people through numerous tragic stories highlights the extent of disability hate crime and the questionable responses of the police (Taylor *et al.*, 2012). The recognition of 'disablism' in law has been highlighted by section 146 of the Criminal Justice Act 2003, which justifies increased sentences for perpetrators in line with other forms of hate crime. Both politically and individually this recognition has provided disabled people with some comfort, not least the condemnation of mental or physical violence against this group. Such law straightforwardly assumes a more useful view of disability, yet such reactions to disablism can be seen as tokenistic because they rely on punishment rather than challenging the deeply held social beliefs that generate such acts in the first place. In adopting a solely punitive reaction to disablism, the cultural norms of society that breed intolerance to difference are left untouched. To tackle violence against disabled people the 'norms that legitimise violence against disabled people in the first place' (Goodley and Runswick-Cole, 2011, p. 614) need to be considered.

In consistently dealing with the symptoms of disability hate, instead of the causes, disability hate crime legislation does little more than scratch the surface of the emotional and physical disablism that permeates our society, whilst creating yet another category of deviance.

References

Goodley, D. and Runswick-Cole, K. (2011) The Violence of Disablism, *Sociology of Health and Illness*, 33, (4), pp. 602–17.

Oliver, M. and Barnes, C. (2012) *The New Politics of Disablement*, London: Palgrave Macmillan.

Taylor, P., Corteen, K., Ogden, C. and Morley, S. (2012) 'Standing' By: Disability Hate Crime and the Police in England, *Criminal Justice Matters*, 87, (1), pp. 46–7.

Thomas, C. (2007) *Sociologies of Disability and Illness*, London: Palgrave Macmillan.

Watch:

X-Men (2000), film, directed by Bryan Singer. USA: Twentieth Century Fox.

40

HOMOPHOBIC HATE CRIME

Karen Corteen

Hate crime refers to prejudicial or biased criminal acts against a person or property that are motivated by a victim's actual or perceived sexuality, race, ethnicity, disability, religion or gender. Although legally, morally and politically this is a contentious area, since the 1980s and 1990s the concept of hate crime has become embedded within law, criminal justice systems, academia, politics and society. Radical social movements campaigned for state action with regard to crime motivated by hatred, resulting in legislation being introduced in the United States and the United Kingdom from the 1990s onwards. Hate crime legislation evokes the violence of the law (law's legitimate capacity to inflict punishment), thus perpetrators who commit a crime that is motivated by hatred, bias or prejudice will be subject to tougher sentences. Other measures include the creation of new offences and changes in policing practices and reporting and recording procedures.

Hate crime not only affects the targeted individual(s) subject to it, it affects those who share the minority or bias status, conveying the message that they 'could be next'. It is also considered an attack on the liberal belief in the tolerance of a diverse society and those citizens who share it. Since the expansion of this contested terrain theoretical and empirical understandings have blossomed, yet there remains much that is unknown or not understood, for example the often ambiguous relationship between the perpetrator and victim (Mason, 2005). Furthermore, whilst there have been changes in criminal justice policies and practices, problems often occur in securing justice.

Homophobic hate crime is concerned with individuals who are victimised due to their (perceived) sexuality. Hence there has been a shift in historical conceptualisations and perceptions of sexual minorities from (deviant) objects of fear to fearful subjects (Moran et al., 2003). Unlike many fears related to possible victimisation, sexual minorities' fears of being victims of crime are more real than imagined. Various studies have demonstrated that globally lesbians, gay men, bisexuals and transgendered individuals (LGBT) are disproportionately victimised when compared with their heterosexual counterparts. A wide spectrum of homophobic violence (verbal, physical, psychological or emotional) forms part of the everyday lived experiences of lesbians and gay men (Moran et al., 2003). Local, national and international studies have also highlighted the fact that such victimisation has particular short- and long-term damaging effects. They illustrate how victims of homophobic hate crime suffer more and suffer for longer than victims of non-bias crimes. This is due to the negatively constructed deviant status that lesbians and gay men still face in many inherently prejudiced societies.

Documentation of such victimisation and its effects and after-effects, together with attempts at encouraging tolerance within increasingly diverse societies, form the backbone of arguments for homophobic hate crime legislation. Other arguments advocate that, since hate crime measures have been enacted to deal with racially motivated crime, it is only fair and just that such measures be extended to other minorities such as the lesbian, gay, bisexual and transgender (LGBT) community. Indeed, failure to put sexual minorities on an equal footing with ethnic minorities reinforces their position as deviant and second class citizens, rendering them as undeserving victims and less worthy of state protection. Another argument for homophobic hate crime legislation is that it would make state actors within and outside the criminal justice system respond to homophobic violence more seriously; this would require the political will of such actors. Whilst there is no evidence to suggest that tougher penalties act as a deterrent, this argument has also been forwarded as a justification of homophobic hate crime laws. One of the more convincing arguments is that of the symbolic and educative role of the law and the power it has to help denounce homophobia and homophobic violence.

Whilst the spectrum of homophobic violence has been acknowledged and condemned, homophobic hate crime legislation (and hate crime legislation generally) has not been embraced by all. Reservations on the grounds of 'freedom of speech' and 'freedom of thought' have been aired in and outside academia. Problems have also been identified with regard to 'outing' and reporting of, policing of and prosecuting homophobic hate crime. The fear of tensions between heterosexuals and sexual minorities being stoked due to the perception of sexual minorities being given privileges in law has also been voiced. Yet ultimately these arguments against homophobic hate crime legislation appear unconvincing given a need for equality of treatment under the law and the need to prosecute crimes motivated by violent sexual bias within communities.

Whether the violence of the law should be resorted to in response to homophobic hate crime depends on one's analysis of the role of the state. For 'critical criminologists', resorting to punitive populism (policies that are shaped by a political interpretation of a perceived punitive stance in society towards crime) and processes of criminalisation serve to bolster state action which is often already draconian and marginalising. Discrimination and crimes based on bias and prejudice do need tackling; however it is well documented that those that come under the gaze of the state and its apparatus (including the criminal justice system) are primarily the poor, marginalised and least powerful members of society.

Whilst responding to homophobes as if they are doubly deviant means that they can be punished more severely, institutional and cultural homophobia remains intact. Sex and relationship education policies in schools still at best normalise heterosexuality and, at their worst, are homophobic. Meanwhile institutionalised religions continue to fight legislation which gives sexual minorities the same rights as other citizens. More problematically, it is unlikely that the harm of not being able to be oneself will be alleviated by creating anti-homophobic hate crime legislation. Similarly, the impact on the wider context of cultural norms and values that shape heterosexual normalcy, heteronormativity and homophobia is debatable. Finally, the extent to which an individual perpetrator can be punished into not being homophobic is questionable, and trying to bring about tolerance through a punitive approach is counter-intuitive and likely to be ultimately counter-productive.

References

Mason, G. (2005) Hate Crime and the Image of the Stranger, *British Journal of Criminology*, 45, (6), pp. 837–59.

Moran, L., Skeggs, B., Tyrer, P. and Corteen, K. (2003) The Constitution of Fear in Gay Space, in E. A. Stanko (ed.) *The Meanings of Violence*, London: Routledge.

Watch:

The Matthew Shepard Story (2002), TV film, directed by Roger Spottiswoode. Canada/USA: Alliance Atlantis Communications.

41

GYPSIES AND TRAVELLERS

Anne Foley

Gypsies and travellers are portrayed with a mixture of curiosity and suspicion in equal measure. TV programmes such as *My Big Fat Gypsy Wedding* have brought renewed interest in the social world of gypsies and travellers, whilst the forced removal of eighty-six families from Dale Farm in Essex in 2011 brought the media gaze on the plight of gypsy and traveller communities to the fore. Despite this, it is fair to say that the lifestyle of gypsies and travellers is often misunderstood by the wider population. The purpose of this chapter is to help put into context the values of gypsies and travellers, and how these have conflicted with the values supposedly embedded in wider society.

Before we move on to discuss the nomadic lifestyle of gypsies and travellers it is helpful to offer some clarification of the different groups that fall within this ethnic group. In general, the designation 'gypsies and travellers' includes groups that share a recent or current nomadic lifestyle, including: English, Scottish and Welsh gypsies, Irish travellers, Roma, fairground travellers and show people, boat dwellers and New Age travellers. It is important to note here that these groups of gypsies and travellers have different cultural lifestyles and as such should not be seen as a homogeneous ethnic group. The one commonality shared by all gypsies and travellers is their desire to live a nomadic lifestyle; for many this means shunning traditional dwellings of bricks and mortar in favour of trailers and barges.

The history of gypsies and travellers is a long one, and in the UK it has also at times been fraught with conflict with the wider society. The first official record of gypsies and travellers in the UK dates back over five hundred years, although it is generally recognised that they have lived here longer than records would suggest; for example, the Showperson's Charter dates back to the twelfth century (Murdoch and Johnson, 2004). Initially gypsies and travellers were welcomed into Britain and were seen to provide a number of essential crafts (Kenrick and Bakewell, 1995). Yet this reception did not last: not long after their arrival in this country gypsies and travellers were subjected to legislation which made it difficult for them to maintain their nomadic lifestyle. It has been widely recognised that in their more recent history the Criminal Justice and Public Order Act 1994, which gave the police in England and Wales greater powers to remove gypsies and travellers from unauthorised sites, has had serious implications for their nomadic lifestyle.

Despite the range of legislation introduced across Europe which has attempted to curb the nomadic lifestyle of gypsies and travellers, it remains an integral part of their culture, offering both an economic and a cultural function. Indeed, for gypsies and travellers, nomadism performs an important rite, allowing them to preserve a significant part of their cultural heritage. Travelling in the main is seasonal, beginning in the spring and finishing in the autumn, during which they move around the country attending fairs and looking for work. In doing so, they are able to establish business contacts and maintain contact with their wider family networks. Pursuing a nomadic lifestyle means that gypsies and travellers seek access to land on either a temporary or permanent basis, and in this way their world can come into conflict with those living a sedentary lifestyle. Indeed, accessing land illegally, albeit for a very short period of time, is often regarded with disdain by mainstream society, which perceives illegal encampments as part of a broader 'gypsy problem'.

By and large gypsies and travellers do not want to access land illegally; this is generally used as a last resort if no other alternative is available. It is worth noting here that in England and Wales all local authorities have been obliged to carry out a needs assessment of gypsies and travellers under their jurisdiction. The outcome from these has highlighted a considerable shortage in legal stopping places, both temporary and permanent, for gypsies and travellers. As a consequence of this, they often have no option but to pull up on to land illegally in order to pursue their cultural rite. Earlier reference was made to Dale Farm, where in 2011 eighty-six gypsy and traveller families were forcibly removed from land which they owned but did not have the appropriate planning permission for. This case received a considerable amount of public sympathy but also condemnation, highlighting the difficulties gypsies and travellers experience in forgoing sedentarists' desire for permanent homes, though the case also gave many in society a better understanding of gypsy and traveller communities and the important role nomadism has within their culture.

Gypsies and travellers adhere to a strict moral code which at times conflicts with the values professed by wider society. This has led to a common image of gypsies and travellers as 'lawless', and yet much of the institutionalisation of a sense of difference between these communities and wider society lies in their desire to live a nomadic lifestyle. Since few legal or culturally appropriate encampments are available internationally this forces a deviant status upon gypsies and travellers, who appear to be departing from mainstream social norms with regard to legal notions of property and the 'right' way to live in particular spaces.

References

Kenrick, D. and Bakewell, S. (1995) *On the Verge: The Gypsies of England*, 2nd edn, Hatfield, UK: University of Hertfordshire Press.

Murdoch, A. and Johnson, C. (2004) Introduction, in C. Johnson and M. Willers (eds) *Gypsy and Traveller Law*, pp. 1–20, London: Legal Action Group.

Watch:

District 9 (2009), film, directed by Neill Blomkamp. USA/UK: WingNut Films.

42

MIGRANTS

Steven Hirschler

Links between criminality and immigration have been propagated for centuries. In the seventeenth century, French Huguenots fleeing persecution were depicted as Catholic spies seeking to subvert English identity. At the turn of the twentieth century, Jewish and Irish immigrants were vilified in the press and blamed for increasing crime levels and rent racketeering. In many countries today, much undocumented migration is considered illegal; one can be culpable of the crime of simply crossing national boundaries. However, the socio-legal construction of the so-called 'illegal immigrant' is a relatively recent phenomenon.

In Britain, the Aliens Act 1793 restricted the entry of some migrants, particularly French refugees, and the Aliens Act 1905 granted individual immigration officers discretionary power to exclude those considered 'undesirable'. Following the exploitation of imported Chinese labour into the United States during the nineteenth century, the 1875 Page Law aimed to reduce the number of Chinese labourers and prostitutes entering the country. Shortly after, the 1882 Chinese Exclusion Act introduced a decade-long moratorium on imported Chinese labour, though certain employment categories were excluded. Erika Lee (2002: 36) explains that the act was the 'first [US immigration law] to restrict a group of immigrants based on their race and class, and it thus helped to shape twentieth-century United States race-based immigration policy'.

In the early twentieth century, the press contributed significantly to the construction of an image of migrants as diseased and threatening, and politicians sought to capitalise on societal fears of apparently dangerous foreigners. Contemporary media representations of immigrants have continued along a similar trajectory, linking migration to criminality and the parasitical exploitation of states' benefits systems. It is now common for the words 'criminal' and 'immigrant' to appear interchangeably in the media and political discourse, a practice that perpetuates fears of identity loss and declining individual security in the face of migrant 'influxes'.

The preoccupation with migrant criminality can be seen as an expression of wider social anxieties about the perceived negative effects of immigration. Tamara Vukov states that 'media spectacles around migration' help develop 'commonsense imaginings of national belonging, of who should be included and excluded in the national community' (2003: 340). Some have argued that the conflation of immigrants with increased crime levels strengthens national identities by creating a simplistic binary differentiation of 'domestic' and the 'foreign' that tends to result in the demonisation of outsiders. This was clearly apparent following the 2011 British riots, when David Starkey claimed during a *Newsnight* interview that 'whites have become black'. This suggested that the acts of rioters were not inherent to native Britons but assimilated from foreign cultures that could themselves be seen as essentially deviant in nature.

Newspaper articles in UK publications like *The Sun* and the *Daily Mail* depict the crimes of immigrants with a particular emphasis upon the foreignness of migrant perpetrators. However, the attention paid to immigrants' criminality overshadows their more frequent capacity for victimisation. Some of the United Kingdom's most vulnerable migrants, such as destitute asylum seekers, have been subjected to racist attacks or have turned to suicide. Racial violence has resulted in the deaths of asylum seekers around the country, but these stories do not seem to resonate with politicians and media outlets seeking to emphasise the immigrant 'threat'. Instead, public policy is designed around the presumption that asylum claims are typically 'bogus' and immigrants seek to take advantage of welfare services.

New immigration laws continually narrow the legal parameters within which migrants can live and operate, and many of the crimes immigrants are charged with tend to relate to their infringement of immigration rules. Offences typically include working illegally, remaining 'in-country' beyond visa expiry or using false documentation upon entry. Sometimes these activities, like seeking illegal employment, are a response to restrictive rules disallowing certain migrants from pursuing legitimate work. While some migrants may be guilty of other crimes, little evidence exists to suggest that immigrants commit more crime than citizens and the relationship between crime levels and immigration rates is weak at best, despite the often exaggerated punitive responses to migrant criminality (Bell and Machin, 2011). Hagan and Palloni (1999) reveal the imbalances Central and South American immigrants face within the US justice system, as they are incarcerated at rates of between two and five times that of US citizens. Immigrants' crimes are therefore significant not because of their degree or frequency, but because of the extent to which the media, politicians and individual citizens seek to highlight and amplify the purported exceptionality of these offences for political gain.

While policy-makers do not hold uniform views regarding the impact of migration, often little is done to contradict publicly representations of immigrants as deviant and dangerous. In the UK, Enoch Powell achieved popular support following his 1968 speech in which he cited a supposed case of immigrants shoving faeces through a pensioner's letterbox to highlight the dangers of an expanding migrant population. More recently, immigration has been closely associated with national security concerns, particularly following the attacks of 11 September 2001, and the state has intensified its punitive approach towards immigration-related offences through the expansion of detention centres intended to control the movements of migrants. Teresa Miller (2005) suggests that US immigration law has become the preferred method of achieving the social control of non-citizens instead of pursuing them via the courts and policing agencies.

Politicians depend upon the continued representation of migrants as an omnipresent threat to justify major investments in costly security systems and to achieve political popularity in often polarised and unsophisticated debates on these issues. The UK Home Secretary, Theresa May, has continually criticised British courts for allowing foreign 'criminals' to remain in the country on the grounds of human rights. In both Great Britain and the USA, lucrative agreements have been agreed between private firms and the Home Office and the US Immigration and Customs Enforcement Agency respectively to manage immigration detention facilities. Given that in Spring 2013, 57 per cent of British respondents viewed immigration as one of the three most important issues facing the country (YouGov, 2013), and three-quarters of American poll participants thought immigration rates should remain static or be reduced (Gallup, 2013), the reaffirmation of migrant otherness through processes of criminalisation continues to offer significant political and economic capital.

Bibliography

Bell, B. and Machin, S. (2011) *The Impact of Migration on Crime and Victimisation: A Report for the Migration Advisory Committee.* Available online at www.ukba.home-office.gov.uk/sitecontent/documents/aboutus/workingwithus/mac/27-analysis-migration/02-research-projects/lse-consulting?view=Binary (accessed 2 October 2013).

Gallup (website) (2013) Immigration, available online at www.gallup.com/poll/1660/immigration.aspx (accessed 23 July 2013).

Hagan, J. and Palloni, A. (1999) Sociological Criminology and the Mythology of Hispanic Immigration and Crime, *Social Problems*, 46, (4), pp. 617–32.

Lee, E. (2002) The Chinese Exclusion Example: Race, Immigration, and American Gatekeeping, 1882–1924, *Journal of American Ethnic History*, 21, (3), pp. 36–62.

Miller, T. (2005) Blurring the Boundaries between Immigration and Crime Control after September 11th, *Boston College Third World Law Journal*, 25, (1), pp. 81–124.

Vukov, T. (2003) Imagining Communities through Immigration Policies: Governmental Regulation, Media Spectacles and the Affective Politics of National Borders, *International Journal of Cultural Studies*, 6, (3), pp. 335–53.

YouGov (website) (2013) Immigration Concern Hits Three-year High, available online at http://yougov.co.uk/news/2013/05/08/immigration-concern-hits-three-year-high/ (accessed 23 July 2013).

Young, J. (2003) To These Wet and Windy Shores: Recent Immigration Policy in the UK, *Punishment & Society*, 5, (4), pp. 449–62. Available online at http://pun.sagepub.com/cgi/doi/10.{1177/14624745030054005} (accessed 18 February 2012).

Watch:

In This World (2002), film, directed by Michael Winterbottom. UK: BBC, Film Consortium, Film Council, The Words, Revolution Films.

43

HOMELESSNESS

Pat Carlen

Homelessness has different meanings in different countries, and according to different legislatures. Here, however, it will refer to the situation of people in Western countries known either as 'rough sleepers' or 'street homeless' because they move from place to place, often alternating between sleeping in the open, on someone's couch, in woods, farm out-buildings, under bridges or in short-term hostels (FEANTSA, 2012). The causes of rough sleeping are various but, historically, the main cause is poverty aggravated by specific economic, political and cultural conditions resulting in lack of access to safe and secure accommodation. Today, rough sleeper populations are comprised of: young single people who have been ejected from state care or their own families; people who have problems relating to mental and physical illness or have been victims of sexual or physical abuse; ex-inmates of penal institutions or ex-members of the armed forces; single adults made homeless as a result of a relationship breakdown; transient and migrant workers unable (as a result of either local welfare legislation or racist landlords) or unwilling (for economic reasons) to take on more permanent housing responsibilities; and illegal immigrants lacking access to basic citizen rights, and frequently exploited by illegal labour entrepreneurs or exploited for criminal purposes by pro-fessional or organised criminals, and especially by those engaged in people trafficking, prostitution or illegal drug importation and distribution.

Being homeless is not, and never has been, a crime, but people sleeping rough have suffered harassment by governments and law enforcement authorities for centuries, as well as being perennial victims of serious physical, sexual or personal-property crimes (Carlen, 1996). On the other hand, rough sleepers themselves have also frequently been driven, by employment policies discriminating against the homeless or by their lack of access to essential living facilities, to engage in crimes of survival, mainly of a trivial nature; though towards the end of the twentieth century, illegal immigrants swelled the numbers of rough sleepers in many European countries and today some of them are also among those who engage in more serious survival crimes (such as drug dealing) if, being non-citizens, they are ineligible for both legal employment and welfare benefits in the jurisdictions in which they are currently living (Sandberg and Pedersen, 2009).

Yet, although being homeless is not against any law, it is almost impossible for street homeless people not to fall foul of laws relating to 'loitering', indecency, vagrancy, public order offences, begging (see Chapter 4) and soliciting. Thus, in the case of more minor law infringements, rough sleepers can be punished for what might appropriately be called 'status crimes'; that is, for situational lawbreaking provoked primarily by their homeless status and to which they most likely would not be vulnerable were they not sleeping rough. These status crimes of the street homeless include some crimes of indecency (urinating in public), drunkenness, minor pilfering (for example, of bottles of milk from doorsteps), soliciting in order to get a bed for the night, trespass (in farms, parks and other sheltered locations) or even meeting together in places (famous tourist sites, say) from which they have been banned by state or local authorities anxious to promote images of public order and affluence. Overall, then, 'homelessness and crime' is indeed an empirically shady and conceptually messy area. From a criminological viewpoint, the main focus of interest lies not so much in the (mainly minor) lawbreaking of people sleeping rough but more in the reasons for the disciplining and harassment of the homeless poor by state, law and citizenry from early modern times right up to the present day. Explanations usually involve analysis of the interrelationships between economy, politics and culture, even though for different writers on the governance of the poor, the primary emphasis may be on: the economy (Wacquant, 2009); the politics of social order (Foucault, 1977); or the cultural construction of anti-poor sensibilities (Young, 2007).

Economic explanations of the spatial regulation of rough sleepers note that in the sixteenth and seventeenth centuries the political concern was not that rough sleepers were without shelter, but that they were masterless men. Yet as Slack (1990) points out, the argument that regulation of the poor has always been related to the control of the surplus labour force should be set against evidence that spatial control and surveillance of mendicancy has continued even during times of labour scarcity. By the first half of the sixteenth century most European countries had local bureaucracies for the administration of poor relief, and then, as now, welfare bureaucracies were concerned with relating entitlement to households and civic responsibility for poor relief to residency of claimants. Economic explanations, therefore, need to take into consideration not only the control of labour but also the political and fiscal incentive to keep local tax burdens for poor relief as low as possible – by ensuring that itinerant rough sleepers were returned to the parishes where they were born. (See Sandberg and Pedersen, 2009 on the lengths to which modern states will go to return illegal immigrants to their countries of origin, and the statelessness that ensues when no country will admit to responsibility for them.) Loïc Wacquant's *Punishing the Poor* not only provides a sophisticated explanation of the acceleration of the punishment of the poor in the United States under economic neo-liberalism; its cultural analysis of insecurity is also a reminder why visible homelessness is such a threat to citizens already made insecure by fragmented labour markets and rightwing portrayals of the threats to social order from marginal populations.

A greater emphasis on the political disciplining of the poor as threats to public order might be derived from Michel Foucault's (1977) *Discipline and Punish*, where the author's writings on schooling and regulation, exclusion and inclusion are directly relevant to attempts to govern homelessness today – for instance, the strategies aimed primarily at getting rough sleepers voluntarily to move into more permanent housing either by withholding welfare benefits from them, by continually moving them on, or by making it impossible for them to be on the streets without infringing some law in relation to loitering (see Levi, 2009).

Finally, a trenchant cultural explanation of why rough sleepers are consistently abhorred not only by governments but also by ordinary citizens can be derived from Jock Young's (2007) *Vertigo of Late Modernity*, where he portrays the late modern condition of ontological and economic insecurity as a fear of falling, of being economically and culturally excluded. Rough sleepers on the streets will arouse pity in some citizens but, at times of global austerity and uncertainty, they are also a living reminder that the feared descent from a higher to a lower income may well result in a nightmarish loss of status, security, home, respectability and civic identity. For governments, of course, the nearer the socially marginal move to the centre, the greater the perceived political threat.

Bibliography

Carlen, P. (1996) *Jigsaw: A Political Criminology of Youth Homelessness*, Buckingham, UK: Open University Press.

European Federation of National Organisations Working with the Homeless (FEANTSA) (2012) Homeless in Europe: The Geographies of Homelessness, available online at http://feantsa.horus.be/files/freshstart/Communications/Homeless%20in%20Europe%20EN/PDF_2012/Homeless_in_Europe_Summer_2012.pdf (accessed 2 October 2013).

Foucault, M. (1977) *Discipline and Punish*, London: Allen Lane.

Homeless Research Institute (2013) *State of Homelessness in America*, Washington, DC: National Alliance to End Homelessness.

Levi, R. (2009) Making Counter Law: On Having No Apparent Purpose in Chicago, *British Journal of Criminology*, 49, (2), pp. 131–49.

Sandberg, S. and Pedersen, W. (2009) *Street Capital: Black Cannabis Dealers in a White Welfare State*, Bristol: Policy Press.

Slack, P. (1990) *The English Poor Law, 1531–1782*, Basingstoke, UK: Macmillan Education.

Wacquant, L. (2009) *Punishing the Poor: The Neoliberal Government of Social Insecurity*, Durham, NC: Duke University Press.

Young, J. (2007) *The Vertigo of Late Modernity*, London: SAGE.

Watch:

Dark Days (2000), documentary film, directed by Marc Singer. USA: Wide Angle Pictures.

44

MENTAL HEALTH AND 'EMOTIONAL DEVIANCE'

Bruce M. Z. Cohen

Whether the aggressive young man you avoid on the way to work, the woman who talks to herself on the bus, your son's problems in concentrating at school or your mother's obsessive hoarding of newspapers at home, there would appear to be more emotionally problematic behaviour in our society than ever before. The public is, in turn, more aware that they may have friends, co-workers or family members who lack appropriate social skills and are not good at interacting with others, or seem unhappy for too much of the time, or are conversely too happy, have too much energy and cannot concentrate on completing any single task. All these behaviours are now designated as symptoms of 'mental illness', a disease that can be treated by the appropriate professionals under the lexicon of psychiatric or psychological treatment. The World Health Organization (2008: 6) estimates the global adult lifetime rate of mental ill-health to be between 12.2 per cent and 48.6 per cent, and it is estimated that from a fifth to a quarter of the population will be suffering from a mental illness at any one time. Yet, rather than see such emotional behaviour as indicating some kind of sickness, or pathology, sociologists of deviance seek to question mental illness designations as highly relative categories of social behaviour which are often imposed for questionable reasons.

A 'mental disorder' is defined by the American Psychiatric Association (2000: xxxi) as a 'clinically significant behavioral or psychological syndrome or pattern that occurs in an individual'. Under such a definition, mental illness is considered to be an objective, immutable fact of scientific medicine. However, this view can be questioned through a brief survey of historical and cultural understandings of madness. In the Middle Ages signs of madness or 'unreason' were often associated with sacred forms of knowledge with the potential to give insight into the human condition. This conception of seemingly 'irrational' behaviour as a sacred otherness remains in many parts of Asia and Africa today, where madness is seen as the visitation of spirits that may be positive or negative and affect the wider community as well as the individual. Since the Enlightenment and the rise of psychiatric medicine in Western society, behaviours categorised as signs of madness have changed as society itself has changed; infamous examples of mental illnesses no longer considered as such include drapetomania (a 'disease' suffered by black slaves in the United States, which induced them to run away from their owners), masturbatory insanity, hysteria and, more recently, homosexuality. Thus behaviour considered 'mad' or 'mentally ill' in a given historical epoch or culture is better understood as *socially relative* and contingent on *social reaction* rather being simply the result of an underlying biological illness (this can be seen, for example, in the context-specific nature of 'hearing voices' – during church services it is acceptable to hear voices from God and even to speak in tongues, yet the same behaviour carried out on the street is viewed as socially unacceptable).

Without any substantiating proof for mental illness (see Kirk and Kutchins, 1997), behaviour so labelled can be conceptualised as a form of social deviance which has been successfully 'medicalised' by psychiatric professionals. As Conrad and Schneider (1992: 1) have noted of medicine's ability to turn aspects of social life into medical conditions, we have witnessed over time 'the historical transformation of definitions of deviance from "badness" to "sickness"'. Focused on the deviant populations of paupers, criminals, lunatics and lepers, the moral focus of the Middle Ages has been replaced in industrial society with an increasing 'medical gaze' on the subject (Foucault, 1994). The dominant scientific discourse on mental illness can be seen as a powerful form of disciplinary knowledge used to control social problems and to police populations considered a threat to the social order. Thomas Szasz (2010: xxvii–xxviii) has been a traditional critic of psychiatric power and theorises the construction of such 'pseudo-scientific' knowledge as a means of controlling deviant groups including the poor, homosexuals, women, ethnic minorities and young people. The disproportion of such groups currently represented in the mental illness statistics would appear to substantiate such claims.

The power of the psychiatric profession to act as moral regulators of deviant behaviour within capitalist society is arguably more prevalent and systematic under neoliberalism than it has been previously. The medical gaze has moved from the confines of the mental institution to be present in the workplace, the school and even the home. Additionally, as the categories of mental illness have proliferated over the past thirty years (see Kirk and Kutchins, 1997: 21–54), the increasing socio-political focus on the individual as a site of responsibility and change means that members of the public are also more likely now to self-diagnose themselves as suffering from some form of mental disorder. Sociologists of deviance have understood this increase in the labelling of everyday emotional behaviour as 'mental illness' as the success of health and welfare capitalism. However the proliferation of new categories of mental illness, such as social anxiety disorder and attention deficit hyperactivity disorder (ADHD), may signify a more specific function – namely, the need to pathologise previously 'normal' emotional behaviour (for example, shyness and introversion, or failing to pay attention in school and hand in homework on time) as no longer acceptable to the needs of capital within the neoliberal marketplace.

References

American Psychiatric Association (2000) *Diagnostic and Statistical Manual of Mental Disorders: DSM-IV-TR (Text Revision)*, Washington, DC: American Psychiatric Association.

Conrad, P. and Schneider, J. W. (1992) *Deviance and Medicalization: From Badness to Sickness*, Philadelphia, PA: Temple University Press.

Foucault, M. (1994) *The Birth of the Clinic: Archaeology of Medical Perception*, New York: Vintage Books.

Kirk, S. A. and Kutchins, H. (1997) *Making us Crazy: DSM: The Psychiatric Bible and the Creation of Mental Disorders*, New York: Free Press.

Szasz, T. S. (2010) *The Myth of Mental Illness: Foundations of a Theory of Personal Conduct*, revised edn, New York: Harper Perennial.

World Health Organization (2008) *mhGAP: Mental Health Gap Action Programme: Scaling Up Care for Mental, Neurological and Substance Use Disorders*, Geneva: WHO Press.

Watch:

The Trap: What Happened to Our Dream of Freedom (2007), TV documentary series, directed by Adam Curtis. UK: BBC.

45

RACISM

Tina G. Patel

Racism is a belief that 'races' (or ethnic groups) have distinctive character-istics, which form some sort of natural hierarchy, giving a select few supe-riority over others. Although racism refers to a varied and complex pattern of discriminations, including inter-group conflict, the most common form of racism is that directed against 'black and minority ethnic' groups by their 'white' counterparts. This is unsurprising given the tendency to view whiteness as being a kind of identity without racial qualities, a non-raced norm, which allowed global expansion and national rule, itself resulting in violent practices of imperialism and colonialism; the African slave trade; immigration regulations; Jim Crow; and the Aboriginal Stolen Generations. Racism and race inequality thrive where we find views that a racial hierarchy is natural and needs to remain in place. Such conditions problematise victims of racism by presenting them as over-sensitive trouble-makers, via a process of victim-blaming. This process involves demonising black and minority ethnic populations, reinforcing ideas about their social deviance, as well as representing white perpetrators as *the* victims of black and minority ethnic presence.

In recent years, racism has moved beyond biologically based essentialist conceptions, such as 'colour' distinctions drawn on biological pigmenta-tions. New forms of 'cultural racism' such as xenophobia, anti-Semitism and

Islamaphobia, have now become popular. These allow racism to occur on the basis of national origin, linguistic differences, religion, dress and cultural traditions (Patel and Tyrer, 2011). They are especially powerful because in particular contexts, for instance within the 'war on terror' context, they move under the radar of race equality legislation and anti-discrimination laws. This happens by allowing perpetrators to deny that race is a sole motivation for behaviour, or by justifying the supposed need to override equality measures.

Racism, or racial discrimination, is widely prohibited by law. However, in reality, intentional and unintentional racial discrimination continues – not only in everyday race-hate attacks and abuse, but also by officials acting in the name of the state. For instance, consider the occurrence of 'institutional racism', which is when a whole organisation's procedures and policies disadvantage people of a particular ethnic background. Similarly 'state racism' refers to the way that racism can be enshrined in law enforcement procedures, such as police use of 'stop and search'. Therefore we still have a situation where there is a marked disproportionality: black and minority ethnic groups are over-represented at all stages of the criminal justice system as a result of this in-built form of discrimination.

In terms of criminal offences, the reporting and prosecution of 'everyday' racial discrimination is low. There is a variety of reasons for this, including the vastly hidden nature of such crimes, which renders them invisible or too common an occurrence to report; a fear of further victimisation; or a lack of confidence in the criminal justice system. Organised racism, such as that of the far right, or the behaviour of violent racist extremists, attract more attention. However, there still remains an inability in society at large to view racial discrimination as a widely occurring crime or something that can be connected to the views of wider society. This allows racist attitudes and behaviours to continue and, more seriously, to become normalised. This situation is worsened when perpetrators of racist violence are viewed as eccentric individuals or as lone psychologically disturbed individuals, not like the rest of us. A similar process of distancing from violence was seen in the case of Anders Behring Breivik who, on an island near Oslo in July 2011, murdered many children attending a camp run by a moderate political party he believed to be responsible for a perceived decline of Norwegian society caused by migration.

Historically, images of 'black criminality' have been constantly presented to us as factual. For example, consider the UK moral panic about mugging in the 1980s. Criminological research has led to the debunking of such myths, highlighting at the same time the underlying prejudicial beliefs that focus on black criminality. However, notions of black criminality continue to be popular and there is a tendency to underestimate levels of racism in society at large. This allows a policy and practice disconnection where we find a failure to act on racial discrimination and to treat it as a serious crime. In some cases there is an unbalanced consideration of victim and offender, in particular excusing racially offensive behaviour and a readiness to treat black and minority ethnic victims of crime as 'suspicious' or as if they were themselves the problem. All this combines to reinforce a deeper racist ideology in which racism can thrive and in some cases be excused.

Work on racism can benefit from critical criminological work that forces us to reconsider the relationship between race, racism and crime/deviance. In particular, there needs to be a focus on racism as a hidden crime and the structures that allow racism to continue without seriously being seen as wrong-doing within our wider culture.

References

Patel, T. G. and Tyrer, D. (2011) *Race, Crime and Resistance*, London: SAGE.

Watch:

Four Lions (2010), film, directed by Christopher Morris. UK: Film4 Productions.

PART VII

Global problems of violence and human harm

This section tackles what perhaps most people would argue are some of the greatest challenges for humankind and for those studying questions of crime and harm. Included in this section is a range of problems and issues that are not simply 'out there', things that simply go on in the world we live in; these problems are built into the 'architecture' of the world system we inhabit. Capitalism, a political and economic system predicated on huge and expanding extraction of natural resources, places massive and ultimately unbearable impacts on natural resources and environments. This system also places heavy pressure to cut production costs and boost profits. These forces place workers in Western countries in jeopardy of their livelihoods (as contracts go to cheaper companies 'offshore') and those of other nations at the mercy of largely unregulated corporations who vie for contracts from Western companies.

The kind of world we live in is one that some celebrate as a place of freedom, consumption and emancipation, while others are deeply critical and angry at the way such a system results in massive destabilisation (through warfare and ecological catastrophe), economic crises, great material inequalities and insecure and low-paid workers who compete for existing opportunities. A major question that binds these chapters together is, how violent, harmful and depleted is the world around us becoming and what impacts is this having on national and local groups and individuals? Critical criminologists focus on these questions and the ways in which superficial impressions of an exciting and liberating economy belie major inequalities and harms to humans, communities and the habitats on which we all depend. Thus we see here not only a focus on ecological harm (often involving negligent and profit-maximising corporate organisations), warfare and state violence, but also thought-provoking contributions on the way that education systems confuse or promote ignorance, the ways in which violence is the daily stuff of the world we live in and problems like gangsterism and trafficking, which are fuelled by the very inequalities and instabilities that the capitalist world economy and the war on drugs have ended up incentivising. Human insecurity is now the default condition for the majority of people globally and this final section presents critical commentaries that offer a tantalising glance at the kinds of consciousness-expanding work being produced by critical criminologists today.

46

EDUCATION AS CRIME

Andrea Beckmann

This chapter is part of a tradition of critical criminology that associates itself with social critique, aligned with the conviction that 'certain ideologies are a danger to the public and need to be identified as such' (Klein, 2007: 19). A critical criminological perspective acknowledges the injustices of the contemporary social system and understands dominant ideologies and discourses as having the potential to limit human creativity, expression and resistance. Neoliberal regimes and ideologies in advanced national economies have established 'conditions of domination' that impose reductionist and socially destructive meanings through their education systems. These systems have become a means of simply producing compliant political actors, eager consumers and unambitious workers; outcomes that can readily be construed as a form of harm.

The neoliberal ideology of globalisation has served to open essential public services to increasingly unfettered conditions in which markets are celebrated as the fundamental means of allocating and winning resources (Beckmann *et al.*, 2009). Consequently the purpose of education has been narrowed by policy makers who subscribe to these values and the economy is seen as almost the sole rationale for schooling. One example of this harmful reductionism is represented in the Browne (2010) Review of UK Higher Education (HE), *Securing a Sustainable Future for Higher Education*. It sees HE as a market and forces the university system to open up to new providers (notably private universities), foster competitiveness and signal an end to public funding for all subjects that are not constituted as 'priority' (science and technology). This poses great dangers to the sustainability of the arts, humanities and social sciences, while indicating a vision of the purposes of education that is catastrophic in terms of the social, emotional and cultural needs of children, citizens and participatory democracies.

Educational institutions are now subjected to the rationale of markets and tormented by externally imposed regimes of testing that put emphasis on quantifiable targets and tables. The increasing surveillance and over-regulation of learning via testing and assessment regimes have had damaging consequences for both educators and the educated (Beckmann and Cooper 2005) by fostering individualist and competitive attitudes. Educational institutions have been transformed into objects of spectacle (via exam performance league tables and government reports) and have become conductors of state surveillance (through attendance monitoring and involvement in UK border checks).

A crucial and corresponding element of neoliberal market governance is what is known as the 'new managerialism'. This form of government represents new forms of organisational control that focus on narrowly defined economic priorities at the cost of alternative sets of values such as ethics, mutuality, criticality, care, trust, empathy and conviviality. Corporate culture and neoliberal ideology operate through disciplinarian modes, such as evaluation regimes (Ofsted, audits, Research Excellence Framework, and so on) and restructuring processes that claim to be able to measure educational processes and outcomes. With schools and universities increasingly subjected to the tyranny of public accountability, excellence has come to be defined almost solely in terms of narrow labour-market outcomes, while the arts and humanities are denied a meaningful place in curricula.

Rather than seeking to understand educational outcomes as being deeply embedded in social inequalities, class cultures and government investments, education is seen instead simply as a product of an individual's willpower or institutional quality. Though appearing to value 'objectivity' and 'neutrality', existing evaluation regimes are actually implicated in the reproduction of inequalities, since they decontextualise and depoliticise the deeper social processes that shape educational achievement and outcomes. But this constant pressure to perform and inspect negates self-aware thinking and destroys creativity in favour of crude performance indicators.

An emphasis on testing of learners fosters modes of passive and non-reflective learning. These processes are accompanied by a restriction of the syllabus and a prescriptive attitude to education at the price of a more holistic and pupil/student-centred approach to education. The implementation of outcome-based curricula in which the educational goals are specified in advance delimit the potential development of individuals and their teachers as well as representing the objectification of our subjectivities on a large scale. As educational institutions and processes mould the minds of those within them, a narrow and prescriptive understanding of 'education' fosters attitudes of compliance instead of critical exploration. The impact of such 'education' is particularly staggering in countries like the UK, where children are forced into formal schooling at an increasingly young age and are among the most tested and stressed in the Western world.

The mindset of today's students is predominantly focused on a technological rationality and the economic mantras of the 'market'. Education within neoliberal regimes fosters the formation of similarly neoliberal mindsets that in many cases internalise the 'logic' of individualism, competitiveness. The result of this is that many students view who they are, their 'self', as being closely aligned to identities of entrepreneurhip while defining consumption as freedom. Education becomes a commodity, the result of the consumption of services, and corresponds with a prevailing and media-reinforced 'having mode' of existence. The marketing of knowledge implies that learning is something that can be branded.

These changes have harmful consequences since they compel people to follow scripts that ensure compliance with an unethical, destructively unecological and frequently 'criminal' social and economic system. They produce compliance to political projects designed to meet the needs of global capitalism, which diminish the ability to engage in critical thought and dissent while permitting the domination of global corporations. Education in this context fosters compliance with the exploitative reign of global capitalism instead of empathy and global collectivity.

Naomi Klein has argued that the crimes committed by openly totalitarian regimes have been addressed but 'the contemporary crusade to liberate world markets? The coups, wars and slaughters to install and maintain pro-corporate regimes have never been treated as capitalist crimes' (Klein, 2007: 20). This chapter's suggestion that 'education' in neoliberal regimes can be understood as constituting a kind of 'crime' has to be understood through the functional relationship of education to formations of power: there is a fundamental interconnection between the polity and its educational system. Current educational systems in neoliberal regimes facilitate the generation of a neoliberal subjectivity, with reduced social empathy, the internalisation of the 'logic' of individualism and competitiveness. This problematic and destructive reductionism could well be interpreted as a 'crime', as a harm in its own right to human potential by restricting human development, and by generating a compliance with the violence of the wider systems around us.

References

Beckmann, A. and Cooper, C. (2005) Conditions of Domination: Reflection on Harms Generated by the British State Education System, *British Journal of Sociology of Education*, 26, (4), pp. 475–89.

Beckmann, A., Cooper, C. and Hill, D. (2009) Neoliberalization and Managerialization of 'Education' in England and Wales – a Case for Reconstructing Education, *Journal for Critical Education Policy Studies*, 7, (2), pp. 311–45, available online at www.jceps.com/ (accessed 2 October 2013).

Browne, J. (2010) *Securing a Sustainable Future for Higher Education*, London: Department for Business, Innovation and Skills.

Klein, N. (2007) *The Shock Doctrine: The Rise of Disaster Capitalism*, London: Allen Lane.

Watch:

Paulo Freire and Critical Pedagogy (2008), video, by The Freire Project, available online at www.youtube.com/watch?v=wFOhVdQt27c (accessed 2 October 2013).

47

ECOCIDE

Rob White

Ecocide has been defined as 'the extensive damage, destruction to or loss of ecosystems of a given territory, whether by human agency or by other causes, to such an extent that peaceful enjoyment by the inhabitants of that territory has been severely diminished' (Higgins, 2012: 3). Where this occurs as a result of human agency, then it can be argued that such harm can be defined as a crime.

Ecocide as a concept has been used to refer to 'natural' processes of ecosystem decline and transformation, as well as human-created destruction of ecosystems. Natural processes of ecocide can be found where, for example, kangaroos denude a paddock of its grasses and shrubs to the extent that both specific environment and the kangaroo 'mob' are negatively affected. The migration and/or transportation of 'invasive' species, such as the crown-of-thorns starfish off the east coast of Australia, or the introduction of trout into the central highland lakes of Tasmania, can lead to diminishment or death of local species of fish and coral – again, a form of ecocide.

The term has also been applied to extensive environmental damage during war, as in the case of the use of defoliants (for example, Agent Orange) in the Vietnam War, and the blowing up of oil wells and subsequent pollution during the First Gulf War in Iraq and Kuwait by Saddam Hussein's retreating army. These actions involved intent to produce environmental destruction in pursuit of military and other goals.

The notion of ecocide has been actively canvassed at an international level for a number of years, at least since the 1960s. For example, there were major efforts to include it among the crimes associated with the establishment of the International Criminal Court, although the final document refers only to war and damage to the natural environment. Nonetheless, environmental activists and international lawyers have continued to call for the establishment of a specific crime of 'ecocide' and/or the incorporation of ecocide into existing criminal laws and international instruments. Recent efforts, for example, have been directed at making 'ecocide' the fifth international crime against peace. The urgency and impetus for this have been heightened by the woefully inadequate responses by governments, individually and collectively, to global warming. Climate change is rapidly and radically altering the very basis of world ecology; yet very little action has been taken by states or corporations to rein in the worst contributors to the problem. Carbon emissions are not decreasing and 'dirty industries', such as coal and oil, continue to flourish.

In responding to this circumstance, reformers argue that the law itself must be radically altered. Indeed, there is growing momentum behind the idea of embedding the crime of ecocide as a 'crime against humanity' as well as other initiatives directed at entrenching certain environmental rights. In recent times, the concept of ecocide has been embraced by the UK Green Party and by Oxford City Council, and is of continuing interest in relevant United Nations and other regional forums.

Potential support for the establishment of ecocide as a crime should be assessed in the light of parallel developments in the legal field. For example, the recent *Manual on Human Rights and the Environment* produced by the Council of Europe (2012) provides a platform for the exercise of both procedural and substantive rights with regard to the environment. Worldwide, public trust and public interest law have been used to establish future generations as victims of environmental crime, with the victims including humans as well as the environment and non-human biota, for which surrogate victims (such as parents or NGOs) have provided representation (Preston, 2011; Mehta, 2009). These developments are adding to the complexity of the law, and challenging many longstanding assumptions about the nature–human relationship.

Progressive developments that are supportive of the notion of ecocide also include recent changes in national legislation and constitutional arrangements, many of which are premised upon the idea of Earth stewardship. For example, in 2008 the people of Ecuador, by a 63 per cent majority, voted for a new constitution, the first in the world comprehensively to recognise ecosystem rights and nature rights.

Article 71 provides:

> Nature or Pachamama, where life is reproduced and exists, has the right to exist, persist, maintain and regenerate its vital cycles, structure, functions and its processes in evolution. Every person, people, community or nationality, will be able to demand the recognition of rights for nature before the public organisms.
>
> *(Constitution of Ecuador, 2008)*

Threats to nature rights can be conceptualised as, in essence, a crime of ecocide, and thus punishable by law. This is precisely the point of a series of recent mock trials, each based upon the concept of ecocide. One trial was held on 30 September 2011 in the United Kingdom Supreme Court on the subject of the Canadian Athabasca tar sands (among other issues). Another was organised by the Environmental Defenders Office in Melbourne on 18 February 2012, dealing with climate change and the provision of 8 new coal mines in Queensland's Galilee Basin. Each of these trials drew upon notions of ecocide, Earth rights and the superior responsibility of corporate managers as part of the deliberations. In most cases, the managers were found guilty of extensive destruction, damage to or loss of ecosystem(s) wellbeing.

An Earth jurisprudence is rapidly gaining traction amongst many of those with an interest in ecological sustainability and environmental justice. A growing part of this is the push for the acceptance of 'ecocide' as a bona fide crime. Institutional structures within which such crimes could be tried will be needed. For this, it may well be that an international environment court (or equivalent) with requisite United Nations support is required. This is especially so if environmental matters such as those pertaining to the international spaces of the oceans (for example, pollution, concentrations of plastic, illegal fishing, transference of toxic materials) and climate change (for example, carbon emissions, victim compensation) are to be dealt with adequately.

Some general concluding observations:

* Ecocide is NOT the same as homicide, even though foreknowledge of consequences combined with anthropocentric causation imply preventable death.

- Ecocide is NOT the same as suicide, even though the agents of harm are themselves included as victims of harm.
- Ecocide is NOT the same as genocide, even though there are clear similarities in terms of disregard by perpetrators of the magnitude of the harm and disrespect of specific collectivities/victims.

Ecocide describes an attempt to criminalise human activities that destroy and diminish the wellbeing and health of ecosystems and species within these, including humans. Climate change and the gross exploitation of natural resources are leading to our general demise – hence increasing the need for just such a crime.

References

Council of Europe (2012) *Manual on Human Rights and the Environment*, Strasbourg: Council of Europe.

Higgins, P. (2012) *Earth is Our Business: Changing the Rules of the Game*, London: Shepheard-Walwyn.

Mehta, M. (2009) *In the Public Interest: Landmark Judgement and Orders of the Supreme Court of India on Environment and Human Rights*, (3 vols), New Delhi: Prakriti Publications.

Preston, B. (2011) The Use of Restorative Justice for Environmental Crime, *Criminal Law Journal*, 35, (3), pp. 136–53.

Watch:

Avatar (2009), film, directed by James Cameron. USA: Lightstorm Entertainment.

48

GANGS

Steve Hall

The most common criminological definition of the 'gang' is a durable and structured group, often territorial and hostile to others, which regards crime and violence as integral to its identity (see Hallsworth and Young, 2004). Yet the study of gangs is characterised by a deep fault line.

On one side traditional criminology is replete with a dizzying array of definitions, typologies and descriptions of different values and norms that are said to distinguish criminal groups from the mainstream. We have learnt from this largely descriptive literature that criminal groups can exist for various periods of time in organised and disorganised forms and temporary networks. There are many different hybrids and sub-types of such organisation but it is important to realise that the 'gang' is only one such form.

On the other side, social reaction theorists refuse to talk above a whisper about 'gangs', or for that matter criminal groups in general. Early social reaction theorists set up an intellectual embargo by warning us that talk of 'causes' always reduces our sense of the complexity of phenomena, thus playing into the hands of systems of social control which tend to seek lazy explanations as a means to justify heavy-handed interventions. Despite the crime explosions in the UK and USA in the 1980s, social reaction theory was taken forward by the 'governmentality' thesis, which claimed that most forms of criminality are socially constructed by power elites and governments to justify increases in repressive control. In this vein Hallsworth (2011) argues that the term 'gang' is a stereotype, an invented category within a wider discourse of what might be described as a 'gang control industry' consisting of politicians and members of the policing agencies.

However, critical realists argue that both traditional criminologists and social reaction theorists avoid the study of the deep structural causes and conditions that underlie more harmful forms of criminality (Currie, 2010), thus placing strict limits on intellectual inquiry. This systematic denial is a product of what Pitts calls 'crime-averse criminologies' (2008: 33). However, underneath this lies a deeper current of *political catastrophism*, in which right- and left-liberals are fearful that attempts to confront criminality's deep causes with interventionist policies will inevitably result in the development of brutal, totalitarian governments. Social science, politics and public opinion are thus paralysed by the constant presence of two pervasive manufactured fears – of the *barbarism of disorder*, represented by images of 'gangs' and other criminal forms in the media, but also of the *barbarism of order*, in which a totalitarian state would invade social life with heavy-handed and pervasive forms of policing (Hall, 2012). These strains of thinking have thus left vulnerable residents of high-crime areas afraid of crime and simultaneously afraid that nobody is there to listen and help.

Before social science can begin to understand 'gangs' and their underlying socioeconomic and cultural currents, it must struggle free from this intellectual straitjacket. The study of media and crime is shot through with political catastrophism. The familiar 'moral panic' thesis argues that the mass media, aiding and abetting the capitalist state, tend to exaggerate the threat crime poses to the 'moral order' to throw the population into a panic. In such a fearful condition they are more likely to vote for authoritarian governments. However, social science has been systematically misreading the crime–media nexus for decades. Most TV or film productions about crime do indeed present criminality in a theatrical mode to raise concerns, but only to set up an initial problem – presented as a strictly individual and ethical phenomenon with all underlying politics, cultural forces and structural conditions largely ignored – that the forces of law, order and individualised welfare can be shown to resolve. This continuous rollercoaster presentation produces complacency, not panic (Hall, ibid.).

Municipal capitalism's image-management agents also play a part in the denial of the reality of harmful crime as they try to attract business and residents to their cities. The dominance of traditional criminology, which downplays underlying socioeconomic conditions, and social reaction theory, which downplays the harmful effects of crime, has made a significant contribution to the anxiety, cynicism and loss of faith in democratic politics that are pervasive sentiments today. Proper critical analysis of criminal gangs has been suppressed by a combination of three powerful forces operating on behalf of liberal capitalism to reproduce the concern/complacency couplet: catastrophist traditional and social reaction discourses, theatrical media stereotypes and governmental image-management.

For Pitts (2011), media exaggeration does not mean that gangs do not exist or inflict real harm on victims and members alike. Youth gangs have in the past thirty years become a real problem in poor locales in Britain, as they have been in the USA throughout its history. They cause harms such as violence, intimidation, weaponisation and the recruitment of young people into criminal activity. Gangs increased in number alongside other criminal groups and networks since the arrival of crack cocaine and structural unemployment in the USA during the deindustrialisation process in the 1980s. Despite the much-vaunted 'crime decline' in the 2000s – a product of artificially leveraged economies, mass imprisonment, hi-tech security systems and other factors – the youth gang problem in the UK, previously of a lesser magnitude, began to 'catch up' and undergo a convergence of form.

For Pitts, the denial of the harmful criminogenic effects of socioeconomic disruption is nothing less than the 'dereliction of our professional duty' (2011: 178) as social scientists. He argues that 'sustained exposure to acute social and economic disadvantage' (2008: 33) creates the conditions for increases in harmful crime. This is echoed by other critical realists who seek to contextualise the criminal shadow-economy and explain its effects on social life. They also remind us that amid the colonial legacy and long-running currents of racism in the West, socioeconomic inequality is racialised. African-Americans and Hispanics still suffer from structural discrimination, cultural disrespect, political marginalisation and disproportionate economic disruption, which were only partially addressed by the civil rights victories in the 1960s. Deindustrialisation in the USA led to the ghettoisation of former industrial workers, some of whom moved into relatively lucrative criminal markets to form gangs and criminal networks of other types as functional units in a hostile environment. This process is currently diffusing across the deindustrialising sectors of the West. Young people in the industrial countries now live in an era of *post-politics*, where traditional, class-based political identities are virtually absent (Winlow and Hall, 2013). As they confront long-term unemployment they are absorbed in consumer culture and feel unrepresented in the political sphere; in these conditions some young people who lack support drift into criminal markets (Hall *et al.*, 2008). Criminal markets are also expanding and gangs and loose criminal networks are emerging in the developing world as neoliberal restructuring disrupts traditional socioeconomic forms and ethical codes (Wiegratz, 2010).

References

Currie, E. (2010) Plain Left Realism: an Appreciation, and Some Thoughts for the Future, *Crime, Law and Social Change*, 54, (2), pp. 111–24.

Hall, S. (2012) *Theorizing Crime and Deviance: a New Perspective*, London: SAGE.

Hall, S., Winlow, S. and Ancrum, C. (2008) *Criminal Identities and Consumer Culture: Crime, Exclusion and the New Culture of Narcissism*, Cullompton, UK: Willan.

Hallsworth, S. (2011) Gangland Britain: Reality, Fantasies and Industry, in Goldson, B. (ed.) *Youth in Crisis? 'Gangs', Territoriality and Violence*, London: Routledge.

Hallsworth, S. and Young, T. (2004) Getting Real about Gangs, *Criminal Justice Matters*, 55, (1), pp. 12–13.

Pitts, J. (2008) *Reluctant Gangsters: the Changing Face of Youth Crime*, Cullompton, UK: Willan.

Pitts, J. (2011) Mercenary Territory: Are Youth Gangs Really a Problem?, in Goldson, B. (ed.) *Youth in Crisis? 'Gangs', Territoriality and Violence*, London: Routledge.

Wiegratz, J. (2010) Fake Capitalism? The Dynamics of Neoliberal Moral Restructuring and Pseudo-development: the Case of Uganda, *Review of African Political Economy*, 37, (124), pp. 123–37.

Winlow, S. and Hall, S. (2013 forthcoming) *Rethinking Social Exclusion: the End of the Social?*, London: SAGE.

Watch:

The Interrupters (2011), documentary film, directed by Steve James. USA: Kartemquin Films.

49

TERRORISM

Scott Poynting

Terrorism is an enormously contested concept. While it is often suggested that 'one person's terrorist is another's freedom fighter' it is also a fact that Nelson Mandela, Gerry Adams and Xanana Gusmão were all branded as terrorists by the states that imprisoned them and where they later became internationally respected statesmen. Conversely, while the Mujahideen of Afghanistan were celebrated (and aided) by the West as freedom fighters when they were fighting a guerrilla war against the Soviet Union in the 1970s and 80s, their progeny the Taliban have, since the US-led invasion of Afghanistan, been defined as terrorists by Western states, in many of which it is a terrorist offence to recruit for them or otherwise provide material support.

Despite the conflict over what constitutes terrorism, the following defining features are widely agreed: terrorism is extreme and unlawful or wrongful violence, strategically aimed at engendering fear and terror in targeted communities for political ends. Those whose behaviours are intended to be affected by the example or threat of such violence extend well beyond the direct victims themselves. Victims are usually innocent, or civilians, or otherwise arbitrary or representative targets. Some more controversially claimed characteristics include that terrorists are sub-national groups by definition, and that their victims are exclusively random. The latter stipulation would rule out targeted political assassinations; the former would arbitrarily exclude acts of terror conducted by the state. A growing literature on state terrorism tends to make the point that state terrorism is in fact far more pervasive, damaging and destructive than non-state terrorism, and this makes it all the more important to recognise it as terrorism.

Terrorism is at least as old as nations and empires, and has, as a rule, been practised more often by states and empires than by those who use political violence to oppose subjugation by them. The Roman flogging of the Iceni queen Boudicca and the rape of her daughters in AD 61 Britain was doubtless intended as public humiliation and a terrifying lesson to warn others against resisting imperial rule. It is clearly an early and famous example of terrorism, by most definitions – and notably one that rebounded, provoking an insurgency. This blowback effect of harsh and violent impositions of power has been identified in the reactions to acts by groups like those responsible for the attacks on the New York World Trade Center, but is also identified by observers in the use of 'extraordinary rendition', torture and abuse of suspects by the USA and UK in the conflicts that followed.

Terrorism was practised in all feudal regimes, and the transition beyond feudalism to capitalism was effected through primitive accumulation that was everywhere enforced with the aid of terror; from medieval looting (including the Crusades) to the enslavement, genocide and dispossession of indigenous peoples in the New World, from the institution of chattel slavery there to the brutal repression and eviction of peasantries in the Old World. Colonialism was almost everywhere reinforced, if not instituted, through terrorism.

Anti-colonialist struggle, though not without its terrorist proponents, has been invariably met by imperialist regimes deploying terror tactics; this is very clear in the political violence of post-World War II decolonisation. The British Empire, in its death throes, was a foremost proponent: in Malaya and in Kenya, for example. In late 2012, three elderly survivors of British colonial terror in Kenya won a High Court case granting permission to claim damages from the British government for atrocities, long denied and recently proven in uncovered documents, committed against them during the counter-insurgency of the 1950s. Paolo Muoka Nzili, now 85, Wambugu Wa Nyingi, now 84, and the now 73-year-old Jane Muthoni Mara were subjected by British officials to what their lawyers rightly termed 'unspeakable acts of brutality' (Cobain, 2012), including castration with pliers used on cattle, repeated beatings almost to death (on one occasion in a massacre that did kill 11 others) and sexual assault including rape with a bottle containing scalding water, causing lifelong injuries. Some 70,000 Kenyans were imprisoned as Mau Mau suspects over the 7 years of the Emergency, and some 2,000 are now expected to sue for compensation. These horrific state crimes were intended to wreak terror, in the classic definition of terrorism, for political ends, in this case the repression of an anti-colonialist rebellion. Many of the 70,000 had little or no connection with the Mau Mau insurgency.

French atrocities in Algeria – and against Algerians in France – were contemporaneous, and involved widespread use of torture, not only for interrogation but as a means of terrorising and thus demoralising anti-colonialist struggle, as well as eliminating its cadres. In Vietnam in the following decade, the USA mounted Operation Phoenix, a counter-insurgency programme targeting what the CIA called the 'Viet Cong Infrastructure', involving torture (often torture to death) during interrogation as well as imbuing civilian terror, along with the mass killing of suspects – over 20,000 of them (Blakeley, 2009). The techniques employed starkly prefigure the atrocities of Abu Ghraib, and other dark places outside the rule of international law in the ongoing pursuit of the 'war on terror':

> Rape, gang rape, rape using eels, snakes, or hard objects, and rape followed by murder; electric shock ('the Bell Telephone Hour') rendered by attaching wires to the genitals or other sensitive parts of the body, like the tongue; the 'water treatment'; the 'airplane' in which the prisoner's arms were tied behind the back, and the rope looped over a hook on the ceiling, suspending the prisoner in midair, after which he or she was beaten; beatings with rubber hoses and whips; the use of police dogs to maul prisoners.
>
> *(Valentine, 2000: 85, cited in Blakeley, 2009: 50)*

One of the ironies of contemporary state terrorism is that it is very often practised in the name of counter-terrorism. Noam Chomsky (2003) shows clearly how those who 'resist direct US aggression' are defined as terrorists and subjected to the full panoply of counter-terrorism technique, from the Vietnam War to the Iraq wars. So-called 'counter-terrorism' can be pre-emptive: Chomsky reminds us that the USA mounted a counter-insurgency intervention by special forces in Colombia in 1962, the fore-runner of similar 'paramilitary, sabotage and/or terrorist activities' (quoting General Yarborough, who did not mince words), that was to be repeated in El Salvador in the 1980s, then Guatemala, then Nicaragua, where Washington sent the Contras to attack 'soft targets'. Rarely is such counter-terrorism openly countenanced as terrorism; only the 'known communist proponents' are 'terrorists'. The transition from Cold War to 'clash of civilisations' rhetoric following the World Trade Center attacks saw former 'known communist' demons increasingly replaced by 'Islamic fundamentalists'. It is clear that deploying the term 'terrorist' has been a strategy used by states to neutralise their opponents by denying their politics, as well as designating unconscionable political violence, including that perpetrated by states. Critical understanding of the roots of such violence must go beyond ideological news media coverage and government manipulation of information and apprehend the deeper histories which have generated ongoing and, in many cases deepening, violence against the vulnerable.

References

Blakeley, R. (2009) *State Terrorism and Neoliberalism: The North in the South*, Abingdon and New York: Routledge.

Chomsky, N. (2003) *Hegemony or Survival: America's Quest for Global Dominance*, New York: Henry Holt.

Cobain, I. (2012) 'Mau Mau Torture Case: Kenyans Win Case against UK', *The Guardian*, 5 October, available online at www.guardian.co.uk/world/2012/oct/05/mau-mau-veterans-win-torture-case (accessed 9 October 2013).

Valentine, D. (2000) *The Phoenix Program*, Lincoln, NE: iUniverse, available online at www.american-buddha.com/phoenixprogtoc.htm (accessed 9 October 2013).

Watch:

Taxi to the Dark Side (2007), documentary film, directed by Alex Gibney. USA: THINKFilm.

50

CORPORATE CRIME

Mark Monaghan

Academic interest in corporate criminality can be traced back to Sutherland's (1949) seminal work. Sutherland's broad thesis was that although crime statistics showed that much crime was committed by offenders from lower socioeconomic groups, this was very much an arte-fact of the way that the statistics were compiled and of the operation of the criminal justice system more generally, which is systematically adminis-tered by those from the upper socioeconomic classes and works to protect their interests. It is the case, therefore, that in comparison to street-based, urban violence, corporate criminality has tended to be of less interest to criminologists.

Part of the problem here is that there is no agreed definition of the nature of corporate criminality. Taking the 'corporate' side of the coin, the first thing to note is that corporations differ in size and scale. They can range from small enterprises to large multinational conglomerates. Some of these are more crime-prone than others. Large conglomerates, for instance, have the ability to shield themselves from the gaze of the criminal justice system and have a greater ability to engage in the systematic obfuscation of potential detection. Since this is the case, and as recognised by Sutherland, much white-collar crime is not defined as crime per se, nor is it handled by criminal courts. As a result, it is absent from the official statistics.

There are, then, a number of grey areas in the definition of corporate crime. Most obviously corporate crime is used interchangeably with the terms 'organisational crime' and 'white-collar' crime. This can create confusion on the grounds that *organisational* crime differs from *organised* crime – the latter of which is usually related to the activities of Mafia and crime syndicates. This is not to say that links between organised crime and some legal corporations do not exist. Indeed, in November 2012 the bank HSBC was fined $1 billion for allowing its accounts to be used for laundering money from Mexican drug cartels and other 'rogue' organisations. For current purposes, although there is a significant degree of overlap, we also need to distinguish corporate crime from white-collar crime. White-collar crimes are usually committed by middle-class or 'high-status' actors acting independently against an employer. This could take the form of theft or embezzlement, for instance. Corporate crime, to reiterate, relates to crimes carried out by individuals or organisations for the intended benefit of the organisation (De Keseredy, 2011: 68–9). Thus, the host organisation or company is ignorant of white-collar crime but complicit in corporate criminality.

Like many kinds of 'suite' crimes, it is difficult to know the extent of corporate criminality. Four main reasons can be cited for this. First, it is widely acknowledged that media reportage has systematically misrepresented the nature and extent of corporate crime by focusing on more conventional or 'lower-class' criminality. Although it is not universally accepted, Box (1983) refers to the 'collective ignorance' of corporate crime in the media. Popular crime-based television series rarely focus on the issue of corporate crime and large conglomerates who own the majority of the media are unwilling to shed light into this murky area of activity. It is clear, then, that reporting of corporate crime does find its way into the popular media, but the reporting of conventional criminality outweighs that of corporate criminality, despite the widespread prevalence and social and economic cost of the latter. Furthermore, whereas conventional crimes are frequently the stuff of headlines and often accompanied by graphic and spectacular images, the same is almost never true of corporate crime, which tends to be 'buried' in more specialist business and finance sections of papers.

Second, unlike many other kinds of criminals, corporate criminals carry out their activities in precisely the locations in which they are expected to be seen – for example, in the workplace. In this sense, some of their activities are not out of the ordinary and they come to resemble legitimate business practice or they involve a specific kind of technical expertise which affords the perpetrator an opportunity to try and implement a cover-up. A high-profile example here is the insider trading of Nick Leeson, which led to the collapse of Barings Bank in the 1990s. Third, because corporate criminality often involves a particular kind of expertise, there is often a blurred distinction between illegality and legality in the corporate world; perpetrators carry out their actions in the course of their routine activities. This makes detecting wrongdoing infuriatingly difficult, so that law enforcement in this context tends to be somewhat insipid. At times the criminality associated with certain acts – for instance, health and safety transgressions leading to the loss of lives – is downplayed and the accidental nature of incidents is reinforced.

Fourthly, a key difficulty in researching corporate crime relates to the advancement of neo-liberalism in the main institutions in society, which has served to silence many voices. For Tombs and Whyte (2002), this can be illustrated by how the university has come to typify the maintenance of the neo-liberal hegemony as research agendas 'have increasingly been defined in terms of that which is immediately relevant for neo-liberal ideologues and their bureaucratic handmaidens'. By way of evidence, they show for example how business schools frequently employ staff who are sponsored by local businesses, and also tender for research grants from the business community. One outcome of such a relationship is a decline of critical research calling into question the practices of elites.

Although there has been increasing academic interest in the area of corporate criminality and public anger around key cases, the area remains something of a cottage industry within criminology and of little interest to the mass media, who remain preoccupied with street-based urban violence.

References

Box, S. (1983) *Power, Crime and Mystification*, London: Tavistock.
De Keseredy, W. (2011) *Contemporary Critical Criminology*, Abingdon: Routledge.
Sutherland, E. (1949) *White Collar Crime*, New York: Holt, Rinehart and Winston.
Tombs, S. and Whyte, D. (2002) Unmasking Crimes of the Powerful, *Critical Criminology*, 11, (3), pp. 217–36.

Watch:

Wall Street (1987), film, directed by Oliver Stone. USA: Twentieth Century Fox.

51

STATE VIOLENCE

Mark Monaghan

In his 1988 Presidential Address to the American Society of Criminology, William Chambliss proposed that:

> The most important type of criminality organized by the state consists of acts defined by law as criminal and committed by state officials in the pursuit of their job as representatives of the state. Examples include a state's complicity in piracy, smuggling, assassinations, and criminal conspiracies, acting as an accessory before and after the fact, and violating laws that limit their activities…State-organized crime does not include criminal acts that benefit only individual officeholders, such as the acceptance of bribes or the illegal use of violence by the police against individuals, unless such acts violate existing criminal law and are official policy.
>
> *(Chambliss, 1989)*

Although this seems like a comprehensive definition and is undoubtedly a useful starting point, most discussions of attempts to define crime – or indeed particular types of crime – are beset with difficulties, as is the task of revealing its true extent. Definitions of state violence are also contingent on how we go about defining the 'state'. Different states have developed at different historical junctures and with different trajectories; they also have varying arrangements whereby power may be concentrated in the hands of the many or the few. In the contemporary era, since many of the functions associated with state formation have become subsumed under supra-state organisations such as the European Union and United Nations, there is little clarity as regards the reach and scope of the nation state. Lister (2010, p18) suggests that whilst there is difficulty in defining the state, we tend to recognise it when it compels us to act in certain ways, for example through paying taxes or sending children to school. Less benignly, we also begin to recognise the state in action when it commits illegal acts and engages in deviant activities for its own ends. Furthermore, we need to recognise that the state is also the prime operator involved in collating and disseminating information about such activities, and so has the capacity to collude in, deny or cover up its actions.

In line with Chambliss, state crime and violence can be said to entail deviance or criminality coordinated by the state or those acting on behalf of the state agencies, which often results in the violation of human rights or contravenes international criminal law or public law. Such deviance or criminality can occur through action or inactivity. The picture becomes more opaque because the terms 'state crime', 'state-sponsored terrorism' and 'political crime' are used interchangeably, whereas some prefer to speak of governmental crime, 'state-sponsored corporate crime', state political crime or state-organised crime. Ross (2003, p4) offers an initial explanation of terminology by suggesting that 'in general, an actor has committed a political crime if he or she has a political or ideological intention or motivation to cause harm, whereas state political crime consists of an action perpetrated by the government to illegally minimise or eliminate threats to its rule.'

A further layer of complexity concerns the victims of state criminality. In their discussion of state violence (or governmental crime, as they term it) Kauzlarich et al. (2001) demonstrate how the victims and perpetrators of state crime generally fall into two categories: domestic and international. Domestic offences are those that fall foul of any nation's criminal laws; international offences are those that are in contravention of internationally agreed codes of conduct, such as United Nations Conventions. This creates a four tier account of different kinds of state violence:

- Domestic–International: occurs within the geographic jurisdiction of a state; entails actions in contravention of international law or human rights standards, for example institutional racism;

- Domestic–Domestic: occurs within the geographic jurisdiction of a state; entails actions in contravention of criminal, regulatory or procedural laws or codes, for example intelligence agencies spying on their own citizens, as in the case of COINTELPRO, or political malpractice, as in the Watergate affair in the US;
- International–International: occurs outside the geographic jurisdiction of a state; entails actions in contravention of international law or human rights standards, for example international terrorism;
- International–Domestic: occurs outside the geographic jurisdiction of a state; entails actions in contravention of criminal, regulatory or procedural laws or codes, for example in the Iran–Contra affair.

Although this typology is useful, it does not allow for an understanding of the extent of state criminality globally. This is because domestic criminal law varies from country to country so an illegal act in one jurisdiction will not be considered as such in another. In terms of international law, human rights violations are open to a number of interpretations and the law is only binding if the international conventions have been ratified by the country in question. Deciphering the true extent of state violence is further hindered by the scant attention devoted to the issue within criminology and related disciplines, but more significantly by the fact that most Western democracies have become accustomed to viewing the state as the protector of citizens and the leading instrument in the fight against crime, rather than as the perpetrator.

Nation states can use various tools to shield themselves from the critical gaze of their citizens and other nations. Consequently, much of this kind of criminality goes unnoticed. For Cohen (2002), a key tactic is to employ a 'spiral of denial', whereby at the point of accusation a state first denies any wrongdoing. If this is untenable, the second stage is to depict suspected criminality as legitimate activity. Finally, and if needed, the last act of denial is to claim 'exceptionalism' is necessary. Here unlawful activity is deemed as being necessary in the interests of national security. It is this last rung of the spiral that has been used by many Western governments to justify various recent actions which would otherwise be labelled criminal. Policies and procedures developed as a consequence of declaring war on terror, including extraordinary rendition, migration camps and various surveillance practices, not to mention the use of internment in Guantánamo Bay and abuses of power at Abu Ghraib prison acquire a veneer of legitimacy through claims of necessity.

References

Chambliss, W. (1989) State-organized Crime: The American Society of Criminology, 1988 Presidential Address, *Criminology*, 27, (2), pp. 183–208.

Cohen, S. (2002) 'Human Rights and Crimes of the State: The Culture of Denial' in E. McLaughlin, J. Muncie and G. Hughes (eds) *Criminological Perspectives: Essential Readings*, London: SAGE.

Kauzlarich, D., Matthews, R. A. and Miller, W. J. (2001) Towards a Victimology of State Crime, *Critical Criminology*, 10, (3), pp. 173–94.

Lister, R. (2010) *Understanding Theories and Concepts in Social Policy*, Bristol, UK: Policy Press.

Ross, J. I. (2003) *The Dynamics of Political Crime*, London: SAGE.

Watch:

All the President's Men (1976), film, directed by Alan J. Pakula. USA: Warner Bros.

52

ENVIRONMENTAL CRIME

Rob White

Environmental crime refers to transgressions against humans, specific environments and plant and animal species. Environmental crime is typically defined on a continuum ranging from strict legal definitions through to incorporation into broader harm-based perspectives. Within 'green criminology' there is an expansive definition of environmental crime or harm that includes:

> transgressions that are *harmful to humans, environments and nonhuman animals*, regardless of legality per se; and
> environmental-related harms that are facilitated by *the state*, as well as *corporations and other powerful actors*, insofar as these institutions have the capacity to shape official definitions of environmental crime in ways that allow or condone environmentally harmful practices.
>
> *(White, 2011: 212)*

The kinds of harms and crimes studied within green criminology include illegal trade in endangered species (such as, for example, trade in exotic birds or killing of elephants for their ivory tusks), illegal harvesting of 'natural resources' (such as illegal fishing and illegal logging) and illegal disposal of toxic substances (as well as pollution of air, land and water).

Wider definitions of environmental crime extend the scope of analysis to consider harms associated with legal activities such as the clear-felling of old growth forests and the negative ecological consequences of new technologies, such as the use of genetically modified organisms in agriculture (for example, reduction of biodiversity through extensive planting of GMO corn). Recent work has considered the criminological aspects of climate change, from the point of view of human contributions to global warming (for example, carbon emissions from coal-fired power plants) and the criminality associated with the aftermath of natural disasters (for example, incidents of theft and rape in the wake of Hurricane Katrina in New Orleans).

There are several intersecting dimensions that need to be considered in any analysis of environmental crime. These include consideration of who the victim is (human or non-human); where the harm is manifest (global through to local levels); the main site in which the harm is apparent (built or natural environment); and the time frame within which harm can be analysed (immediate and delayed consequences). Many of the main features pertaining to environmental harm are inherently international in scope and substance.

The detection and origins of some types of environmentally related harm may be unclear due to significant time-lags in manifestation of the harm. Here it is important to acknowledge the notion of cumulative effects. For example, this could refer to the way in which dioxins accumulate in fish over time. It could also refer to the cumulative impact of multiple sources of pollution, as in cases where there is a high number of factories in one area (such as places along the USA–Mexican border). Diseases linked to asbestos poisoning may surface many years after first exposure and this, too, provides another example of the long-term effects of environmental harm. Persistent use of pesticides in particular geographical areas may also have unforeseen consequences for local wildlife, including the development of new diseases among endemic animal species.

Extensive work on specific incidents and patterns of victimisation demonstrates that some people are more likely to be disadvantaged by environmental problems than others. For instance, studies have identified disparities involving many different types of environmental hazard that especially adversely affect people of colour, ethnic minority groups and Indigenous people (Bullard, 2005). There are thus patterns of differential victimisation that are evident with respect to the siting of toxic waste dumps, extreme air pollution, chemical accidents, access to safe clean drinking water, and so on. It is the poor and disadvantaged who suffer disproportionately from such environmental inequalities.

Environmental crime frequently embodies a certain ambiguity. This is because it is not only located in frameworks of risk (for example, the precautionary principle) or evaluated in terms of actual harms (for example, the polluter pays), but is also judged in the context of cost–benefit analysis (for example, licence to trade, pollute, kill or capture). This goes to the heart of why environmental crime itself is consistently under-valued in law. The label of environmental crime tends to be applied to specific activities that are otherwise lawful or licensed (such as cutting down trees or pulling fish from the ocean), since these are viewed as not being intrinsically criminal or 'bad'. It is the context that makes something allowable or problematic. To take another example, harm to the environment is, in many situations, considered to be acceptable (for instance in certain circumstances we are prepared to allow pollution under licence or authorisation) because it is an inherent consequence of many industrial activities which are seen to provide significant benefits.

From an eco-justice perspective, environmental harm is evaluated in terms of justice, which in turn is based upon notions of human, ecological and animal rights, and broad egalitarian principles. Environmental victimisation is considered from the point of view of transgressions against humans, specific biospheres or environments and non-human animals (White, 2011). This is conceptualised in terms of three broad areas of analytical interest: *environmental justice* (where the main focus is on differences within the human population: social justice demands access to healthy and safe environments for all, and for future generations); *ecological justice* (where the main focus is on 'the environment' as such, and to conserve and protect ecological wellbeing – for example that of forests – is seen as intrinsically worthwhile); and *species justice* (where the main focus is on ensuring the wellbeing of both species as a whole – such as whales or polar bears – and also individual animals, which should be shielded from abuse, degradation and torture).

Recent years have seen greater legislative and judicial attention being given to the rights of the environment per se, and to the rights of certain species of non-human animal. This reflects the efforts of both eco-rights activists (such as conservationists) and animal rights activists (for example, animal liberation movements) in changing perceptions and influencing laws, in regard to the natural environment and non-human species. It also reflects the growing recognition that centuries of global exploitation of resources are negatively transforming the world ecology – and that environmental crime affects us all, regardless of where we live.

References

Bullard, R. (ed.) (2005) *The Quest for Environmental Justice: Human Rights and the Politics of Pollution*, San Francisco: Sierra Club Books.

White, R. (2011) *Transnational Environmental Crime: Toward an Eco-global Criminology*, Abingdon: Routledge.

Watch:

Erin Brockovich (2000), film, directed by Steven Soderbergh. USA: Jersey Films.

53

VIOLENCE

Simon Winlow

In 2012, the psychologist Steven Pinker published *The Better Angels of Our Nature* to popular acclaim. The book marshals an incredible amount of data, and contains within it a range of interesting observations about the occurrence of violence in human societies. The book's central claim is admirably straightforward. Despite the constant mediatisation of violence, despite the ubiquity of the terrorist threat, despite the persistence of war and political conflict, and despite the deep fear and social antagonism that pervade Western cities, Pinker claims that violence is in fact falling, and that we are locked on a long-term trajectory away from the barbarism of the past and towards a civilised future in which 'the better angels of our nature' triumph in their long-running battle with our 'inner demons'. The book appears to have become popular because it contradicts our immediate, common-sense understanding of contemporary social reality. Surely violence and conflict must be rising? Don't we see its social effects every day on our news broadcasts? If, as many social scientists now claim, we are more anxious and emotionally defensive than at any point in our recent history, is this not a reaction to a world in which potential threats and dangers appear to lurk around every corner? Pinker's argument is that, despite all of these things and much else besides, human violence is falling.

In many ways Pinker's book is a popularised extension of the more sophisticated work of Norbert Elias (1994), albeit accompanied by a range of additional empirical data. In this discussion I want to challenge Pinker's core thesis in the hope of suggesting a deeper complexity that must be acknowledged by those seeking to offer a coherent and thorough account of contemporary forms of violence.

First, we must think carefully about what violence is and how it can be defined. There is of course a basic logic that surrounds our understanding of violence: violence involves bodily activity and the intent to harm another. We can see this form of violence in activities that range from domestic assaults to war; we can call this violence *subjective violence*. However, to understand violence truly we must go a good deal further than this. What other forms of violence can we see in the world today, and what might Pinker have omitted from his account of falling rates of violence and increases in human civility?

A second form of violence we can define as *structural violence*. This is a destructive, more abstract form of violence that is beyond our immediate comprehension. For Slavoj Žižek (2009), this structural violence is the violence that needs to occur in order to create the impression of order and civility within society. Today, in a global economic crisis precipitated by an ideological attachment to free markets, it makes sense to connect the dominant forms of structural violence to the onward march of global capitalism. There are numerous aspects to this. We might claim, for example, that the Western attachment to cheap consumerism exerts a powerful structural violence on developing countries and our shared natural environments. In the West we often fail to grasp the connection between our aesthetic appreciation of cheap consumer products and the suicides and child labour associated with their production. In order for us to live the way we do, violence must take place, even though this violence is beyond our immediate comprehension.

We can also identify a deeply corrosive *symbolic violence* at work in contemporary society, the violence that hides behind smiles and polite conversation. It is a violence of language. With symbolic violence, the raw energy that drives physical violence is re-channelled into ostensibly non-aggressive social conduct. A common form of symbolic violence might leave one feeling belittled and aggrieved, and that one's social identity has been mocked or attacked in some way. Despite the fact that the victim remains *physically* unharmed, we should not underestimate the harms that can result from what is essentially a cultural form of violence.

Symbolic violence is integral to our consumer economy. We can best elucidate this by acknowledging that much of our formal economy is driven forward by envy and social competition. The ultimate power of consumerism lies in its ability to bestow status and, in so doing, to address individual anxieties relating to social identity. This kind of social distinction is made meaningful by the envy it generates in others.

We can relate economically functional envy to symbolic violence. In a cultural world dominated by mediatised consumer fantasy, the hyper-consumption of others reveals our own inability to consume at the same level. Being poor in such societies is to be subject to constant messages that remind one of one's abject economic failure and cultural inconsequentiality. A bountiful feast is laid before the poor, but they are denied the opportunity to eat. This form of exclusion serves to reiterate the fundamental failure of the poor to earn enough, to achieve enough, to strive enough, and it also encourages the poor to throw themselves back into the sphere of social competition in order to try to gain admittance to the banquet. This process of rubbing the noses of the poor in their own failure can be understood as an act of symbolic violence.

Pinker's account of the fall of violence and the onward march of civilisation omits these other dimensions of violence. We may be killing each other a little less than we were ten years ago, but our cultures are suffused with aggressivity, competition and naked self-interest. Authentic forms of community life have disintegrated, and the positive social substance of modernity appears lost. Pinker fails to recognise that the raw energy of popular violence did not simply vaporise and disappear into the ether. Rather, Western societies underwent a complex process of pacification in order to allow capitalism to develop. The energy of that violence was then re-channelled to drive further the competition and acquisitiveness needed to expand markets. Now, in the apparently less violent twenty-first century, symbolic violence has been democratised and we fight for cultural recognition with all others attempting to follow the same path. This breeds deep social anxiety and enduring social antagonisms as we find pleasure and advantage in the downfall of others. So, Pinker may be right about the decline of violence, but he is only addressing physical violence. One only needs to look at the drive to accumulate among new financial elites, and our technocratic politicians who cheer them on, to develop a keener sense of the kinds of systematised aggression, hate, envy and antipathy that run through our apparently civilised culture.

References

Elias, N. (1994) *The Civilizing Process: Sociogenetic and Psychogenetic Investigations*, Oxford: Blackwell.

Pinker, S. (2012) *The Better Angels of Our Nature: A History of Violence and Humanity*, London: Penguin.

Žižek, S. (2009) *Violence: Six Sideways Reflections*, London: Profile Books.

Watch:

The Corporation (2003), documentary film, directed by Mark Achbar and Jennifer Abbott. Canada: Big Picture Media Corporation.

54

HOMICIDE AND WAR

Nathan W. Pino

Homicide refers to the act of causing a person's death. Whether or not the act of killing is considered criminal depends on the eye of the beholder, but powerful segments of society usually dominate the social construction of criminal killing. The most commonly thought-of type of homicide is murder, including serial and spree murder. Serial murder refers to the killing of two or more persons over time, while spree murder involves going on a rampage and killing multiple people at one time.

Though there are a few exceptions, countries with more economic inequality and underdevelopment tend to have higher murder rates, which are measured by the number of murders per 100,000 persons in the population. For example, in general terms, homicide rates are higher than average in Sub-Saharan Africa, South America, the Caribbean and Central America, while countries in Asia, the Middle East and Northern Europe enjoy lower than average rates (United Nations Office on Drugs and Crime (UNODC), 2011). Many countries in Asia, North America and Europe have seen declines in their homicide rates since the mid-1990s, but in the Caribbean and Central America homicide rates have been climbing over the same period, owing in part to increased competition by gangs over control of unstable illicit drug markets, and high young male unemployment rates. In any case, both victims and perpetrators of murder are more likely to be members of marginalised populations – such as the poor and minority ethnic groups – and live in impoverished urban areas.

Men are much more likely to be murder perpetrators and victims (roughly 80 per cent) than are women, but there are other important gender differences in murder victimisation. While men are more likely to be killed in a public place during a dispute with another male, women are more likely to be murdered by a current or former intimate partner or a relative, demonstrating that patriarchal intimate partner violence is a major factor in the murder victimisation of women. In parts of the world where gang violence is less common, the proportion of female victims of murder increases. Firearm availability is another key factor affecting rates of murder, with around 40 per cent of all murders involving firearms. However, in the Americas around three-quarters of murders involve a firearm, while in Europe only one in five involves a firearm (UNODC, 2011).

All that being said, if we concentrate solely on the homicides committed disproportionately by the poor and the marginalised, including street gangs and terrorists (as much of mainstream criminology tends to do), we neglect the massive amounts of killing committed by corporations, militaries, private mercenaries, police and other governmental and private agents. Wilful killing occurs when corporations knowingly make dangerous or harmful products, cause pollution or create unsafe working conditions; and when hospitals and medical workers deny life-saving care or engage knowingly in various forms of medical malpractice that lead to death. Throughout human history governments have engaged in killing via police and other government security officials (for example, police shootings and torture that leads to death), state terrorism, capital punishment, targeted assassinations, genocidal activities and war. Many of these killings will be legitimised by the state and are therefore not labelled as criminal, but if there are prosecutions it is often the case that lower-level officers are punished rather than the high-ranking officers who gave them their orders. In war killing enemy soldiers is often considered heroic, but rules of war based on international norms and codified by the United Nations prohibit the indiscriminate killing of civilians, or the killing of enemy soldiers who surrender or are taken prisoner.

Theories of violence and murder in mainstream criminology tend to separate typical murders from spree and serial murders, police shootings, atrocities and the like. Theories of typical murders, for example, focus on social learning, hyper-masculinity and subcultures of violence originating in impoverished neighbourhoods that generate gang activity, as well as the routine situations people find themselves in that spark violence. These theories would obviously not be able to explain fully activities such as genocide, war crimes and serial murder, but a wider perspective on these different forms of killing is needed to examine what they have in common.

Atrocities committed in war and serial offending, for example, involve similar behaviours, including torture, rape, the belittling of victims before killing them and the keeping of trophies, such as the body parts of the depersonalised victims (Shanafelt and Pino, 2012). In addition, these victims tend to be members of marginalised groups including, but not limited to, sex workers, the homeless and racial, ethnic or religious minorities. However, police torture and atrocities committed during times of war and political oppression are often conducted by 'normal' men trained to engage in extreme forms of violence and depersonalisation in normalised group settings, while serial offending is almost always committed by individual offenders that develop pathological belief systems and fantasies over time. That being said, all of these forms of killing involve social learning and the development of ideologies and personae that allow a person to engage in these behaviours; and these ideologies are shaped by larger structural economic, political, educational and cultural forces that support patriarchy, the idea that violence is a way to solve problems, and the dehumanisation and 'othering' of marginalised groups (Shanafelt and Pino, 2012).

These observations will hopefully encourage future critical scholarship on homicide and other forms of violence. However, as Michalowski (2009, p. 303) points out, mainstream criminology focuses on crimes committed by the marginalised and gives little attention to transnational forms of violence committed and normalised by 'structures of power' such as governments. Conventional criminologists primarily focus on individual criminals committing private acts the state defines as criminal (such as murder) against other individuals, without critically examining why certain harms are defined as criminal while others are not. We must instead study the aetiology of all forms of killing, as well as the processes by which only certain forms of killing are criminalised.

References

Michalowski, R. (2009) Power, Crime and Criminology in the New Imperial Age, *Crime, Law and Social Change*, 51, (3–4), pp. 303–25.

Shanafelt, R. and Pino, N. W. (2012) Evil and the Common Life: Toward a Wider Perspective on Serial Offending and Atrocities, in Winlow, S. and Atkinson, R. (eds) *New Directions in Crime and Deviancy*, New York: Routledge, pp. 252–73.

United Nations Office on Drugs and Crime (2011) *2011 Global Study on Homicide: Trends, Context, Data*, Vienna: UNODC.

Watch:

Salvador (1986), film, directed by Oliver Stone. USA: Hemdale Film Corporation.

55

VIOLENCE AGAINST WOMEN

Walter S. DeKeseredy

One of the key lessons of this volume is that deviance takes many shapes and forms. Nonetheless, some violations of social and legal norms are more common than others. Furthermore, some transgressive acts are far more harmful to individuals and society in general than are others. Violence against women in intimate relationships is one prime example of a worldwide, highly injurious social problem. Indeed, the number of females affected by this devastating shade of deviance would, in the words of former Canadian politician and current human rights activist Stephen Lewis, 'numb the mind of Einstein' (cited in Vallee 2007).

Defining violence against women is subject to much debate. Many people restrict their focus to only physical abuse (for example, beatings) or sexual assaults involving forced penetration. There are major problems with this narrow, legalistic definition because scores of painful assaults on women behind closed doors never involve acts that cause bodily harm. Consider coercive control. This entails psychologically and emotionally abusive behaviours that are often subtle and hard to detect and prove; these seem to be more forgivable to people unfamiliar with violence against women and its traumatic effects. The main goal of coercive control is to restrict a woman's liberties, for example through the use of threatening looks or frequent verbal 'put downs'.

It is also important to note that, despite the severity of a beating or sexual assault, many women deem psychological abuse to be far more hurtful than physical attacks. I have conducted studies of numerous types of woman abuse for nearly 30 years, and large numbers of women have repeatedly told me (and many other researchers) that most of their physical wounds heal, but the damage to their self-respect and ability to relate to others caused by emotional, verbal and spiritual violence affects every aspect of their lives. As a consequence of this, and because of other significant accounts from female survivors of male violence and those identified by an international cadre of feminist social scientists, many people use broad definitions of violence against women.

Regardless of whether women find non-physical acts to be more damaging than physical ones, female targets of intimate violence are seldom victimised in only one type of assault. Rather, they typically suffer from an array of cruel male behaviours that include physical assault, psychological abuse, economic blackmail, the denial of money (even if a woman earns a wage), harms to pets or possessions to which she has attachment, coercive control or stalking behaviour. Roughly 80 per cent of the women I interviewed or who completed a questionnaire in the woman abuse studies I have conducted reported they experienced two or more of these variants of abuse, with numerous other studies showing that violence against women is multidimensional.

Violence against women can also be seen as a world-wide public health problem, as demonstrated by the World Health Organization's multi-country study of the health effects of gender violence. Over 24,000 women living in urban and rural areas of ten countries were interviewed. The percentage of women who were found to have been physically or sexually assaulted (or both) in their lifetime by an intimate partner ranged from 15 to 71 per cent, with most research results ranging between 29 and 62 per cent (Garcia-Moreno *et al.* 2005). In addition we can turn to the numerous surveys of North American women enrolled at institutions of higher learning (such as colleges and universities) that routinely show that at least 25 per cent of them are sexually assaulted each year.

What type of man would hit or rape a woman he is attracted to, or with whom he is romantically involved? A common answer to this question is that it is someone who is 'sick' or mentally ill. The truth is that less than 10 per cent of male batterers and rapists are pathological in this sense. Obviously, a sizeable portion of men assault women and thus it is necessary to examine carefully broader social and social psychological forces in societies around the world that contribute to this kind of deviance. Some of the key sociological determinants identified in the scholarly literature include men's adherence to the ideology of familial patriarchy (male dominance within the family unit), membership in sexist all-male peer groups and frequent consumption of Internet pornography. To be sure, however, it is impossible simply to pick out one 'reason' and announce that it covers all cases at all times.

Violence against women occurs in all demographic and social groups, but not all women are equally likely to be victimised. Those at the highest risk are separated or divorced women, women in cohabiting or common-law relationships, women between the ages of 16 and 24, impoverished women and those who belong to certain ethnic groups, such as women of colour. Intimate violence, of course, is certainly not restricted to these groups of women. Pregnant women, elderly women, women in same-sex relationships, homeless women and women with disabilities are also vulnerable groups.

Male violence against female intimates has existed for centuries and will not be sharply reduced soon. Sadly, thousands of women will continue to be killed, beaten, sexually assaulted and stalked until the major social, political, cultural and economic causes of such abuse are recognised, understood and addressed by the mainstream mass media, politicians and general public.

References

Garcia-Moreno, C., Jansen, H., Watts, C., Ellsberg, M., and Heise, L. (2005) *WHO Multi-country Study on Women's Health and Domestic Violence against Women: Initial Results on Prevalence, Health Outcomes and Women's Responses*, Geneva: World Health Organization.

Vallee, B. (2007) *The War on Women: Elly Armour, Jane Hurshman, and Criminal Violence in Canadian Homes*, Toronto: Key Porter Books.

Watch:

Flirting with Danger: Power and Choice in Heterosexual Relationships (2012), documentary film, directed by Sut Jhally and Andrew Killoy. USA: Media Education Foundation.

56

HUMAN TRAFFICKING

Sarah L. Steele

Human trafficking, also referred to as trafficking in persons, involves the illegal trade in people for their exploitation, either in the sex trade, labour market or in other contexts such as forced marriage, adoption, soldiering and the removal of organs. The core differentiation between smuggling (procuring illegal entry into a state) and trafficking is that the latter requires the coercive movement of people, usually for the purpose of their incorporation into illegal activities and exploitation when they arrive. Human trafficking can therefore take place within and across countries. Upon arrival trafficked persons are not permitted to leave and are held against their will, often with the threat of violence, or are deceived. Trafficking, then, involves conceiving of people as products and treating them like other illicit goods to be bought and sold.

The central legal instrument on trafficking remains the *Protocol to Prevent, Suppress and Punish Trafficking in Persons, especially Women and Children* (also referred to as the Palermo Protocol). It was adopted by the United Nations in Palermo, Italy in 2000, and attaches to the United Nations Convention against Transnational Organized Crime. It sets out an agreed definition of trafficking in persons and aims to facilitate international cooperation in investigating and prosecuting the crime by guiding states to protect and assist the survivors with full respect for their human rights. The Protocol entered into force on 25 December 2003, and by December 2012 the Protocol had 117 Signatories and 154 Parties, making it internationally influential.

Estimates suggest that trafficking is the fastest growing crime in the world, accounting for significant global profits. There is great controversy over the extent of trafficking in persons and its annual revenue, with some experts suggesting that it accounts for as much as $31.6 billion per annum from the movement, sale and exploitation of 2.4 million men, women and children, while others suggest much lower estimates, in the range of a few billion (Pemberton Ford, 2012). Much of the disparity relates to how organisations define trafficking and whether they observe the Palermo definition or engage a wider understanding. Other commentators argue that many statistics are inflated to aid the agenda of advocacy groups and to inspire greater anti-trafficking efforts by governments. Regardless, it is clear that significant numbers of vulnerable persons are subjected to this callous and violent trade.

There is also great contention about the definition of trafficking and how it relates to sexual exploitation. Two views emerged from the debates over the Protocol. One view was that prostitution remains legitimate work and, therefore, only 'forced' prostitutes can be viewed as trafficking victims. The other view promoted is that prostitution is something that should be abolished because it is harmful to all women. From this perspective the idea that women are capable of consenting as individuals to prostitution is essentially rejected, as it is a clear violation of basic human rights (both of adult women and of children), and therefore fundamentally exploitative. While the Protocol's definition only includes sexual services obtained via force, threat, coercion, deception and bondage through forced debt, a continued discussion remains around trafficking and prostitution and what different national and legal communities consider to be a crime. The two phenomena are often conflated, without the deeper issues involved in these harms being opened up for public debate and scrutiny.

Furthermore, both in law and popular culture, discussion of human trafficking has largely focused on prostitution and failed properly to profile the large percentage of cases pertaining to child trafficking, exploitative labour, begging, petty crime, benefits fraud, adoption and pornography (Pemberton Ford, 2012). Despite popular culture focusing on the sex trade, it remains the case that labour trafficking is ubiquitous across low-paid and poorly regulated industries, including fisheries, agriculture and leisure, and the textile, leather and construction industries, affecting men, women and children across the globe.

Human trafficking encompasses a wide range of exploitations that have various physical and psychological effects on survivors. Research suggests that trafficked persons suffer high levels of mental health problems as a consequence of the violent and inhumane treatment they experience, resulting in anxiety, depression, sleep disorders and post-traumatic stress disorder, as well as phobias and panic attacks. Beyond mental scars, survivors often suffer physically with bruising, muscle degradation, scarring, chronic back and joint problems, reduced hearing and vision, cardiovascular or respiratory problems, diabetes and even cancers. While most of these physical impacts diminish with treatment and recuperation, the mental health impacts are enduring and severe (Zimmerman *et al.*, 2006). They are only further compounded when survivors themselves are made to face criminal sanctions for their acts when trafficked, and the court or deportation processes come to further traumatise the trafficked person.

Even when returned home without charge, though, many survivors experience great difficulty in reintegrating. It may be that there is a threat of re-trafficking to pay off continued debts accrued from the initial 'deal' made with traffickers. Also, trafficked persons may face social alienation, stigmatisation and intolerance as a result of what they were forced to do while trafficked. Successful reintegration is difficult and requires comprehensive engagement by governments, non-governmental organisations and communities. Also, there must be partnerships with existing anti-trafficking actors from around the world, as international cooperation can lead to the creation of tested models and the implementation of campaign programmes which have already proved effective.

Addressing the driving factors of trafficking requires that we know more. In the face of a lack of data and a failure comprehensively to understand the trade in people, urgent research must be undertaken to inform the direction of resources and education campaigns. Such education campaigns need to be directed, not just at at-risk populations, but also at government agencies, police and other officials. Counteracting current stigmatisation requires multifaceted campaigns that highlight the plight of trafficked persons and drive reporting and support. One of the opportunities for this form of education could be to take advantage of global sports events (where at some points half the world's population tunes in to watch the apex of human sporting achievement) and cascade information across national sporting federations – a route so far neglected

(Pemberton Ford, 2012). Just as traffickers have used technology and travel, so too can anti-traffickers. It is integral that we consider multiple ways of addressing trafficking both within and beyond the law. Trafficking is intrinsically linked to systemic and enduring inequalities, and thus a key response to trafficking lies in a more equitable distribution of wealth and a robust application of human rights to address this latest and invidious form of enslavement.

References

Pemberton Ford, C. (2012) *Human Trafficking, Sporting Mega Events and the London Olympics of 2012*, London: IbixInsight.

United Nations (2000) The Protocol to Prevent, Suppress and Punish Trafficking in Persons, Especially Women and Children, Supplementing the United Nations Convention against Transnational Organized Crime, 15 November, available online at www.unhcr.org/refworld/docid/4720706c0.html (accessed 28 January 2013).

Zimmerman, C., Hossain, M., Yun, K., Roche, B., Morison, L. and Watts, C. (2006) *Stolen Smiles: A Summary Report on the Physical and Psychological Health Consequences of Women and Adolescents Trafficked in Europe*, London: London School of Hygiene and Tropical Medicine.

Watch:

Not My Life (2011), documentary film, directed by Robert Bilheimer. USA: Worldwide Documentaries.

CONCLUSION

Engaging your criminological imagination

Rowland Atkinson

This book is only a starting point or series of waymarks to other contributions and debates. Learning about crime and deviance is an exciting and dynamic area of study. Some readers will be about to embark on a degree programme, or already studying at a higher education institution. These final comments are intended for those students, but also for those who see themselves as students of crime in the sense of trying to build their personal knowledge and analytic skills around these issues. For some the study of crime is a vocation and a means of working in a particular job (youth worker, journalist, police, prison guard, social worker, law courts and so on); for others the question of human harm is an intrinsically interesting area for reading and learning. For anyone learning about a particular area of interest it is essential that you take charge of your own learning and, to ensure that your excitement about your chosen area of study is matched by active learning, keep up with key debates about crime and justice, as well as engaging with your peers to fine-tune your understanding of the issues. So, to round off, here are nine things you can do to help make yourself an effective student of crime, deviance and harm, whether you are a citizen, police officer or university student:

1   Be critical – be self-aware and self-critical, ensure that you are open to new ideas, hold up your own values to scrutiny and do not take others' perspectives for granted.

2   Be informed – make sure that you expose yourself to a wide range of news media on a daily basis; have a time when you will watch or listen to the day's news. Without this knowledge it is difficult to apply concepts or be able to apply your thinking seriously to the world around you.

3   Keep a notebook – it is well worth ensuring that you make notes of issues, readings, news items, books and articles that you have found interesting. This isn't about bookmarking or keeping notes, but about going further and writing notes to yourself about your under-standing of concepts and issues. Return to these later and see how your thinking has become more sophisticated, but also log impor-tant information that you can build up into hunches, ideas and directions for your understanding of the issues.

4   Read books – book-length contributions are essential, in-depth statements of research and thinking. Ask others which books have influenced their thinking. Read as much as you can: this is the life-blood of learning about crime, and will not only help you to have a command of your field but also improve your writing as you observe how good writers work their own craft.

5   Always look up words and concepts when you do not understand them – a simple tip that will generate an authoritative command of concepts and definitions.

6   Read journal articles – academic journals are, relatively speaking, the quickest way of accessing new research. They are relatively short and contain insight into the cutting edge of your field. Don't rely on your textbooks – or indeed your lectures – as being anywhere near the universe of information you require. This will seem daunting at first but you can start by setting up content alerts for the key crimi-nology and related journals so that you can keep up to date with the issues. There is a world of (very expensive) subscriptions to data and information through journals that is a large part of your university fees – don't waste it! See the university as a point for generating a self-reliant and exploratory attitude towards criminology.

7   Search out good literature and film media on complex issues – there are many important contributions to thinking about crime and social harm that don't come in the form of a lecture or a book. Films, popular literature and other statements offer you new ways of being presented with ideas and guides to issues. The films allocated to each entry here are an indication of this, but starting to watch a

series like *The Wire* (sixty hours of unparalleled ruminations about crime, city life, poverty and drugs, among many other issues) can and should be seen as part of your development and thinking. See all ideas, forums, information, data, journals, newspapers, and so on as important ways of learning, but never allow yourself to confuse careful scholarship with lazy and populist media representations of crime and its impacts.

8   Seek to understand how knowledge is produced and what values and distortions it introduces – always offer thoughtful analysis without allowing yourself simply to become cynical or unsophisticated in your responses. Being critical also means being constructive: ensure you are always engaging actively with the people you discuss issues with; be generous in your contributions while ensuring you hold to your views and values (when you have the evidence to do so).

9   Get involved – join one of the penal reform, human rights or grass-roots organisations involved in dealing with issues of crime or human harm. Their briefings are often cutting-edge and essential to thinking about how we might promote better social outcomes and reduce the risks of crime.

INDEX

CPSIA information can be obtained
at www.ICGtesting.com
Printed in the USA
FFHW022248090719
53528245-59174FF

SHADES OF DEVIANCE

Written in a unique format, *Shades of Deviance* is a turbo-driven guide to crime and deviance, offering 56 politically engaged, thought-provoking and accessibly written accounts of a wide range of socially and legally prohibited acts. This book will be essential reading for undergraduate students in the fields of criminology and sociology, and those preparing to embark on degree courses in these fields, as well as general readers.

Written by field-leading experts from across the globe and designed for those who want a clear and exciting introduction to the complex areas of crime and deviance, the book provides a large number of short overviews of a wide range of social problems, harms and criminal acts. Offering a series of cutting-edge and critical treatments of issues such as war and murder, paedophilia, ecocide, human experimentation, stalking and sexting, it also features a guide to further reading and suggestions for other media, to develop the reader's understanding of these issues.

Shades of Deviance requires readers to reconsider critically their ideas about what is right and wrong, about what is socially harmful and which problems we should focus our attention on. It also provides careful analysis and reasoned explanation of complex issues in a world in which sensationalist headlines, anxiety and fear of crime permeate our lives – read it to be prepared!

Rowland Atkinson is Reader in Urban Studies and Criminology, and Co-director of the Centre for URBan Research, at the University of York, UK. His research has focused on the experience of poverty and social exclusion, and applied research around urban affairs and housing issues. He is the author, co-author or editor of over 80 articles, chapters and reports on urban social problems.